Eclectic Thoughts
of a
Rational Mind

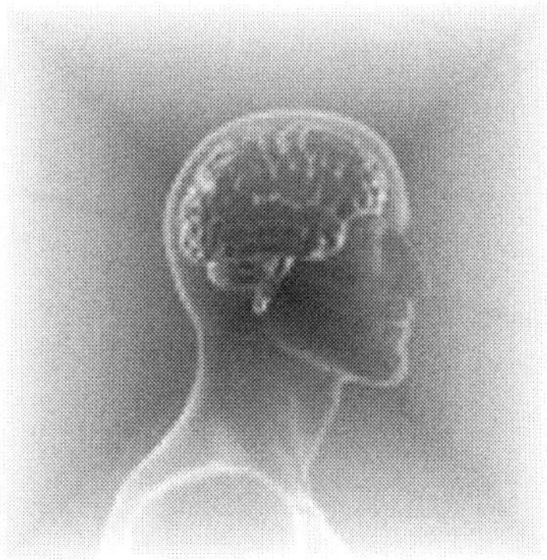

A Potpourri of Seminary Papers

By
Dr. Gordon E. Necemer

Gordon E. Necemer,

10122 - 125th Street,
Surrey, B.C. V3V 3B5

Email: necemer@aol.com

ISBN: 978-0994858337

Published in Surrey, BC Canada
By

Table of Contents

Chapter 1: Factors That Influenced My Theological Convictions 15

My Parents 16

Foster Parents 19

influence of Pastors 20

Frank Dyck 20

Art Bell 21

Ross Wightman 23

High School and College Teachers 25

Martha Lowndes 25

Larry Kronstrom 26

Ron Wright 27

J. I. Packer 27

Journals 28

Books 28

Pilgrim's Progress 28

Humble Apologetics 29

Cheap Grace 29

Systematic Theology 30

The Gravedigger Files 30

Films, Videos, DVD's 31

The Passion of the Christ 31

The Flywheel 32

Regularly Associating with God's People 32
Chapter 2: Abortion 35
Definition of Abortion 36
Types of Abortions 36
The History of Abortion in Canada 37
The Case against Abortion 41
Abortion from a Biblical Perspective 46
Conclusion 47
Chapter 3: Sally's Quandary - Is There an Alternative to Abortion? 49
Introduction 50
Questions and Challenges 51
Challenges 52
Interaction with Society 54
Interaction with the Church 55
Sympathetic Acquaintance with Others 55
Underlying Concerns - Hopes and Fears 56
Clarification of Issues 57
Admission of Guilt 58
Defense against Abortion 59
Action 63
Chapter 4: Child Abuse 67
Introduction 68
Definition of Physical Abuse 69
Major Causes of Child Abuse 69
Risk Family Settings for Child Physical Abuse 70
The Results of Child Physical Abuse 76
Theological Rebuttal to Child Abuse 78
The Church's Responsibility 80

Conclusion 83
Chapter 5: Guilt 85
Definitions of Guilt 86
Types of Guilt 88
Impact of Guilt 90
Release from Guilt 90
Theological Implications of Guilt 92
Chapter 6: Proposed Safeguards Against Secularization for Christians 97
Introduction 98
Tenants of Secularism 99
Historical Progression of Secularization 101
Biblical Wardship against Secularization 105
The Believer's Response to Secularism 112
Chapter 7: Age Integrated Church Worship 117
Introduction 118
Age Integration throughout Scripture 119
Problems with Age Segregation in the Church 121
Recommendation for Age Integrated Ministry 125
Chapter 8: Authorship of the Fourth Gospel 127
Disputations about the Authorship of John 129
Internal Evidence 135
External Evidence 137
Implications for the Faith 139
Personal Persuasion and Conclusion 141
Chapter 9: Christ's Missional Church 143
Implications for Missional Churches 155
Chapter 10: Eternal Security 159
The Context of Eternal Security 161

God, Initiator of Redemption 162
The Preservation of the Saints 164
The Assurance of the Saints 167
Perseverance of the Saints 168
Conclusion 171
Chapter 11: Francis of Assisi 173
Introduction 174
Background 174
Conversion 176
The Triune Calling 176
Francis and the Three Orders 179
The Death of Francis 181
Francis, "Mirror Of Christ" 181
Conclusion 184
Chapter 12: The Pietists 185
Introduction 186
The Origin of Pietism 186
Background to Spener 188
Tenants of Pietism 190
Conclusion 198
Chapter 13: Liberation Theology 199
Introduction 200
A Brief Historical Overview of Latin America 201
Ground Work for Liberation Theology 202
Definition of Liberation Theology 204
Model for Liberation Theology 205
Praxis – Catalyst for Change 208
Problems with Liberation Theology 211
Conclusion 213

Chapter 14: MS PowerPoint 215

Introduction 216

Value of PowerPoint 216

Discredit of PowerPoint 218

Conclusion 223

Chapter 15: Baptist Pastoral Leadership Training in Post-Communist Romania 225

Introduction 226

Background to the Romanian Baptist Union Fellowship 228

Clergy Training during Pre-communist Times 229

Clergy Training during Communism 230

Pastoral Leadership in Romania Today 233

Pastoral Leadership Problems 234

Conclusion 238

Endnotes & Bibliography 239

Chapter 2 239

  Endnotes 239

  Bibliography 241

Chapter 3 243

  Endnotes 243

  Bibliography 244

Chapter 4 246

  Endnotes 246

  Bibliography 249

Chapter 5 252

  Endnotes 252

  Bibliography 254

Chapter 6 256

  Endnotes 256

Bibliography 260
Chapter 7 263
Endnotes 263
Bibliography 264
Chapter 8 264
Endnotes 264
Bibliography 268
Chapter 9 270
Endnotes 270
Bibliography 271
Chapter 10 273
Endnotes 273
Bibliography 275
Chapter 11 277
Endnotes 277
Bibliography 280
Chapter 12 282
Endnotes 282
Bibliography 284
Chapter 13 286
Endnotes 286
Bibliography 288
Chapter 14 290
Endnotes 290
Bibliography 291
Chapter 15 292
Endnotes 292
Bibliography 296

Preface

Since graduating from Semiahmoo Senior Secondary School in White Rock, British Columbia in 1969, I have been blessed to procure seventeen years of academic study at secular and religious colleges and seminaries. In 2015 I was blessed to receive my Doctor of Ministry degree from Providence Theological Seminary in Otterburne, Manitoba.

Although I immensely enjoyed completing my studies at all levels, I found it cumbersome and stressful to write the hundreds of essays, book reports, reflective journals and essays that were demanded. Because of God's goodness, strength and enlightenment – especially when doing research – I successfully completed all the assignments on time, and with a high grade.

For years the papers have "sat idle" in two or three of my filing cabinets, being of no further value to me, or anyone else. One day, as I was looking for an article on leadership, I decided others may be blessed by reading some of the papers stored here. Because of this "illumination," I have selected a number of my "better papers" and assembled this compendium by which I desire, and trust other believers will be blessed.

To provide fluency and ease in reading the articles, I have placed the endnotes and bibliographies of all the chapters at the end of the book. Some of the citations – especially the journal entries – are incomplete. The explanation for this is I didn't keep all the documents I early photocopied, and some of the citations cannot be found on the internet. I ask you to kindly and graciously overlook the few errors you might find throughout this work – if there are any – and enjoy what I present. If you have any concern about the opinions expressed within this work, please email me at Necemer@aol.com. God richly bless you. My hope is that you will be edified in the Lord by what you read.

Chapter 1

Factors That Influenced My Theological Convictions

I have been a born-again Christian for over sixty years. Because of the many, God ordained influences on my life I believe I have enjoyed a strong, unwavering and mature faith walk with God.

My Parents

I was born on December 10th, 1947 in Powell River, British Columbia. At my birth the family consisted of nine children – seven boys and two girls. In 1961, when my mother died of cancer, the family consisted of sixteen children - eight boys and eight girls. I am the middle child among the siblings.

My dad escaped from Yugoslavia in 1939. During his early adult years, while living in Belgrade, he trained as a Roman Catholic Priest. For a short time – about three years – he did parish ministry under a Bishop in Belgrade. He escaped from Yugoslavia in 1940, with five other young men, to avoid fighting in World War 2. On arriving in Canada, he came to a personal faith in Christ as Lord after reading and meditating on the scripture, "And call no man your father on the earth: for one is your Father, which is in heaven" (Matt 22:9).

Throughout my childhood my dad worked as a tree faller for MacMillan-Bloedel in several logging camps on Vancouver Island. Because he was away from home for lengthy periods of time, his influence on my life was limited. However, whenever he was home, he reminded me of the need to be "connected with God" in the same trust relationship he possessed.

As I reflect on his influence on my faith, I recognize he had two impacts on it. First, he encouraged me to "seek and honour the Lord constantly, regardless how I felt, or what I faced. Second, he admonished me to be ready and willing to answer and follow God's call on my life regardless what vocations others might suggest because, "obedience is better than sacrifice" (1 Sam 15:22). I was deeply moved when he, in August 1968, recognized God's call on my life for gospel ministry, and encouraged me to attend Bible College instead of apprenticing as an automotive mechanic with MacMillan-Bloedel, Port Hardy Division.

At this time I was concerned I would not have adequate finances to cover my tuition for the upcoming September enrollment at Western Pentecostal Bible College in North Vancouver, so I asked him if he could lend me the money I desperately needed. In responding to my request, he reminded me of my need to trust God to supply the need stating, "Go ask your Heavenly Father to intervene. If He wants you to attend college, He will supply the funds." His encouragement fixed within me the confidence God hears and answers prayer when we ask with a pure and upright heart according to His will.

My mother was born in Roblin, Manitoba. Between my dad and her, she provided me the stronger theological influence. As a child she had attended the Romanian Orthodox Church through which she had gained a deep faith in God, and the teachings of the Church which she taught her children. Throughout my earliest childhood she taught the family the need of honouring God in everything we did, obeying His word, and submitting to His will as we prayed, read scripture and fellowshipped with fellow believers. To empower us to develop this worldview, she encouraged us to pray and read scripture daily, to trust God for our daily needs, to regularly attend church, and to be willing to share our faith whenever an opportunity arose. And with this she reminded us we were beloved children of the living God. If we honoured Him above everything else, He would adequately provide our physical and spiritual needs.

Mother lovingly counseled us of the need to be born-again so we could know forgiveness of sins, become God's children, and enjoy the abundant life – spiritually – He provides for those who trust Him. By her daily, godly example and witness I discovered the joy she possessed when, in May, 1961 I accepted Christ as Savior, Lord and Redeemer Friend. Since then, I have never been disappointed.

After I was saved, mother encouraged to me be ready, at all times, to share with others the gift of salvation I had received. After all, she would say, Jesus gave His very best for us. Because of this, witnessing for Him should not be a burdensome task for those who are one of His children. To empower me to share my faith, she often took the family to Vancouver's East Side Skid Road where we handed out gospel tracts, sang hymns, and gave sandwiches and soup to the needy. Announcing Christ's love to others was an opportunity, not an option according to mother. She taught us to take every opportunity that came our way, even if it meant saying nothing more than, "I thank the Lord for saving and keeping me." This early training in evangelism could well be the reason I am proactive today in sharing my faith with others.

Living for Christ as Lord and Savior was a significant teaching mother also instilled within me. Regardless where we went or what we did, she reminded me I was God's child. My actions, therefore, should clearly reflect His character so others would never have cause to speak unbecoming of God and His salvific work in my life. According to her, I should live different from the ungodly – not peculiarly or strangely – because God had transformed my focus on life to a godly standard of conduct. Instead of pleasing self by embracing the philosophy and lifestyle of this world, I should love and please God to the best of my ability as I submit to His Word and the direction of the Holy Spirit.

Because of this wholesome teaching, I was not ashamed – during my high school years – to carry my Bible with my textbooks, to ask my grade eleven high schoolteacher to allow me to read portions of the Bible for credit in English 30, instead of reading secular books, and to attend the Interschool Christian Fellowship meetings, instead of participating in many sports activities for which I was well qualified.

So significant was my mother's desire that I live for Christ, regardless what I faced, her last comment to me before dying was, "Whatever you do, Gordon, don't forget to continue living for Christ; you'll never be disappointed!"

Foster Parents

Within a week after my mother's death on August 31st, 1961, a younger sister and I were placed in the first of three foster homes. Mr. & Mrs. Williams were a middle-aged couple who were devoted Christians, and who displayed godly compassion to us during this grieving period. It was from them I discovered God's unshakable love, compassion and sustaining grace during the darkest "night of the soul."

Mr. & Mrs. Williams accepted me as their son within minutes of arriving at their home. They unashamedly informed to me they were devoted Christians. Daily they treated me with the highest esteem physically, mentally and spiritually as they read scripture and prayed with me regardless of the hour I approached them if I were depressed about my mother's passing, or concerned about being separated from my brothers and sisters. And after providing this godly care, they wisely assured me God had everything under control, and He would carry me through the difficult time of sorrow if I trusted His promises and rested in His faithfulness.

I lived with this family for two weeks, and then moved on to a second home where the foster father was an abusive alcoholic. If I had not received the encouragement and the teaching the William's provided, I am sure I would have had a difficult time remaining faithful to God's call on my life. But, because I understood God's loving care, His sustaining grace, and His promise, "He will never leave me nor forsake me" (Heb 13:5), I was empowered to accept my mother's death, and gain strength daily. Every time I drive by the Williams' home I rejoice in God's goodness for allowing me to live with these godly and caring people, even though this was for a few days.

Influence of Pastors

Throughout my 'faith walk' the influence and teaching of my pastors has been extremely valuable. Although each pastor had his special ministry focus, each one imparted to me godly, biblical principles I still value immensely today.

Frank Dyck
Pastor at Cloverdale Pentecostal Church, 1953-1961

Pastor Dyck was an elderly pastor who began his ministry during the depression years. He, during his youth, had gone through the "waters of testing" many times. Despite being tempted often to abandon God and the faith, he remained faithful to his call, and was "marked a faithful, devoted and directed servant of God." From his ministry I gained appreciation of the following biblical teachings.

First, God's love towards His people is for their immediate and eternal good. Second, Christ's church is a welcoming community of faith that loves the brotherhood. Because of this, it readily invites others to know God through Christ as Savior so they, too, can be part of this great, loving and caring community. Third, Christ's church is comprised of talented and gifted individuals who are welcome to use their gifts for the edification of the church as they are empowered by the Holy Spirit, and endorsed by the leaders of a local fellowship (Rom 12:1-8; 1 Cor 12 & 14).

Regardless what ability, talent or gift a brother or sister possessed, Reverend Dyck readily invited him or her to use it during the public worship services. He, for example, encouraged me as a teenager, to usher during the morning services because he recognized I enjoyed welcoming people to church. And I also recall he invited my older brother to play in the orchestra because he owned a steel guitar and played it well.

Fourth, Christ's church is a caring community of faith touching the marginalized, the poor, and the sick. Whereas other churches within the community held an in-house midweek Bible Study and Prayer meeting, Pastor Dyck encouraged the congregation to weekly visit the patients at the Scenic View Seniors' Home, where it sang hymns and read scripture to the patients. As I participated in these services, I quickly learned God's love is always welcomed and appreciated by believers, regardless how aged or sick they may be. Going to this care centre was one of the best learning experiences of my youth, and I thank God for the opportunity to have ministered there.

Fifth, Christ's people are to be steward managers of the material blessings they possess. Therefore, they should prudently guard them from wanton waste so they can be invested liberally in God's work as He directs them (1 Cor 16:2). This teaching was clearly reinforced in 1956 when the Board decided the congregation needed additional space in the church for the Sunday school, and should build a new Fellowship Annex in which the classes would be held.

At this time the congregation possessed a small cash reserve to pay for the construction of the annex's foundation, but it lacked adequate finances to complete the project. Despite this, in faith the money needed could and would be provided by the Lord's people, the project was started in the spring of 1957. When the funds ran out, Pastor Dyck asked everyone – including the children – to enable the completion of the project by contributing twenty-five cents – or multiples thereof – each Sunday, for the purchase of bricks. As the congregants began to understand the joy of sacrificial, stewardship giving, within three months all the bricks were purchased. Within eight months, construction of the annex was completed, and in use.

The church was blessed to have Pastor Dyck direct it to build this structure. During the period of 1958-1964, the regular Sunday school attendance was two hundred to two hundred and fifty. If the congregation did not build the annex, there would be no way to handle the immense growth with which the Lord blessed the church.

Art Bell
Pastor at Cloverdale Pentecostal Church, 1961-1964

Reverend Bell, like Pastor Dyck, was an older man who had also experienced difficult times during his early years of ministry. But he had seen God do several miracles for his family. Because of this, he regularly affirmed to the congregation God could and should be trusted regardless how difficult life may look. Through his ministry I learned the following valued principles.

First, God is sovereign and can be trusted to bring His children to a promised good end if they trust and obey Him wholeheartedly and unreservedly. Pastor Bell was totally convinced God, and not man, brought him to pastor our congregation even though he often faced difficult and discouraging times. When hard times arose, he would remind me of God's provisional, sovereign call stating, "I don't have to know why I'm here, or for how long. All I need to know," he would continue, "is who has brought me here, and remain faithful to the call regardless of the cost." He faithfully pastored the church until June 14th, 1964 when he had a heart attack during a morning service, and died a week later because of a second, major heart attack.

Second, church membership is important because it signals believers are committed to a local church as part of the family that makes ministry goals, plans and decisions together. Before his arrival in Cloverdale, the congregation was comprised of adherents who allowed the Board to decide and direct the church's ministry focus. On arriving at Cloverdale, Pastor Bell immediately encouraged church membership because, "The local church is comprised God's people who gather as fellow citizens of the commonwealth of grace (Eph 2:10-14), as brothers and sisters in the Lord (Jn 17; Acts 2), and as co-workers with one another and with God" (2 Cor 6:1). Within a year church membership was established, the congregation became closely knit together as family, and the church grew in love and care one for the other.

Third, God cares about His people (Matt 6:20-33), and His people should mirror Him by lovingly and excitedly caring for one another. This principle was demonstrated by him clearly one day when I was distressed by problems I was facing at school. Although I didn't want to distress anyone with the problems, Pastor Art was sensitive how I was feeling, and invited me to his home for fellowship so I could share these with him. What was very noteworthy during our discussion was this, as I talked with him he showed a sincere interest in what I was saying. As I left his home I was confident he possessed a deep, loving concern for me and my future.

Fourth, as a Christian I needed to be sensitive to the "gifts of the Spirit" (1 Cor 14), and willingly submit to His counsel and leading. His eagerness for me to understand this became apparent when he invited me to accompany him, at the Cloverdale Legion, for a special meeting with Nicholas Bengu, the Billy Graham of South Africa. During this service, Pastor Bell was convinced God desired to give me the "gift of evangelism," and wanted to have prayer for me. Despite my hesitancy to allow this, Pastor Art arranged for he and Brother Nicholas to pray for me. By the time the service ended, because I heard and heeded his counsel I received the "gift," and my life was radically changed. Whereas prior to this service I was shy, backward, and lacked confidence in sharing my faith, afterward I knew that "I would never be ashamed of the gospel of Christ for it is the power of God unto salvation" (Rom 1:16). My ministry of evangelism over the past sixty years would not have been as exciting, and as profitable as it has been had Art Bell ignored obeying the "leading of the Spirit" that day.

Ross Wightman
Pastor at Cloverdale Pentecostal Church, 1965-1971

Rev. Wightman was the youngest of the pastors that influenced me while I attended Cloverdale Pentecostal Church. He, like other pastors, was sincerely devoted to God, and concerned about the spiritual growth of the congregation. It was during his ministry I received coaching in theological dogma and spiritual maturity. From his ministry I learned.

First, God had a special, unique, personal call on my life and I would discover it if I accepted pastoral care and counsel. Prior to Pastor Ross' coming to the church, I attended the services as one "putting in time" to please others. But as Pastor Ross encouraged and instructed me to discover God's "call," I started attending church because I earnestly desired to grow in the knowledge of the Lord Jesus Christ (Eph 2:13-15), and know the "good, the excellent and the perfect will of God (Rom 12:1-2). Sunday after Sunday, regardless of the weather, I walked six miles to church so I could be nurtured in the Word and discover what God wanted me to do! Within three years of this change in my attitude I knew, with certainty, God wanted me to attend Bible School and train for pastoral ministry. An immediate confirmation to this "call" came from Pastor Ross seconds after I mentioned to him what I felt God wanted me to do.

Second, God had endowed me with special ministry gifts – the gift of encouragement and the gift of leadership – and if I developed them under godly mentoring, later I would be able to impart these to others (2 Tim 2:2) as Paul did to Timothy.

Shortly after recognizing these gifts, Pastor Ross invited me to co-pastor with him. In this role I looked after the Sunday school, the weekly prayer meetings, and shared in pulpit ministry by speaking, once in a while, during either the morning or evening service. In September 1968, when I left Cloverdale to attend Western Pentecostal Bible College, Pastor Wightman held a special meeting during which he prayed over me that these two gifts would never decrease or cease, and they haven't. Because of Pastor Wightman's encouragement in this area, I have met many, who through my witness, have come to faith in Christ. Four years of approval and encouragement by Pastor Ross turned into a lifetime of extended and excited ministry on my part. Like Elisha, I received a double portion of Pastor Wightman's encouragement which, I trust, I will be able to pass on to someone else if the Lord so wills.

Third, I needed to maximize the time I spent in prayer and meditation on scripture. Pastor Wightman reminded me the marks of a devoted, directed, disciple of Christ were that he prayed regularly, and he had a deep love for scripture. In the second year of his ministry I, under his guidance, began a life of prayer and meditation by meeting with him twice a week for an hour of prayer before attending my classes at Lord Tweedsmuir Senior Secondary. During these years I noticed a marked spiritual growth in my walk with the Lord, and the influence God allowed me to have on the lives of many with whom I had contact.

High School and College Teachers

I am convinced my life, during my teen years, was strongly influenced to discipleship by the godly high school and college teachers, under whose instruction I sat. Space allows me to comment only on three or four that enabled me to discern and discover God's plan for my life. I will be eternally grateful for their instruction and encouragement in the Lord.

Martha Lowndes
Grade 11 French Teacher

Martha Lowndes was a devoted Christian teacher who attended Glad Tidings Church in Vancouver. Noticeable in her class, which I visited three times a week for French, was a Bible she always had a on her desk next to her Daybook. Whenever a discipline problem arose during class, before disciplining the student, she would read from 2 Corinthians 13, and then consult with the student what might be the appropriate action she should take as discipline.

I took French from Miss Lowndes for three semesters. One day I gained courage to ask her why she always consulted scripture before applying discipline. She responded, "I want to ensure I'm making a decision based on thoughts that 'are true, that are honest, that are just, that are pure, that are lovely, that are of good report; and that are virtuous' so I can show grace like Christ did, instead of being vindictive like many would expect."

Through this discussion with Martha I learned that Christians need to be clay in the potter's hand allowing Him to "transform them by the renewing of their mind "(Rom 12:2), so they can know the joy of returning good for evil (Rom 12:21) regardless how difficult this might be. Her example enabled me, many times throughout the years, to show kindness when people have offended or abused me, instead of being vindictive.

Larry Kronstrom

Grade 9 Chemistry Teacher

Larry, so he told me years after I graduated from high school, was an agnostic. Nothing – absolutely nothing – was going to move him towards believing in God. God, however, was going to use Larry to teach me no one is too obstinate, proud, or difficult to understand, appreciate and accept grace, faith and mercy (1 Tim 1:12-13) when the Holy Spirit woos his or her spirit to Christ.

Larry returned an essay to me unmarked because I had expressed a strong belief that God was the Creator and Sustainer of the universe. Since my opinion did not concur with his, he detained me after school to rewrite it. Explaining to him I could not change my opinion because it reflected my deepest convictions about God, he failed me on the assignment. Minutes before my detention ended, a colleague of Larry's – a music teacher called Bob Ferguson – arrived to visit with him. On seeing me, he started to ridicule God and my faith. I kindly warned him his low regard for God should be guarded against, for he might be in God's presence that day. Fifteen minutes later we received news he had been killed in a car/train collision a short distance from the school.

In August 1977 I received employment teaching in the same school district in which Larry was employed. On meeting him at a staff luncheon, I discovered that after praying for him - the espoused agnostic - for twenty-four years, he had become a Christian.

Often I meet Larry for coffee. Each time he states, "I was the foolish one for refusing to believe in God like you did, but you never gave up. I'm sure you thought I, like Saul, was a chosen vessel unto the Lord (Acts 9:15), and you never gave up on me - thank you so much!"

Ron Wright

Professor at Western Pentecostal Bible College 1968-1970

Of all the college professors I've met, Ron Wright influenced my theological thinking the greatest. This may have happened for two reasons. First, he taught all the Theology courses offered at the college, and second, he regarded me as being teachable, and desperately desirous to grow in the knowledge of the Lord.

It was because of this second trait he gave me personal tutoring on the doctrines, the creeds and the traditions of the church. And with this – while he worked graveyard for Safeway – he provided me with a bibliography of books and journals I should read so I could gain an appreciation for scholarly religious writings. During my last year of studies at Western, because of his guidance, I read Calvin's Institutes, Hodge's Theology, and other such books so I could be well versed in the doctrines of the church and equipped "to give an answer in love for the hope that lies within me" (1 Pet 3:15). The encouragement I received from him is greatly appreciated; I am much the better for knowing him!

J. I. Packer

Regent College Professor of Theology 2004-2007

During my studies at Regent College I had the privilege of taking "Introduction to Theology," taught by J. I. Packer. Indeed, this was a great privilege, and learning experience.

J. I. Packer made Theology come 'alive' through his clear, and simple, yet knowledgeable explanation of the issues about God, redemption, the work of the Holy Spirit, and the return of Christ. Like Ron Wright of Western Pentecostal Bible College, he also took a personal interest in my understanding of theological issues. Of particular note was his strong determination that I, with the rest of the class, understood the issue of the Trinity. To make this clear he explained the Trinity as dancing partners viewed from three different perspectives, stating, "Regardless from what angle one sees a dancer, he or she retains the same personhood, value, charisma and importance during the whole dance." From this explanation I gained an understand that the members of the Trinity are equal in personhood, in ministry, and in worship regardless of the name attached to their role in one's spiritual formation. Further theological knowledge was gained in reading his book, *Knowing God,* and by reading a few articles written by him that have been published by *Christianity Today, Church History,* and other Christian journals.

I value greatly meeting personally with J. I. Packer on two or three occasions, during which I discussed some of his theological opinions and could voice my personal convictions. Many times we did not agree on several issues, but he treated me with a welcome dignity I appreciated.

Journals

The following Journals have been helpful in forming my theological persuasions: *Charisma, Christianity Today, Crux, Leadership Journal, Psychology Today* and *Sojourners.*

Books

Pilgrim's Progress by John Bunyan

This was the first "classical book" I bought and read after graduating from high school. It remains a significant reminder of justification and sanctification in the Christian life that occurs on the pilgrimage from earth and despair, to heaven and glory. What remained significant as I read the book was the reminder, "except the branch abide in the vine it cannot bring forth any fruit" (Jn 15). It was by reading this book I learned my "faith walk" needed to be one of complete, unreserved surrender to God that included a complete reliance on Him to help me remain faithful to Christ and His church.

It was clear, from reading this book, unless I followed Him in humble obedience, I could easily succumb to temptations that would make my earthly pilgrimage extremely stressful and unprofitable (Rom 6:23). By reading the book, I also learned the vastness of God's love, mercy, grace, and forbearance shown to His children whenever they stray from the path of righteousness. This assurance enabled me, at an early age, to be fully "persuaded, that neither death, nor life, nor angels, nor principalities, nor powers, nor things present, nor things to come, nor height, nor depth, nor any other creature, shall be able to separate me from the love of God, which is in Christ Jesus our Lord" (Rom 8:37-38), as God preserves me until the day of Jesus Christ (Phil 1:6).

Humble Apologetics by John Stackhouse Jr.

Through taking three or four courses, at Regent College, taught by John Stackhouse, Jr., and reading this book, I discovered the importance of being taught and grounded in Orthodox Biblical Doctrines so I can adequately articulate the truth of the gospel to others in rational, reasonable and understandable terms. The purpose of the book is to introduce believers to the process of integrating the truth of the gospel with everyday life situations. As this is faithfully done, the ungodly will see Christ love, and then ask pertinent questions that will lead to a discussion around the matters of Christ and the gospel.

Although Dr. Stackhouse does not present a clear evangelistic thrust in the book, the book is beneficial because it affirms Christ as God's heaven-sent Savior. And with this, it further calls Christians to provide a sound, coherent, well-argued biblical defense of God and Christianity to the inquiries posed by those who do not yet know Christ as Savior. The book has inspired me to be more exact in presenting a defense for biblical truth, instead of casually, carelessly, and callously presenting it as unquestionable truth.

Cheap Grace by Dietrich Bonhoeffer

From reading this book I was reminded of my responsibility to live before God and man as a diligent, directed disciple of Christ, instead of living as a carnal and self-centred "heathen". Realizing this afresh, I immediately started following Christ regardless what joy or distress I might face. As I studied scripture I further recognized Christ has called me to be His servant, His ambassador, His witness, and to walk humbly in obedience to His commands as a mature son who is not ashamed of Christ or His church.

The book provided me a clearer understanding of Christ's Lordship over my life, and instilled within me a stronger passion to love, honour, obey and follow Him regardless of the cost. At times this has been a very difficult and disconcerting demand. But, through reading scripture, and contemplating Bonhoeffer's sincerity in what he wrote, I understand doing anything else will make Christ's redemption "cheap grace" which is an abomination to Him, and my witness of what He has done for me and others for whom He came to die.

Systematic Theology by Henry Thiessen

This was the first book on Systematic Theology I read after graduating from high school in 1968. Being instructed by my pastor(s) that being rooted in sound doctrine (1 Tim 1:9; 2 Tim 4:3; Titus 2:1) was imperative if I was to take on public ministry, I read the book two or three times during my first and second year of study at Western Pentecostal Bible College. Wanting to ensure gained a deep, and clear understanding of what the author was presenting, I underlined those things I thought were pertinent so I could be established in the faith and come to maturity in Christ.

Just recently I reread two or three chapters of this book, and I was encouraged by the simplistic, yet intelligible way Thiessen presented Systematic Theology in a clear manner that empowered me to learn the things of God. Since 1968 I have read many others systematic theologies by Hodge, Kuyper, Milne, and others. Each of these has been of immense value in providing me growth in knowing the doctrines of the church, and in my love for Christ and the gospel.

The Gravedigger Files by Os Guinness

This book was read while I was attending Regent College in 2007 for a course on Contemporary Theology. In this book Guinness suggests that the Western Church is being gravely influenced by a ruinous conspiracy based on the philosophies of modernity and postmodernity. His thesis contends because of the Church's tolerance of pluralism, deceptive, humanistic philosophies, and tolerance of other religious teachings which has cause it to lose its credibility, authority and legitimacy in the world. The conspiracy is ramped within the Western Church, and without an immediate, decisive reaffirmation and recommitment to the primacy of the teachings of

Christ and stalwart obedience to His commands, eventually the purpose, and the effect of the Church will be eroded.

As Guinness develops his plot, the outlook for the Church becomes bleaker and bleaker to the extent many believers conclude the Church no longer has any valued, redemptive influence on the ungodly. Guinness' redemption for the Church is "The Third Fool," who is a committed believer who understands the Directorate's unwholesome plot, but will not succumb to his oppressive tactics because he is fully committed to scripture and kingdom advancement regardless of oppressive schemes. This conviction will guarantee the "fool" will never "be spoiled by philosophy and vain deceit, after the tradition of men, after the rudiments of the world" (Col 2:8), so as he continuously "holds fast the faithful word as he has been taught, that he may be able by sound doctrine both to exhort and to convince the gainsayers" (I Tim 1:9).

This book impacted my life in two ways. First, it reminded me how my spiritual formation is constantly being influenced by worldly, cultural and cultic dynamics. Second, it stirred me to recall that the things I have learned of God through the instruction of godly men "who came in the wisdom of the Holy Spirit, rather than in human wisdom" (1 Cor 2:1-9), must be prime importance for my spiritual growth. In light of these two teachings I have immerse myself in the Apostles Doctrines and the established traditions of the Church" so I may be established "in the unity of the faith, and of the knowledge of the Son of God, unto a perfect man, unto the measure of the stature of the fullness of Christ" thereby guarding myself against the possibility of "being tossed about by every doctrine, by the sleight of men, and cunning craftiness, whereby they lie in wait to deceive" (Eph 4:13 & 14).

Films, Videos, DVD's

The Passion of the Christ by Mel Gibson

This presentation unquestionably is one of the most sobering presentations of the life, death and crucifixion of Christ. Although this film was very graphic in its presentation, it reaffirmed for me the bitter, mental agony, the intense physical suffering, and the immeasurable "struggles" Christ faced as He willingly laid down His life for the sins of the world. By seeing this presentation I got a clearer understanding of what John means when he writes, "For God so loved the world that He gave His only begotten son" (Jn 3:16). Christ's death, burial and resurrection demonstrate God passionately wanted His fallen creation to be reinstated into fellowship with Him. Because of this, there was no sacrifice too great, even if it meant sending His only Son to die on the cross for humankind's redemption.

The Flywheel

The plot centres on a "Christian" car salesman – Jay – who, despite claiming to be born-again and devoted to Christ, purposely sells over- priced vehicles to his customers – including his pastor. As the Holy Spirit, through a number of circumstances, speaks to him about his shameful, hypocritical actions, he ends his unethical business practices, repents, and recommits his life to Christ. By doing this, and doing business "God's way," the business, instead of being a loss, becomes a financial success.

Theologically, the film presents the teachings of repentance, restoration of that which was unjustly taken, reconciliation to God, family and society, and a relentless trust in God for one's daily bread. Strongly implied in this movie is the principle of being responsibly accountable to the family of God as one lives out his/her Christian commitment so he or she can be Christ's disciple as he/she willingly "denies himself or herself, takes up the cross, and follows Christ unreservedly" (Lk 9:23).

Regularly Associating with God's People

Understanding that "scripture is not of any man's private interpretation" (1 Pet 1:21-22), I regularly attended Sunday public worship, weekly Bible studies, and Bible seminars so I could be taught, by godly instructors, the things of Christ in a systematic way.

Coming together regularly proved to be very beneficial for me in a number of ways. First, it gave me a solid grounding in the basic teachings of scripture (Heb 6). With this, it also empowered me to move on to a deeper understanding of biblical precepts such as the gifts of the Spirit, the high priestly ministry of all believers, and the second coming of Christ, to name a few. Second, it provided me correction and reproof from the brethren when this was needed. Third, it formatted my thinking so I could provide a reasonable, rational, logical, and loving answer to all men for the hope that lies within me (1 Pet 3:15). And fourth, it provided me with boundaries so I could prudently, and intelligently discriminate between biblical truth (Jn 17:17), and worldly vain, empty and futile philosophy (Col 2:8-10).

Because of this training, I received two benefits. First, I became equipped to enjoy times of "table talk" about the things of God with fellow believers during home or restaurant coffee fellowships. And second, I became empowered provide a defense for the teachings of scripture to the unsaved I met from time to time.

I am appreciative and thankful to God for the fellow believers He allowed me to meet throughout the years. Through their instruction, counsel, and encouragement I have been equipped to "rightly divide the word of truth" (2 Tim 2:15), and admonished not to neglect my "call to evangelism" which was "imparted to me by the Holy Spirit, and by the laying on of hands of the presbytery" (1 Tim 4:14), in Canada and abroad.

Although I have been a Christian for over sixty years, and have received extensive academic training, I know I have not attained or apprehended all the things of Christ. Understanding this, "I hold lightly the accomplishments, and reach forth unto those things which are before, as I press toward the mark for the prize of the high calling of God in Christ Jesus" (Phil 3:12-14) so I will be protected from being "carried away with strange and divers doctrines which have not profited others who have been preoccupied with them" (Heb 13:9). May God be richly blessed for each of these factors that influenced my life to mold me in what He planned me to be while I was created in the secret place of my mother's womb (Ps 139:14). All glory, and praise, and honour goes to His name, for without His intervention in my life, I would be nothing.

Chapter 2

Abortion: A Woman's Right?

I'm a rather conservative person, who is willing to go "with the flow" rather than exasperating a situation by strongly, and openly opposing it.[1] There are, however, one or two social issues which agitate me, and against which I will protest vigorously regardless of the cost. One of these is abortion.

Definition of Abortion

Abortion may be defined "as the termination of a pregnancy by any spontaneous or induced method.[2] Miscarriage is most commonly recognized as the only "non-induced" abortion.

Types of Abortions

Medically, there are six types of "induced abortions." First, the "morning after pill" which, when taken, inhibits the fetus from attaching itself to the uterus, thus dying.[3] Second, vacuum suction technique, whereby the fetus is dismembered and sucked out of the uterus. Third, the saline infusion procedure, whereby a saline solution, 'protogleden', is injected through the abdomen into the amniotic fluid cavity within the uterus, causing the fetus to be expelled within twelve hours after the injection.[4] Fourth, partial birth abortion where the fetus is aborted just before full birth. Fifth, the live birth abortion whereby labour is induced and the baby it is left to die.[5] And sixth, therapeutic abortion, whereby the pregnancy is ended because of maternal medical complications by doing a dilatation curettage,[6] or scraping of the uterine cavity which removes the fetus from the womb.

Besides the aforementioned types of abortion, there also exists "back alley abortions." These usually are performed by untrained and unskilled individuals who employ unsafe methods to induce labour and terminate the pregnancy. Since 1980 "back alley abortions" have reduced considerably because of the availability of abortions being performed in hospitals and funded through Canada's Medicare. Regardless which method of abortion is used, the primary purpose is to destroy the fetus, terminating the pregnancy.

The History of Abortion in Canada

Before 1960 abortions, in Canada, were forbidden under the threat of imprisonment. However, in 1960 Pierre Trudeau, Canada's then Justice Minister, liberalized Canada's position on this issue by allowing women to apply for special permission for an abortion, "from a Therapeutic Abortion Committee of three doctors at a hospital, who would judge whether her health or life was in danger."[7] Permission to get a therapeutic abortion could be granted if "the abortion were performed by a qualified medical practitioner in an accredited hospital, after approval by a majority of that hospital's therapeutic abortion committee which must certify that continuation of the pregnancy would probably endanger the life and health of the mother."[8]

Through this legislation, opportunity for obtaining an abortion was increased. Doctors, however, if they could not justify the abortion for medical reasons, could still be imprisoned. Therefore, most Therapeutic Abortion Committees refused to accept applications for abortions.

In 1967 Dr. Henry Morgentaler, a family physician from Quebec, lobbied the federal government for further changes in the 1960 abortion law. His reason: women have a basic right to an abortion, and the decision in this matter should be left to the individual's conscience. In his letter to Pope John Paul II in March of 1966 he writes:

> Like the assassination of Prime Minister Rabine, violence against medical workers who perform abortions implicates the violent language in which some religious leaders condemn them. You speak of abortions 'as murder, crimes which no human law can claim to legitimize, careless destroying . . . the killing of an innocent and defenseless human being, etc.' Continuous exhortations in such terms inevitably incite unbalanced and impressionable minds. Spurred on by religious leaders, among whom you are the foremost, these people direct their hatred and violence against people like me who not only provide abortion services to women, but also believe abortion to be a woman's right. I would like to point out to you that many people, including liberal-minded Catholic theologians and other Christians, believe that abortion is a difficult moral dilemma and the decision whether to abort should be left to the individual conscience. When such a decision has been made, it should be, in my opinion, the duty of the state to honour it and the duty of the medical profession to provide it under the best conditions to ensure safety and dignity for women.[9]

Morgentaler expected the Federal Government, once again, to immediately enact changes in the Canadian Criminal Code, and remove abortion as a criminal offense. When the government did not promptly comply with Morgentaler's demands, in 1970 he opened his first abortion clinic in Montreal. Within the first year of operation he performed over eleven thousand unlawful abortions.

Morgentaler was arrested and charged under the Criminal Code of Canada, Section 251. But before he could be brought to trial, Pierre Trudeau was reelected as Prime Minister. Within a year of his reelection Parliament enacted changes to Section 251 whereby homosexuality and abortions were no longer regarded as criminal offenses.

In Quebec, however, abortion remained a crime. When, in 1974 Morgentaler brought TV cameras into the abortion clinic and televised abortions, he was arrested one more time. However after being arrested and found guilty by the lower Quebec Court, he appealed his conviction to the Supreme Court of Canada. At that trial he was found guilty and sent to a minimum security nursing home for a short incarceration.[10]

Public sympathy towards Morgentaler and his cause increased after each arrest and trial. Within a short time thousands of women, who believed abortion is a personal choice and a personal right, marched on Parliament Hill lobbying Trudeau to extend the right of abortion to women "no strings attached."[11] By 1975 the Supreme Courts of Quebec and Canada jointly had given up trying Morgentaler on charges that had been laid. During the period of 1980-1989 Morgentaler opened three abortion clinics and performed over 350,000 abortions, with no criminal charges being laid against him from the Federal Government.

In 1988 Pierre Trudeau resigned as Prime Minister. Much to his discredit no legislation had been introduced or enacted about the legality of abortion in Canada. In 1991 Canada's Justice System, by not upholding and enforcing the law of 1969, opened the door to freelance abortion. That, which was regarded earlier as a criminal offence, is now considered to be legal and right. Today, Canada has no legislation forbidding abortion. Therefore, hundreds of thousands of abortions are done yearly in hospitals and abortion clinics.

The Case for Abortion

Supporting or opposing abortions is a dilemma which has become complex and controversial in light of recent relaxed legislation and ethics in Canada. There are two militant "schools of thought" about abortion, these being Pro-choice and Pro-life. A woman's decision to have or to bypass an abortion rests on two major issues, these being a woman's rights as carrier of the fetus, and the ontology of the fetus.

Proponents of 'pro-choice' may agree with the 'pro-life' movement God is the creator and sustainer of life. But, they do not agree that every occasion for reproducing life is of God. Therefore they strongly contend that in circumstances such as rape and unplanned or unwanted pregnancies, women should not be "saddled" with the obligation of bringing the pregnancy to completion. Rather, they should have the recourse of terminating the pregnancy by having an abortion should it be their desire. With this, proponents of pro-choice also argue that in situations where there are large families and an additional child might be a psychological or financial burden to the family, abortion is the most reasonable and compassionate alternative available.

And then they ask, "What about women living in the slums, who suffer from acute mental illness, social deprivation or who lack education. Because of these conditions they may not adequately protect themselves from getting pregnant. "Is it right, fair, or godly," they strongly argue, to force them to "carry the pregnancy to completion?" And then they continue to ask, "Would any compassionate human demand that these incapacitated women have another child when they are already strained beyond capacity to look after themselves?" The obvious answer is, "no." Charles Hartshorne comments:

> I share something of the disgust of hard-core opponents of abortion that contraceptives, combined with the availability of abortion, may deprive sexual intercourse of spiritual meaning. For me the sacramental view of marriage has always had appeal, and my life has been lived accordingly. Abortion is indeed a nasty thing, but unfortunately there are, in our society many even nastier things, like some children are growing up unwanted. This, for my conscience, is a great deal nastier, and truly horrible. An overcrowded world is also nasty, and could in a few decades become truly catastrophic.[12]

So now the argument is based on pragmatics instead of the value of life. What will work best for protecting the woman from an unwanted child, and the uncontrolled circumstances of life? In its simplest form abortion has become a form of contraception by which not the unneeded, but the unwanted are mercilessly, yet conveniently disposed of. As a rebuttal to Hartshorne's position Francis Schaeffer writes:

> At first we hear much talk of compassion for the unwanted. The discussion moves on to "rights," then to "my rights," and soon to pure "economics." The discussion of life must be

brought back to where it belongs, - not emotional extreme examples, not to expedience, and certainly not to economics. This matter should be discussed in terms of right and wrong."[13]

What is mysterious about the occurrence of abortions is most requests for abortions do not come from women with oversized families, or from those suffering from socioeconomic privation. Rather, they come from middle class professionals who feel that a pregnancy may be an infringement on their freedom, and future career development. Such being the case, abortion is the most feasible alternative.[14]

The Case against Abortion

In response to these concerns, pro-life proponents respond with the following claims:

First, several forms of contraceptive pills and devices are available free to women of all socioeconomic levels, and should be used regularly by women who are not ready, or willing to carry a pregnancy to completion. There is an a-priori responsibility on those who are sexually active to safeguard themselves against pregnancies. If no protection is used, the suggestion that a woman should carry the pregnancy to completion, instead of aborting it, stands as being reasonable.

Second, bringing a child into an unhealthy economic situation may "be nasty," but is there anything nastier than a woman, willfully, knowingly, and purposely dispensing with a life for convenience and self-gain? No, for in so doing, this degrades her to being barbarous, or elevates her to being God as she assumes what will or will not be on the morrow. Both, the author feels, are dangerous conjectures by which one might live.

Third, pregnancies, wanted or unwanted, "planned or unplanned," are a temporary situation in a woman's life. The choice to allow the pregnancy to complete is a choice with lifelong effects, and responsibilities that should not be taken lightly, but so is the decision to abort.

Although aborting the fetus may bring instant and gratifying relief to the carrier, it can also ignite "post-abortion syndrome"[15] which can be manifested by feelings of guilt, shame, despair, and mistrust.[16] With this, abortions may create physical complications such as breast, cervix, ovarian and liver cancer. Elizabeth Liston comments:

> I have met the 'super confident, cool, everything's under `control' type, the 'hard, blank faced, leave me alone' type, the 'quiet, retiring, timid, that's just my lot in life' type, as well as the "blasé, couldn't care less'' type. Appearances differ, but I have found that many are experiencing or have experienced suffering, pain, bitterness, anger and unresolved grief following an abortion.[17]

Fourth, although rape is ugly, terrifying, and demoralizing, conception in rape still is a gift of God. As born-again disciples of Christ, we believe all life is a gift from God, "who is the Creator, and Sustainer of all things" (Col 1:16). The shameful condition in which the pregnancy might have occurred does not necessarily degrade the mother or the fetus's worth. Dignity can be regained by the mother if she becomes surrounded by a community of loving people who will compassionately care for her during, and after the pregnancy.

Even as drugs, smoking, and emotional stress can cause the mother and fetus distress during a pregnancy,[18] a caring and loving community can influence them to good health. Women, turning to abortion as a solution to psychological apprehension, because of trauma during pregnancy, need to avail themselves of helpful, clinical and remedial care so they will not make an abrupt, and irrational decision by destroying the fetus in the womb.

Fifth, regardless what the woman's opinion is of her pregnancy, more than just her welfare needs to be considered when she is contemplating whether to have an abortion or carry the pregnancy to completion. According to pro-life proponents, she is unjust in her decision if she does not also consider the welfare of the fetus. If she is anxious and fretful about socioeconomic crisis that might befall her with the birth of the child, she could make provision for it to be adopted by a loving and caring family who will raise it with great love and dignity. By taking this alternative – instead of aborting the fetus - good for the woman and the fetus can be guaranteed.

The second matter of dispute between the pro-choice and the pro-life groups is the question whether the fetus possesses personhood. Both groups agree the fetus is a living entity composed of cells with a non-duplicable, gene pool, regardless of what it is called. Whereas 'pro-life' advocates are willing to regard the fetus as a human being with personhood because "they have both a human mother and father,"[19] 'pro-choice' supporters are not willing to go that far. They suggest the fetus is nothing more than a collection of genes in the becoming of personhood which will be fully realized after birth, when the collection of billions of cells is uniformly compacted into one whole identifiable human construct. Charles Hartshorne clarifies the point:

> The fertilized egg is an individual egg, but not an individual human being. For such a being is in its body a multicellular organism - a metazoan - to use the scientific Greek, and the egg is a single cell. The first thing the cell does is to begin to divide into many cells. For some weeks the fetus is not a single individual cell at all, but a colony of cells. During the first weeks there seems to be no grounds for about the fetus as an individual animal. Only in possible or probable destiny is it an individual. A possible individual is one thing; a person is another thing.[20]

In response to Hartshorne, the 'pro-life' group suggests personhood is exactly what he is describing because even after birth, the individual is nothing more than a "collection of cells" interlocked as one entity allowing the person to live with integrity, identity, meaning, value and purpose. Grobstein, an embryologist and Professor Emeritus at the University of California, San Diego, also denies personhood to the fetus. He writes:

> Extending full personhood to an individual cell that is barely visible makes no more sense than declaring acorns to be an oak tree and selling them as oak trees. At conception only genetic individuality, a set of hereditary properties that define an individual is present. But there are still five other essential aspects of individuality to come: developmental, functional, behavioral and social.[21]

Grobstein cannot see the fetus having personhood until it has fully developed and possesses total independence from the mother. Responding to Grobstein, the 'pro-life' group remarks that he is correct when he concludes the fetus is not an independent entity, but he is wrong to suggest it is person afterbirth because it has independence functionally, socially, and behaviorally. Jean Garton responds to Grobestein stating:

> The unborn child, of course, is not the same as the child sleeping in the crib or playing in the sandbox. Yet, if someone were to say he or she had at home an infant and an adolescent, we surely would not wonder if that person was referring to different kinds of pets or plants. Infant and adolescent are terms that describe human beings at different stages of development. That is all the word "fetus" does. It tells us where a child is on the life spectrum. Is the adolescent less human than an adult? Is the infant less human than the adolescent? Is the fetus less human than the infant? They are different only in terms of development and dependence.[22]

All infant children remain dependent on their mother for some time afterbirth; they are fed, dressed, bathed, carried, and nursed sometimes up to the age of two. And, occasionally, individuals at age twenty-five, because of illness or mental disabilities, are still dependent on their parents or others; Grobstein would need to deny these, even as he does the fetus, personhood.

In response to Grobstein's suggestion that the fetus is only a representation of what is becoming, and therefore cannot be granted personhood, pro-life groups respond that he has missed the point. Before his thesis was published, it was an idea "barely visible", yet he considered it of value, otherwise he would never have published it. Likewise, with the fetus, even though it does not have visible and measurable value, it has worth - worth we call personhood. Professor Judith Thompson agrees with the pro-life movement the fetus is a human being with personhood, and possesses an inalienable right to life. But according to her, "this does not mean that a woman must be forced to use her bodily organs to sustain its life."[23]

The welfare of the fetus, despite the mother's hesitancy to carry it to maturity, remains the right to be born, the right to be known, the right to know life and develop into the person it is intended by God to be. Even the unwanted fetus can be nurtured to birth, and given opportunity to develop as a valued part of humanity as time and opportunity is afforded it.

Three replies the aforementioned claim are provided:

First, her suggestion the value of a fetus as human life decreases when interdependence is added to the equation is laughable. Every day in every way individuals, afterbirth, are interdependent for survival, but we do not kill them because of it. Why, then, would killing the fetus be acceptable?

Second, her suggestion the woman is forever tied to the fetus to preserve its life is inaccurate. Pregnancies usually last for nine months after conception. After discharge from the mother's womb, the fetus no longer needs a woman's internal organs for existence. She may be responsible for caring and nurturing the newborn child, but this "infringement" on her organs will end until she – willingly or accidently – becomes pregnant again.

Third, her suggestion the woman "must be forced to use her bodily organs to continue life" is simplistic and crude in that it overlooks the obvious implication of every pregnancy. The fetus, by design, must use the woman's body to continue its life; there's no other way for the fetus to develop.

The problem with Thompson's suggestion the fetus should be aborted is twofold. First, it is subjective; that is, every woman must decide in and of herself whether the fetus is parasitic. Second, it places punitive blame on the fetus for doing what it was created to do.

Abortion from a Biblical Perspective

Although there is no single ecumenical view of abortion[24] available presently, and no biblical directive about this matter, there are biblical guidelines which "drive" Christians to frame strong objections against abortion.

From a Christian viewpoint it is concluded that human life is God ordained and created (Gen 1:27). With this, Christians further assert the fetus is more than "just a lump of jelly or a blob of tissue, or a growth in the mother's womb which may, therefore, be extracted and destroyed like teeth, tumors or tonsils."[25]

Further it is suggested that every fetus, immediately after conception is a person with a body, spirit, and soul that is created in God's image with an temporal and an eternal destiny which is known to God (Genesis 2:7 Ecclesiastes 11:5; Psalm 139:11-16).·Life, because of this, is sacred and any human being, well or sick, desired or undesired, must not be disposed of like one might do with a cow or hog, fit for the slaughter.

God's injunction to Adam and Eve immediately after they were created was to "go forth and multiply and replenish the earth," (Gen 2:27-28). This He commanded as a witness that human life is a "heritage of the Lord and the fruit of the womb is His reward," (Ps 127:3), given creation as a gift of Divine blessing for the continued procreation of humanity. Hannah recognized Samuel as a gift from God (1 Sam 1:7), and in worship offered him to serve the Lord continually.

Christ specifically displayed God's love and care for children by taking them on His knee and blessing them (Mark 10:14), even though the disciples were frustrated with their presence. Nowhere throughout scripture do we find any command that life should be destroyed, except as a direct judgement of God for a nation's collective sin, and this judgement comes directly from God.

The Ten Commandments are clear about the value of life! The sixth commandments states, "Thou shalt not kill" (Ex 20:13), or you shall not take life without just cause for it is the Lord, God, who is gives and takes life (Job 1:21). Anyone, therefore, who promotes abortion, could be equating himself or herself with God. If this is not happening, he or she could be suggesting he or she has privileged insight about God's will for the not yet born fetus. This is a dangerous position to be in, for the power of life-and-death belongs only to God!

Conclusion

Any form of abortion, therefore, is deplored by Christians and the Church of Jesus Christ. This undebatable, and unshakable position is held because not only does it destroy life, it also robs society of future gifts that may be resident in those that may be indiscriminately destroyed for convenience, or for other self-serving reasons. Who knows, whether the next aborted fetus might be the research scientist who will find the cure for cancer, the next Beethoven who composes a great symphony, or a great evangelist under whose ministry hundreds of thousands of people may be brought to salvation through Christ?

The distasteful and shameful factor about abortion is the value of life and the reasons for destroying it have no connection one with the other. No woman, in her right mind, would ever think of killing her son or daughter. This, to her, would be murder! But, when it comes to the matter of aborting the fetus, many women have no reservations about the matter, for this to them is liberty! This cold, callous, and careless attitude by "pro-choice" women may facilitate a women's desire to be freed from carrying the fetus to completion, but it will never release her from the possibility of guilt and shame about of how she dealt with a life she was gifted to carry. Because of this, abortion can never be tolerated by those who believe life, as a fetus or as a fully developed human, must never be destroyed to accommodate one's probable, immediate and self-centered needs![26]

Chapter 3

Sally's Quandary

"Is There an Alternative to Abortion
and
Can This Be Soundly Demonstrated?"

Introduction

Sally[1] was a twenty-three year old secretary living in Toronto, with a dream to become the secretary to the Chief Executive Officer of Grandall Motors - a luxury car exchange depot - in Flatmouth, Ontario. To fulfill this dream, she enrolled in Toronto's most prominent business school.

Three months after starting the program, Sally started a casual friendship with the president of the college, thinking he might have "connections" that would help her secure the position at Grendall Motors. What was intended to be nothing more than a casual meeting over coffee, within a very short time, became a regular convergence.

Emotionally Sally was becoming attracted to the president. He was a caring, kind, and affectionate character who, she felt, had only her best interests at heart. Unexpectedly, during one of the meetings, she willingly had unprotected sex with him. Much to her dismay, shock, and horror, three months later she discovered she was pregnant.

At the next "get-together" she confronted her paramour with the situation. On hearing about her plight he responded, "I'm married, I have three children, and you just can't have that child. You will have to get an abortion!"

"But just get an abortion" was not the answer Sally expected or needed. She was a born-again Christian who strongly believed abortions were wrong. But she also feared exposing the president's untoward involvement with a student. If he were to be "found out," his marriage and his career, most likely, would be finished. Sally was now in a quandary what she should do. After a couple days of considering her alternatives, she decided to visit a Christian clinical psychologist in Missassauga to gain advice what her best recourse of action might be; should she have an abortion, or should she carry the fetus to completion?

Questions and Challenges

Sally comes to her crisis with several questions to which she desperately needs answers so she might make the right, and honourable decision for her and the fetus..

She questions "how God could have allowed this to happen to her." It is difficult for her to understand how she, as a longtime Christian and a prominent member in the church, with a devoted love for her Lord, could be allowed by God to get into this predicament. God should never have let this happen - there's absolutely no acceptable reason for her dilemma!

Closely associated with this question is, "Why is God punishing her?" Sally accepts she is pregnant. Recent pregnancy tests have corroborated it! Now, in her state of anxiety, fear, frustration, and increasing shame, Sally is beginning to believe God might be punishing her for some earlier, hidden sin she has not confessed.

Sally confronts her pregnancy questioning the teachings of scripture about abortion. She wants to know whether scripture directly teaches against abortion, or whether this is something the Church has inferred from scripture over the years. "The answer to this question," Sally states, "will have a great impact on her decision for, or against having an abortion."

Public opinion is highly important to Sally at present. She questions how her family, friends, and members of her church will treat her because of her pregnancy, and her decision for or against having an abortion. Sally does not want to be an offense, or a stumbling block to anyone in the church. But now her primary concern is about having a strong support base, regardless what her decision might be.

Sally – based on many articles she has read - questions whether the fetus is a human being with personality and worth. She has been taught, through the church, that from the moment of conception the fetus has immeasurable worth to God because it is part of his creative power. But, she has received, through secular institutions, information that suggests the fetus is nothing more than a "blob of flesh" with no value until it is born. Which of these views is true, and how can she be certain she will know how to make the right choice with all the "voices" begging for her attention? Of all the questions confronting Sally, she is haunted by the question, "If I have an abortion, will God condemn me to hell for what I've done?"

But Sally has one more perplexing question to which she is desperately searching for an answer, without immediate resolve. She wants to know why the president is seemingly getting off so lightly, when he was involved in getting her pregnant. And then she questions whether she should reveal the truth about his involvement, and put him at risk of losing everything, or if she should handle the decision on her own. "After all," she says, "this baby is his as much as it is hers."

Sally is open to carrying the fetus to completion if many of her questions are answered to her satisfaction. But one further question remains for her, that being, what choices are open to her if she carries the fetus to birth.

Challenges

A few pressing challenges about abortion have been presented to Sally since she discovered she is pregnant by her pro-choice associates in the workplace.

Few, if any, within society, confront the male involved with the pregnancy about what his responsibility towards "caring" for the fetus and its destiny. Everyone, on the other hand, attacks the woman as being the negligent participant. But, if the man has freedom of choice, so shouldn't the woman. It's her body, and she has a privileged right to decide for herself whether she shall be a mother of the unwanted child. The decision she makes will affect every part of her life. Because of the "rights she holds," the directive for action will be determined as she holds consultation with her doctor to determine what's best for her and the fetus. Pro-choice exponents contend that forcing a woman to have an unwanted child is punishment for enjoying sex. Since the sexual act has hurt no one – considering that the fetus is not a human being – no one has the right to punish the participants. Enslaving a woman to carry an unwanted fetus by placing taxing and unethical demands on her is the cruelest of punishments, especially when the child could be aborted.

Pro-choice advocates might be convinced that their moral standards are suitable guidelines for their choices. But they must remember different people have different ethical foundations for life, and these people should not be coerced into accepting religious morals by religious benevolent despots, who think they have the 'right answer' about abortion.

Pro-choice proponents contend that pro-life advocates are not willing to cover the expenses entailed in raising all the children that would be born if abortions were prohibited. Because of this irresponsible and uncaring attitude, pro-live advocates should have nothing to say about fetus that are aborted. When they are willing to financially commit themselves to adequately caring for children alive today, then they should speak up. Otherwise, they should say nothing.

Pro-choice advocates see a contradiction in the value of life that pro-life advocates have. They suggest that pro-life followers say little about the thousands of children who die yearly because of mass starvation, war, disease, and murder, but "scream to high heaven" whenever an abortion takes place.

Pro-choice advocates suggest antiabortion groups are often irrational which is demonstrated by their militant action that has put the lives of doctors and their associates in great danger. To the pro-choice, there is a distinct contradiction of values - killing the abortion provider to save the life of the fetus does not reflect rational behavior.

Antiabortionists, say the pro-abortionists, cannot agree on when life begins. Some say it begins at conception,[1] some say it begins after twenty days when the spinal cord fully develops, and some say it begins when the child breathes independently of the mother.[2] Besides, some religions condone abortion in the first trimester,[3] while others forbid it.[4] Muslims recognize and protect a fetus in the womb as a human life,[5] but the Qur'an does not give any detailed explanation about the religion's openness to aborting the fetus, although it does state, "Kill not your offspring for fear of poverty; it is We who provide for them and for you. Surely, killing them is a great sin."[6]

Interaction with Society

Within a week of discovering she was pregnant, Sally went to the local abortion clinic, and acquired pamphlets and booklets through which she could gain insight about having an abortion. She is familiar with the major arguments for abortion. She understands a woman should have full, unrestrained right to do with her body whatever she thinks is best. When faced with an unwanted pregnancy, only she can choose whether she should carry the fetus to term. Governments, churches, friends, and family have a right to suggest what she should do, but in the end, it remains her sole decision.

She has also been told the fetus, in its first trimester, has no real value as a human being, and it cannot be regarded as having personhood because it is only in the developmental stage. Ending the "life of the fetus" at this stage, would be no different from killing a snail. With this, she has also been warned that keeping the child would be nothing more than yielding to undue pressure of family, friends, and the church. Her decision for or against the abortion needs to come from herself as she rationally assesses the obligations she will face because of her decision to carry the fetus to birth. Regardless of the path she takes, it must be affordable for her present and future welfare.

Sally has been "charged with fear" of not fulfilling her career goals should she "carry" the pregnancy to completion. In this twenty-first century "consumer" oriented world, Sally has been conditioned she has to lay a solid foundation for success first, and then think about marriage and family. If the pregnancy is going to inhibit her from attaining her career, it should be terminated. She could always "try again" when circumstances look better for her.

The most significant message Sally gets from society is she must not allow herself to be obligated as a slave to her reproductive organs. No one can legitimately expect her to nurture, for a whole lifetime, an unwanted child. She made a grievous mistake. But there are ways of solving it, that being having an abortion.

Interaction with the Church

Sally is a born-again Christian who is intensely devoted to Christ. She has attended church since she was a teenager. She has taken catechism, and she has been accepted as a full member of her church. Throughout the years she has heard messages on the sanctity of life from conception, and of life being a gift from God which needs to be honoured and protected from conception until natural death (Psalm 139:14).

Sally understands that most Protestant and all Catholic Churches forbid abortion regardless of the circumstances because "fetus is a full human being, with a right-to-life, from the moment of conception."[7] She is also aware that, should she have an abortion, her local church may discipline her severely, up to and including disfellowshipping her from the congregation.

Sally honestly wants to honour God by doing what is godly, honourable and right, but being pregnant out of wedlock, has thrown her into a "tailspin" over which she has no control. She would like to talk to her pastor about the issue, but she is too afraid and embarrassed.

Sympathetic Acquaintance with Others

One of Sally's close church friends got pregnant, and was planning to have an abortion. After viewing a documentary on abortions, the friend, in spite of the many difficulties faced, carried the pregnancy to term, and adopted the child out. Her friend told her she felt better enduring the physical pain and social embarrassment for a short time, and then adopting the child out, rather than having an abortion and feeling guilt for a lifetime. As far as she was concerned, it was a better choice to let a caring couple enjoy the child, than to destroy it for some fleeting, selfish, and frightening reasons.

A couple weeks after discussing the issue with her friend, Sally, at work, met two young women who had abortions. Both mentioned to Sally that they are bothered whenever they see young women of their age playing with, and enjoying their newborn babies. "There is something mysteriously wonderful to see the human likeness of the mother revealed in that bundle of flesh," is often their comment. This overriding sense of sorrow, for not having carried the fetus to birth, is very bothersome to Sally. Hopefully this will compel her to seriously entertain second thoughts about having an abortion.

Underlying Concerns - Hopes and Fears

Sally, despite the great number of fears she holds, hopes she will be able to find godly, professional counsel from her pastor and doctor to help her make the right decision at this critical time. She wants to carry the fetus to term, and be the kind, caring and loving mother she has always dreamt of being if the circumstances were different.

With having these hopes, Sally possesses several fears. She fears carrying the fetus to term without having adequate support from the father, she fears she will not have enough financial resources with which to care for herself and the child, and she fears being condemned as a "second-rate" Christian by her friends. Sally is concerned about developing future relationships with other men later in life. Her concern is other men – like the president – may not carry through with their parental responsibilities, and she will not be able to build a much-needed trust with them. Sally also fears if she has the abortion, she might subtly be supporting advocates of other life terminating venues such as euthanasia, and doctor assisted suicide. Others, she thinks, might befittingly suggest since she attached little dignity and value to the fetus as a human being, she may also consider the elderly, the mentally challenged, the crippled and the terminally ill in the same manner, and also advocate the termination of their life.

Clarification of Issues

Throughout Sally's conversation with her counsellor she has made it clear that although she does not believe in having abortions, she is considering it as a viable option. But, she is still open to discussions about bringing the pregnancy to completion, if she can be persuaded she will not be abandoned by her family, friends, and the church. Sally has expressed her sincere desire to do the right, honourable, and godly thing, but she desperately needs guidance at the moment.

The main issues for clarification for her include understanding the term "abortion," the possibility of "potential life," and the personal responsibility for one's act. Once these three factors are clearly delineated, the pros and cons for abortion can be more intelligently assayed.

Noting she is at the point of decision about having an abortion, the counsellor skillfully, yet clearly, clarifies the issues by defining abortion as "The planned and willful destruction or termination of a pregnancy by any spontaneous or induced method.[8] Realistically, although cruel in its intent, the prime purpose of any abortion is to "end development the fetus" and free the "carrier" from responsively bringing it to birth.

Having clarified this point, she continues to define, "potential life" as the plausibility of the fetus to live on its own after birth. However, potential life is conditional on developed, sustainable life being present as the life line to the fetus, so it's independent, potential may be realized. Potential life starts at conception; whether the fetus is fully human with personhood is not the question; the matter to be considered is whether the fetus has life.

The matter of Sally's responsibility in the pregnancy needs to be clarified. She needs to take full responsibility for her actions. She willingly, and knowingly entered into an unprotected sexual relationship with the president with the "extended hope" that by doing so she might obtain the position of Executive Secretary. Although one may want to empathize, and sympathize with her in her plight, she cannot escape her responsibility for being entangled in the "web" of her pregnancy. Aborting the fetus may, at the moment, rid Sally of the haunting fears of carrying the child to term, but it will never free her from the responsibility of conceiving the child. William Werpehowski comments:

> Autonomous choosers may take life or discontinue, or refuse to provide assistance to the other in the case of grave and proportionate threat to the person's well-being (self-defense) and the autonomous need not as a matter of duty provide burdensome assistance requiring the use of one's body, even if that assistance is necessary for life itself, but no one can be autonomous to the point where he or she can claim that she has no participation in 'seeding the life' that needs burdensome care.[9]

Sally, once the relationship moved beyond friendly encounters, should have used contraceptives to protect herself from getting pregnant which is a first-place responsibility on those who become sexually active. If no protection is used, the suggestion that one needs to carry the pregnancy to term stands as being reasonable. But, carrying the pregnancy to term has a second, major benefit. It provides a woman to fulfill her God given passion for motherhood which eventually adds pride, dignity, and value for her purpose in life that is not gained by any other means.

Admission of Guilt

Pro-life advocates have several wrongs for which they need to admit and apologize towards society. First, they need to apologize for scathingly attacking every woman who has had an abortion as being a 'murderer'. Often the evidence has not been fully known. Occasionally, for example, women have had an abortion because the mother's health would be severely risked if the fetus was carried to completion. Also, in cases of rape and incest, an abortion is often necessitated because of the intense risk of genetic imbalance in the fetus, which may cause the child to be physically deformed or mentally deranged at birth.

An apology also should be made for the arrogant "Hitlerian" control pro-life advocates have attempted to place on women. Women do not have absolute, independent control over their body, but they have the 'right' to decide how they will treat it. If women choose to abort the fetus, it's their choice. But, with this choice comes the responsibility to handle the results of that decision without expecting remedial intervention to relieve guilt, shame or any other trouble.

Pro-life organizations must apologize for the militant action it has taken, on many occasions, that has led to the threatening, the injury, and the killing of abortion providers. Regardless how wrong an abortion might be to pro-life advocates, no one has the privileged position of endangering another's life in a vindictive and punitive manner as this. If pro-life advocates want to get their message across, they should turn to the arena of public opinion and the courts. If their convictions are not accepted immediately, they may need to accept that, for the time, nothing can be done to change the pro-choice attitude by society.

The Christian Church needs to apologize to society for not showing a caring, loving, and accepting attitude towards those that have chosen abortion as the best alternative. Its first choice must never be condemnation. Rather, it should offer, as its primary focus, redemptive hope for everyone, regardless of the sin. In so doing, Christ's church will reduce the possibility of alienating many who need godly help and counsel in similar distressful choices. Although the Christian community places a high value on the potential of life within the womb, it must also retain its respect for the life of the woman who has had an abortion. Despite her uncomely action, she still possesses the full dignity of God in whose image she was made. Anything less than this by the God's people could be regarded as bigotry by the church by the ungodly.

Defense against Abortion

In response to the suggestions pro-choice advocates make about the value of abortion, pro-lifers offer the following response to Sally.

Sally is concerned about bringing a child into an unhealthy economic situation which may be cumbersome for her. Bringing a child into a harsh, economic situation is "nasty," but is there anything that could be nastier than a woman willfully, knowingly, and purposefully dispensing with a life for convenience and self-gain? The author suggests there isn't, for by choosing to abort the fetus, she may degrade herself to being barbarous. Francis Schaeffer writes:

> At first we hear much talk of compassion for the unwanted. The discussion moves on to 'rights', then to 'my rights' and then to pure 'economics'. The discussion must be brought

> back to where it belongs - no emotional extreme examples, not to expedience, and certainly not to economics - this matter should be discussed in terms of right versus wrong.[10]

Sally is concerned about her future economic status, instead of soberly and rationally considering her present welfare. In so doing, she might be elevating herself to being God by inferring what will or will not be on the morrow. To ease her pain about her financial stability, she needs to remember that in Canada there are government child tax credits, family allowances, one year paid maternity leave benefits, and other social based programs,[11] to which she can appeal in time of need. Sally may have forgotten to give consideration to family, friends, and church members who regularly offer aid to others by providing financial support when one of their colleagues faces financial difficulties. As Sally seriously considers carrying the fetus to maturity, she needs to accept God's enduring promise, "I will never leave you or forsake you" (Heb 13:5), neither "will He withhold any good thing from her if she diligently seeks Him, and walks uprightly before Him" (Heb 11:16).

Sally is concerned about the shameful condition in which the pregnancy occurred, and about the possibility of bringing into the world a child that has no father for financial or moral support. But neither of these factors destroys the mother's or child's dignity. Sally needs to retain her dignity by surrounding herself with a community of loving people who will care, nurture, and sustain her, to the best of their ability, for her during, and after the pregnancy.

Sally has been told by the pro-choice advocates the fetus she is carrying is nothing more than a piece of matter with no personality or value. In light of this, they further suggest, having an abortion, during the first trimester, should not be of any concern to her. According to their view, the fetus is nothing more than a collection of genes "in the becoming" of personhood which will have value only when the collection of billions of cells is uniformly compacted into one whole identifiable human construct. Charles Hartshorne writes:

> The fertilized egg is an individual egg, but not an individual human being. For such a being is, in its body a multicellular organism, a metazoan, to use the scientific Greek, and the egg

> is a single cell. The first thing the cell does is to divide into many cells. For some weeks the fetus is not a single individual at all, but a colony of cells. During the first weeks there seems to be no grounds for regarding the fetus as anything more than an individual animal. Only in possible or probable destiny is it an individual. A possible individual is one thing; an actual person is another thing.[12]

In response to Hartshorne, the pro-life group says that he is describing personhood, because even after birth, the individual is nothing more than a "collection of cells," interlocked as one entity allowing the person to live with integrity, identity, meaning, value and purpose. Responding to Harstshorne and Grobstein[13] who both deny the personhood of the fetus, Jean Garton suggests that Hartshorne is wrong to conclude the fetus is only a person afterbirth because it has independence functionally, socially, and behaviourly. She writes:

> The unborn child, of course, is not the same as the child sleeping in the crib or playing in the sandbox. Yet, if someone were to say that he or she had at home an infant or an adolescent, we surely would not wonder if that person was referring to different kinds of pets or plants. Infants and adolescents are terms that describe human beings at different stages of development. That is all the word 'fetus' does. It tells us where a child is in the life spectrum. Is the adolescent less human than an adult? Is the infant less human than the adolescent? Is the fetus less human than the infant? They are different only in terms of development and dependence.[14]

But the question of personhood should not be the primary concern of Sally; her a-priori question should be whether the fetus is "life." If the fetus is human life, could aborting it be regarded as murder? From a Christian perspective all human life, regardless of the circumstance in which it was conceived, is God ordained and created and, at conception the fetus is more than "just a lump of jelly or a blob of tissue, or a growth in the mother's womb, which may, therefore, be extracted and destroyed like teeth, tumors, or tonsils.[15] Furthermore, from a Christian perspective, human life is created in the 'image of God' and has both a temporal and an eternal purpose which is fully known only to God (Psalm 139:11-16). Because of the significance human life has both to God and to society, it must not be disposed of callously and carelessly like one might do with a cow or hog which is fit for the slaughter.

The Church, for centuries, has taught life begins at conception and an abortion is an abomination. Tertullian, (ca 223) for example, writes:

> We acknowledge, therefore, that life begins with conception because we contend that the soul begins at conception. Life begins when the soul begins. For us [Christians], murder is once and for all forbidden; so even the child in the womb, while yet the mother's blood is still being draw on to form the human being, it is not lawful for us to destroy. To forbid birth is only quicker murder. He is a man, who is to be a man; the fruit is always present in the seed.[16]

John Calvin comments further about the atrocious activity of this thing called, abortion:

> The fetus, though enclosed in the womb of its mother, is already a human being and it is a monstrous crime to rob it of the life which it has not yet begun to enjoy. If it seems more horrible to kill a man in his own house than in a field, because a man's house is his most secure refuge, it ought surely to be deemed more atrocious to destroy a fetus in the womb before it has come to light. Man, (human procreation), is both the image of God and of our flesh. Whereas if we would not violate the image of God, we must hold the person of flesh sacred - if we would not divest ourselves of humanity, we must cherish our own flesh.[17]

From the preceding citations one may conclude that aborting the fetus has never been a matter of light concern for the Early Church, and it should never be a light matter for God-fearing believers today. An abortion may be the quickest and most accommodating means available by which Sally may rid herself of her pregnancy. But before she follows through with it, she should seriously consider the many physical and psychological problems that could be incurred afterwards. Dr. Ron Hiller[18] states, "Although aborting the fetus may bring instant and gratifying relief to the carrier, it can also ignite post-abortion syndrome which can be manifested by feelings of guilt, shame, despair and mistrust. With these post-abortion syndromes, abortions can create physical complications such as breast, cervix, ovarian and liver cancer."[19] With this, Elizabeth Liston adds the following observation for consideration.

> I have met the "super confident, cool, everything's under control type", the "hard faced, leave me alone type", the "quiet, timid, that's just my lot type", as well as the "blasé, couldn't care less type" who all appear to be handling abortion as if they have been unscathed by the event. Appearances differ, but I have found that many are experiencing, or have experienced suffering, pain, bitterness, anger, and unresolved grief following an abortion.[20]

Sally, whatever she does, needs to be aware her decision will not only affect her; it will also directly and permanently affect the fetus about its right to be born, its right to know and experience life, its right to be known in community, and its right to develop into the full person God intended it to be at the time of conception. She needs to consider her personal worth, her fulfilled dreams, and her hopes for the good life and consider the value of her "child" in light of these factors. An impulsive, irrational act of abortion to relieve one of an unwanted pregnancy may satisfy an immediate solution to the problem, but the long term consequences can never be fully known. Before a woman has an abortion, serious professional and godly counsel needs to be sought. Although this may be a tremendously difficult step for her, it may be the best, and most godly move she might make as she ponders her next important move in the crisis.

Action

Sally's life appears to be "falling apart at the seams." She appears depressed, and supposes the only "door open" for her is to have an abortion, even though this is contrary to the teachings of the church and her conscience. Sally, however, does not need to remain in this state of confusion. There are several alternative actions she can consider and implement instead of having an abortion.

First, Sally needs to enroll in prenatal classes as soon as possible. By doing this, she will learn valuable parenting skills, and gain access to social resources that may help during her pregnancy. She might also consider reading books on the joys of childbearing and child rearing. She should also take time to visit young mothers who are enamoured with the children God has entrusted to them. Being involved with these people might motivate her to look beyond her present crisis, and see the bright future that children bring to parents.

Second, Sally could apply to live in a home for unwed mothers. Such a setting could provide her with physical and emotional support and counselling during the pregnancy, and up to three months after the child is born.[21] This community of peers will provide Sally with encouragement to carry on despite her difficulties, and will be of great value in providing her with professional contacts through which she will find medical, psychological, emotional and spiritual counsel when needed.

Third, Sally needs to stay in close community with her church. Although some in the fellowship might condemn her for her pregnancy, genuine, caring and loving Christians will give her loving and insightful support. Sally could associate with other women within the church who have gone through childbearing, and inquire if one would be willing to be her confidant during this time. She might also consult with elderly couples who have no grandchildren to see if they would be willing to become "adopted grandparents" to the expected child. She might be pleasantly surprised to discover how many elderly couples would be more than pleased to take on this role.

Fourth, Sally needs to consider adoption. Throughout Canada and the United States there are hundreds of couples who would be willing to sacrifice their time, and their finances to ensure Sally's child would be raised in a loving, caring and godly setting as they provide for it the amenities of life she thinks that she is unable to supply. Sally does not need to "dead end" her child's life by having an abortion. She, on the other hand, needs to bridge a future for it by entrusting the stewardship of its life to others if she cannot cope with doing it herself.

Fifth, Sally needs to consider consulting with her parents about becoming co-guardians of the child once it is born. Such an arrangement might mean Sally would have to move into the parent's home. During the day, while Sally worked, her mother would care for the child. During the evening, and during times when Sally is not working, Sally could care for the child. By this arrangement, both Sally and the child would have a strong family support base to "fall back on."[22] As Sally gains emotional strength, she might decide to move out on her own, but keep her mother as a care provider for the child as circumstances warrant it.

Sixth, Sally might want to consider the Canadian Government Supplemented Day Care Program which is provided across the country. Cost for this service to parents is based on one's monthly income. Through this program, approved clients pay a minimal amount daily for child care, while the government covers the remaining costs. In so doing, the government attempts to insure that no child, regardless of the parent's income, is abandoned to looking after children without adequate, funded child care provisions.

Sally does not need to have an abortion. She needs to consider the numerous positive and beneficial options available to her during the pregnancy and afterwards. If she commits herself to this, both she and the expected child will enjoy life as God intended it to be. Any other choice will bring immediate and long-term devastating outcomes her way. No one, not even her worst enemy, would wish these on her!

Chapter 4

***Child Abuse: An Act of Disgrace & Disdain Among Believers*!**

Of the many despicable and shameful crimes in Canada – and other parts of the world – child physical abuse may be regarded as the most repulsive. Statistics Canada recently reported that 12.1 % of Canadian children have suffered abuse at some point in their life.[1] Because of these statistics, child abuse, whether it be physical, sexual, emotional, or neglect should be of concern to all Canadians for, as well as causing immediate harm, it also causes latent immeasurable and irreversible consequences. Kim Oates comments:

> Child abuse, as well as being a family concern, may also be considered as a community influencing concern, influencing as it does the subsequent development of the next generation, and having important implications for the community. These implications include the cost to the community of treatment programs, the cost in terms of inadequate functioning of families where there has been a background of child abuse, and the problem this causes the next generation when adults

of child abuse are at risk for repeating this in their own children.[2]

Throughout this paper it is my intent to discuss child abuse, and to show, from a theological perspective, that child physical abuse cannot be overlooked or condoned by followers of Christ.

Definition of Physical Abuse

Although no common, fully agree definition of child abuse has been developed, several definitions, based on the nature of the act, its frequency, its severity, and its effect on the abused, have been postulated. The simplest definition of child physical abuse "is a terrible act that causes terrible hurt to an undeserving child for unsubstantiated reasons."[3] Human Resources, Canada Child Protection Branch defines child physical abuse as:

> Any intentional, non-accidental act, including hitting, biting, kicking shaking, or willful neglect of the necessities of life, whereby the child is traumatized or subjected to physical deformation as a result of the abuse.[4]

The New York State Act of 1979 states child physical abuse occurs when:

> Any parent, or other person legally responsible for the care of a child younger than eighteen years old, inflicts or allows to be inflicted on that child, hurt other than by accidental means. Child physical abuse may also be considered to have occurred where a care giver knows that another person is inflicting hurt on a child, but does nothing to intervene to stop that abuse.[5]

Regardless how one may define the act, it is reprehensible and cannot be tolerated by common sense, rational and caring people within society.

Child physical abuse is most often precipitated towards the abused because of anger of the caregiver in reaction to an unwelcome situation, or to a multiple of stressors that affect family relationships. The greater the number of stressors incurred at any one time, the greater likelihood child physical abuse will occur. Parents do not always premeditate the time, place, or circumstance for child physical abuse. Burgess and Conger, 1978, after studying child abuse concluded "parents do not plan to inflict hurt on their offspring, but it usually is reverted to as a last resort under situations of stress and cognitive factors such as limited child rearing knowledge, lower tolerance for common demands such as crying, and misattributions for misbehaving.[6]

Risk Family Settings for Child Physical Abuse

Perpetrators of child physical abuse are parents, stepparents, brothers or sisters, baby-sitters, friends or relatives of all socio-economic, ethnic and religious backgrounds. Because child physical abuse is most often done in secret towards vulnerable and helpless children who never expose the abuser under fear of further hurt, it is often difficult to discover who the perpetrator is. However, evidence suggests "most incidences of child physical abuse occur inside the family home at the hands of the victim's parents who use their power to cause unjust suffering to those around them."[7]

Families in which child abuse is known usually exhibit an insecure, transitory lifestyle that are disrupted often because of moves, fragmented relationships, unmanaged aggressive punitive control, lack of personal respect and tolerance one for the other, and threatened by uncontrolled, harmful risk causes. Although there are militating socio-economic pressures that may 'drive' parents to abusive practices, none of these release them from responsible parenting that protects their children from intentional, undeserved hurt. Remedial, helpful resources need to be made available to curb abuse that seems so ramped in many of today's families.

The mitigating reasons that influence parental child physical abuse are as diverse as the home settings in which the act occurs. Child abuse is prominent in families where "sets of dysfunctional relationship patterns, or lack of child coping skills are notable,"[8] because of problematic influences which are beyond the family's control. Families in which there is domestic violence, especially towards the wife, often are risk settings of child physical abuse. Wife batters usually are emotionally unstable, and thrive on control over others. Therefore, when their demands are not met, they inflict physical abuse on their wife, the closest and most non-intimidating member of the family. When, however, children also threaten their need for control by not fulfilling their demands, they react with negative behaviour towards them.

"Preliminary evidence shows children in violent homes are at increased risk for all maltreatments, including child physical abuse"[9] often, because families in which domestic violence occurs, there is a lack of family cohesion and adaptability to change, or because the abuser, himself, suffered extended abuse when he was a child. A history of child abuse may induce within the parent a lack of self-esteem, anger, and bitterness about experiences which may further instill a latent, "get even" hostility towards his wife and children. Lyle Larson comments:

> Abusive parents often have reported being abused as a child. Although abusing parents are always psychotic, they may show high rates of psychiatric and neurotic problems and of social behavioural deviancy. Many studies have found these parents to be narcissistic, immature, rigid, compulsive, lacking in empathy, and hostile, with low self-esteem, and with poor control over their impulses. Often such people know nothing more than to display physical abuse towards those that cannot or will not fulfill their expectations.[10]

Families which suffer from poverty and impoverished socio-economic conditions because of separation, divorce, unforeseen family illness, or the death of the income earning member of the family, are risk settings for child physical abuse. Families that relied on social welfare displayed a higher level of child maltreatment than families that did not. Where child abuse was reported, "once counselling was received, and a better economic foundation was established, there was a noticeable decrease in child abuse."[11]

Evidence indicates that under severe and irreversible financial economic pressures parents may become depressed and apprehensive about the family's future.[12] As this increases, the parent often turns to alcohol or drugs which disables him or her from rationally coping with the stress of child raising. In this state of mind, managed and suitable forms of discipline often turn into a venting of anger through inappropriate and hurtful physical abuse on the most vulnerable of the family, the children.

In families where the husband is unemployed, and left as the caregiver, there is a possibility of a "radical increase in the maltreatment of children left in his care"[13] as the husband is shamed and humiliated he cannot fulfill his role as the main income earner for the family. Lack of earning power threatens the unemployed father's 'control' over the home financially, and may decrease other controls he values. Therefore, when stressors such as child noncompliance with his demands occur, he reverts to abuse both of the spouse and of the children in his charge.

In family settings, where parents, because of early marriages, lack understanding of child development, or because of unstable mental health, place distorted expectations on child behaviour these become high risk settings for child abuse. Child behaviour that is expressed wrongly often is interpreted as a "child's refusal to comply with demands as an affront to authority with malice."[14] Parents then react unbecomingly to the child through acts of undeserved physical, emotional or psychological distress. When this occurs, children rarely understand the basis for maltreatment. Because of this, "the more brutal the punishment, the more children begin to feel self-blame for causing a problem, and believe they deserve the punishment received."[15] As this mind-set is accepted by children, reporting of the abuse to authorities rarely takes place. Some psychologists believe children don't report abuse as a protection from further, unwelcome abuse that would befall them. As reporting of the abuse goes unattended, punitive parents believe their punishment on the child was justified. The longer the abuse remains unreported, the more intense the maltreatment becomes.

Aboriginal families in Canada are high risk settings for child physical neglect and abuse. Many of these family units have been fractured and 'robbed' of parental guidance and educational opportunities because of church managed residential schools. Once these schools were closed, parents entrusted with child care were not adequately equipped with essential care skills. When their children reacted with untoward behaviour towards the parent, severe abuse often was inflicted on the child.

Other "etiological drives" that increase the probability of child maltreatment in Aboriginal homes include factors such as poverty, unemployment, substandard housing, and a lack of culturally based prevention services."[16] Child physical abuse increases in homes where there is an excessive use of alcohol and drugs, where there are single parents – usually a single mother – and a lack of interfamily support groups to aid abusive parents overcome the problem. Instead of being provided with wholesome, non-abusive parenting skills, most native household become stigmatized with child abuse being the regular, "run of the day" discipline for their children.

Young parents who suffer from mental health problems such as "substance abuse, a history of maltreatment, domestic violence, or extended life stressors, are highly susceptible to dish out excessive and continued child physical abuse."[17] Mental health may instill within a parent excessive, uncontrolled mood swings. This may cause the parent to become more irritable and less tolerant of disobedience or unwelcome behavior. The result, the parent responds to the child's conduct with more frequent and severe abuse.

Where alcohol and drugs are extensively used in a household, valuing children is often distorted. As this increases, withdrawal from interfamily activities, by which parent and children bonding is nurtured, becomes severely fractured. Children that should be loved and cared for, become intruders in the life of the abuser. This may cause children and parents to disassociate one from the other. As this happens, parental care often degenerates into parental dominance and control over children. In many situations this familial detachment leads to contempt of the child by parents, and breeds maltreatment towards them. Maureen Marcenko adds:

> Various findings suggest that it may be more helpful to thin of addiction as *interfering* with responsive and responsible parenting, rather than as rendering women incapable of good *parenting.* From this perspective, women who are addicted can be seen as having capacities for parenting similar to those of non-addictive women, particularly when they are compared with women whose life circumstances are shaped by poverty,

trauma, and oppression. As addiction progresses, however, these capacities are increasingly compromised or undermined. A major conceptual, methodological, and interventive challenge, however, is to disentangle women's capacities as parents from their behaviour while they are actively abusing drugs or alcohol.[18]

Recent research suggests abusive male parents use alcohol and drugs, before inflicting abuse on their children, "to diminish feelings of guilt, shame, or to assist in denial of their acts."[19] Until preoccupation with drugs as a necessary part of one's survival is sufficiently dealt with, regardless how intense a parent may love his or her children, there is a high likelihood that child abuse will remain a contiguous part of the family structure. Drugs, such as heroin, continue to inhibit the mother from displaying appreciative, loving and caring discipline towards her children.

Parents who have suffered from sexual perversion and abuse are known to afflict abuse on their offspring more than those who have not. Sadistic parents thrive on "taking control over their victim(s) by restraint, blindfolding, whipping, caging, spanking, raping, cutting, electric shocks, mutilation or killing."[20] They also find great pleasure in seeing their victims suffer, and may use inflicting pain on others to sedate their deep settled, latent anger about what they endured as a child. Sadists are addicted to their need for control. This prevailing preoccupation "to get revenge" often represses feelings of guilt that should be obvious in normal violent maltreatment situations. About the psyche of the sadistic parent, Lloyd DeMause adds the following:

> Sadists live their daily lives full of terrible anxieties about being independent and active. Any success in their lives is fearful, producing regression to infancy and a need to merge with mummy. But merging also means losing one's self – being annihilated. To avoid this, it is necessary to inflict on someone else all the traumas one has had, plus all the fantasies of revenge against the prosecuting parents. Only by reenacting cultic rituals can these deeply regressed individuals avoid

castration and engulfment fears and reassure themselves of their potency and separateness.[21]

The anguish of children maltreated by sadistic parents is indelibly imprinted on their minds. It has lasting, negative, and irreversible outcomes on family relationship. Often, victims of sadistic abuse rebut their attacker by killing them. They justify the murder as "the only right course of action" because no authority figure intervened to release them from the abusive situation they were encountering.

Families, with strong religious convictions, are regarded as "extremely high risk settings" for child abuse. Parents, in such homes, often have legitimatized physical child abuse on the premise "the immediate, strong handed and authoritative affliction of pain" will deter their progeny from straying off the path of righteousness. As a defense for their abusive conduct, these parents appealed to scripture which say, "Withhold not correction from the child: for if thou beatest him with the rod, he shall not die (Prov 23:13). Throughout the early twenty-first century, untrained and insensitive "godly parents" used what the Bible offered as a loving, corrective discipline as a treatise for relentless, unchecked and irresponsible child abuse. Like Daniel Gottlieb Schreber (Physician 1808-1861) many religious parents applied corporal punishment on children, believing that "the most important thing is that the [child's] disobedience should be crushed to the point of regaining complete submission."[22] Unfortunately, they regularly did so without consequences being imposed on them for their brutish conduct. Linda Nelson comments further:

> A 'poisonous pedagogy' within the Christian tradition stresses the absolute obedience of children to their parents, the sinful nature of children, and the need to 'break their wills' at a very early age with harsh physical punishment.[23]

Families with cultist affiliations are known to inflict child physical abuse on their progeny, and sanction it by claiming "it is God's will"[24] for the children. Extended, intimidating and punitive control of the victim is often gained and enforced by convincing it if he or she rebels against the "corrective abuse," or reports it, he or she will be rebelling against God who has delegated the leaders to be caretakers of their souls. Fear of alienation from group identity, hospitality, and physical care may also be used to gain unquestioned submission to the many perverted, abusive techniques used by cultist religions.

The Results of Child Physical Abuse

The impact of child physical abuse is multifaceted. The primary and most noticeable result is physical disfigurement through irregular bruising, welts, burning of the flesh, fracturing of bones, inordinately large lacerations to the face or mouth, or damage to the abdominal regions. Such physical condition should cause concern by anyone who notices them, and they should be reported to the appropriate authority immediately.[25]

Beyond these observable, physical results there are a number of emotional results that may befall a child. First, physically abused children often gain a strong disdain and dislike towards the abuser. Although the child often cannot run away from the abuser, as the punishment increases, the abused often will display signs of detachment through hiding, retreating into lengthy times of solitude, or by associating socially with nonfamily members more than he or she does with his parents. If extended, severe abuse continues, the child may revert to suicide to find release from the haunting dilemma that oppresses him.

Second, abused children are often overcome with acute depression, and "suffer from low self-esteem, exhibit cognitive impairment and abnormal anxiety thresholds, and often lack necessary social skills"[26] which are foundational to successful adulthood relationship in later years. Educational psychologists suggest children from abusive family relationships display an increased absence from school than those from non-abusive families, and they "usually perform at a lower academic achievement score."[27] This possibly occurs because of a constant subconscious reflection on past abusive encounters, or worrying when the next degrading and painful battle will occur. These contemplations often deter students from focusing on the tasks at hand. Because of this, they do not perform to their fullest capacity, and their academic achievement scores remain low.

Third, abusive children exhibit posttraumatic stress disorders which are revealed with fear and an excessive sense of helplessness in their plight. Parents are physically larger and stronger than children. Their loud, demanding and authoritarian voice is intimidating to children. A parent's threat to a child he or she might be removed from the home by Social Services if the situation is reported to authorities engenders, immeasurable fear within the child he or she might be deprived the needs of life. These factors cause the child to view the parent as holding unquestioned and unrestrained power over him or her. Parents, in a fit of rage, often use this power in a completely arbitrary and capricious manner.[28] There is little or nothing the child can do to avoid being inflicted with inhuman abuse as the parent acts like an autocratic despot who has full, and unaccountable control over him or her.

Fourth, abused children often exhibit psychological disorders of "depression, anxiety, abnormal sleep patterns, hyperactivity, and neurosis."[29] When punishment cannot be reasonably justified by a parent, those who been unjustly abused may become physically aggressive towards their siblings or peers. They justify and excuse their behavior with claims they are mirroring their parent's behavior. If this aggressive behaviour is not "held in check" at its earliest stages, abused children, when they have reached adolescence, retaliate to their parent's abusive behaviour by murdering them in the "get even syndrome."[30]

Fifth, abused children (especially young women), may develop gastrointestinal and severe eating disorders such as bulimia nervosa, anorexia nervosa, or binge and purging during their later years. Tamas Treurer comments:

> When, during the working through process after physical abuse, patterns of lack of identification or rejection appear, the victim of physical abuse, herself can become an abusive parent, and depending on her own personality, coping patterns, family conditions, and interpersonal skills, can behave more harshly within herself by imposing self-

destructive behaviour and torture by developing an eating disorder.[31]

Sixth, children who have endured both past and current intense physical abuse, evoke feelings of depression, display lower self-esteem, and regard life more negatively than children who have undergone limited or no physical abuse.[32] Abused children also appear to be lethargic, regressive, and nonproductive in their work. In such circumstances, children need to be affirmed by stable and caring family members, or friends, as possessing value, worth, and dignity despite what has occurred. If this is not received at an early stage of depression, the child may develop dysfunctional emotional responses, and begin to believe "the odds are stacked against him ever to achieve his full potential."[33]

Theological Rebuttal to Child Abuse

From a biblical, theological and a Christian ethical perspective, child physical abuse should never be entertained, never mind enacted, by those who are Christ's disciples. Children, like other members of humanity, are the creative image of God fashioned in his image and likeness (Gen 1:26). As such, from the moment of conception, "they are fearfully and wonderfully made" (Ps 139:14) possessing emotional and physical elements that need to be nurtured towards health through loving and caring parental and child relationships.

There is no passage in scripture that belittles or advocates abuse of children. However, there are strict injunctions to God's people not to "avenge, nor bear a grudge against them (Lev 19:8). Paul, the Apostle, recognized the possibility of internal family strife and abuse. As a safeguard against this he instructs the people at Rome, "Not to think of himself more highly than he ought to, but to think soberly in accordance with how God has given unto everyone a measure of faith" (Rom 12:3). When parents think soberly towards their children, they will honour them by not inflicting physical abuse on them, regardless of the stress or undesired behaviour displayed.

In scripture parents, who have large families, are regarded as being blessed because their children "will act as power in their hand, and they will speak well of them in the gate" (Ps 127:3-5). The

Christian family is God's nurturing ground for spiritual, physical, and social health as the family collectively submits itself one to another in the fear of Lord (Eph 5:21-15). God's desire for His people is unity, prosperity, righteousness, and love one for the other. As these principles are manifested in the family, dignity and welcome worth is instilled within its members, instead of abuse – emotional, physical, or sexual – that destroys many children's lives. Fathers are instructed by Paul they are not to "provoke their children to wrath by abusive words or actions. Instead of reverting to this, they are to bring them up in the nurture and admonition of the Lord" (Eph 6:4). Even as Jehovah has been a kind, patient, accepting, and welcoming Father to those who often disappoint Him by willfully and headstrongly disobeying His commands, earthly fathers are to be of the same tenor in their behaviour before their rebellious children. Although it might be easier to return evil with evil, godly parents "walk a higher path" showing love, kindness, gentleness and forbearance" (Col 3:13) so bitterness and disdain, by the children to the parent, will not be birthed.

Regardless how disrupted, confused, or fractured the home setting might be, or how disruptive a child's behaviour might be, no parent has the right to inflict physical abuse on his offspring. Rather parents – mother and father alike – are to inculcate family settings in which godly loving, caring, righteous, and edifying counsel is offered. When a parent attempts to break a child's "beastly and abhorrent will" by inflicting brutish, inhumane, and unjust physical punishment on it, a wedge of hostility is placed between the parent and child. But, when he or she pursues to mold the child's will by "the sweetness of the gospel," and not the harshness of the law, a bridge of love, acceptance and respect is built between the parent and child.[34] This is the first proactive and profitable step parents can take towards enabling their children to honour their father and mother which is right in the Lord (Eph 6:1). Abusive, controlling and psychotic parents command respect by reverting to physical, emotional or sexual abuse! Godly, compassionate, and caring parents, on the other hand, commend respect by appealing to "sacrificial, servant love."

Children, regardless whether they are the offspring of "unplanned" or "planned" pregnancies, regardless whether they were conceived in or out of a marital relationship, and regardless of their physical or emotional deficiencies are a good gift of God on loan to the family.[35] Each gift is distinctly unique, possessing limitless worth, strength and protection to the home and community as is suggested by God comparing children to valued, needed and appreciated arrows in the hands of a warrior (Ps 127:3-4), and as olive plants round the table (Ps 128:3-4) which is regarded as Israel's most valuable and most coveted plant because of the immense social prestige it brings to the owner.

Whenever children are regarded as less than God's gift to society, they become regarded as "nothing more than a blob of flesh and blood equal to a farm animal that can be battered about if one's demands are not complied with."[36] No one would treat a gift from a friend with disregard and disdain. Why, then, would anyone impose indignation on a child – God's gift to humanity – by physically abusing it to such an extent that it becomes physically and emotionally negatively scarred or permanently physically disfigured?

The Church's Responsibility

Far too often, Christians, because they believe they are "people of grace," permit suspected or known cases of child abuse to bypass inspection. This is an extremely careless and serious oversight because of the physical, emotional, psychological and social consequences that could befall the abused. Believers – regardless of their relationship to the abuser or abused – must take every suspicion of child abuse seriously, and notify authorities – pastors, teachers, social welfare agents and the police – to intervene immediately so remedial, protective action for the abused can be implemented. As has been stated earlier, child physical abuse is ramped in Canada, and possibly in Canadian evangelical churches. Although it is painful and shameful for Christians to accept and admit this, dealing with the issue in a godly and constructive way is essential. The following recommendations are suggested.

First, although the local church cannot be fully aware of "every incident of child abuse" that occurs within families that attend week by week, it has a responsibility to "subscribe to and teach the care and respect for the innocence of the child, and their rightful expectation to be treated with utmost dignity and esteem as they are raised in a loving environment."[36] At no time must congregants be allowed to think or to ascribe that godliness can be attained or maintained through abusive physical beatings of children. Nowhere in scripture are believers given such indicators.

Second, when child abuse occurs, fellow believers need to remember the perpetrator(s) are humans, oftentimes "controlled by the deeds of the flesh" (Gal 5:19). Because of this, Satan may exchange a parent's desired love for his or her offspring to anger and hatred when it does not comply with a "reasonable demand." This possibly is why he counsels believers to "give no place to the devil" (Eph 4:27). With this, Christians also need to remember that the perpetrator of abuse, like the Apostle Paul, often falls into the pit of doing what he or she does not want to instead of the things he or she desire to do (Rom 7:23-24). Because of this individuals may afflict their children with painful abuse despite their strong, godly desire not to do so. Fellow believers, if they are to be of help in resolving child abuse, need to uphold those who are weak through prayer, counsel, and corrective, provisional care instead of standing aloof from the transgressor, and gossiping about his or her problem (Rom 15:1-3).

Third, pastors, elders and attendees of the church need to be observant of the physical, emotional and psychological condition of children under their care. If there is a sudden, unexplained change in a child's behaviour or appearance, a notation about this should be made. If the condition worsens, serious questions regarding the child's condition need to be imposed on the parent and child – independent of each other.

"Speaking the truth in love" (Eph 4:15), means the caregiver will not accept superficial responses such as, "I fell" from the child, or "I accidently slapped my son or daughter" from the parent when the evidence indicates abuse has occurred. Rather, he or she will probe the issue until he or she – along with other ministry staff – is sufficiently satisfied the child's change in appearance or behavior is adequately and honesty explained by the child and parent. If the parents are apprehensive and resistant about participating in the dialogue about the issue, authorities, outside the church, may have to be notified. Regardless how difficult this might be, it will be the first step towards protecting the child from future abuse, and long term physical, emotional and spiritual damage.

Third, if an indisputable case of child abuse becomes known to the church staff, it – in collaboration with members of the fellowship – needs to hold the felon(s) accountable for his or her uncomely and ungodly act. Scripture instructs believers to "love one another," and to "forgive one another even as God for Christ's sake hath forgiven them" (Eph 4:32). But before scripture counsels this, it adjures believers to set aside "all bitterness, wrath, anger, clamour and evil speaking" (Eph 4:31) so they can live godly and upright regardless of the pressures they face from time to time. The perpetrator cannot be shown grace and acceptance by Christians until he or she is willing to admit to the charge of abuse, repent of the deed, and come under remedial pastoral, or professional therapeutic treatment to overcome the problem.

Until treatment suitable treatment for the perpetrator is procured, the leadership team should place him or her under the care of a spiritual director. The "director" would assist the abuser "to clarify what God wants in the person's life, and discern between the evil and good spirits creating movement in the person's emotional and spiritual life." If the member refuses to come under "instruction, correction and reproof to righteousness" (2 Thess 5:17), after a time the fellowship may have no alternative other than to regard him or her as a heathen man and a publican (Matt 18:17) and then "deliver such an one unto Satan for the destruction of the flesh, that the spirit may be saved in the day of the Lord Jesus" (1 Cor 5:5). If the church – leaders and congregants together – think this action would too severe of a reproof for the perpetrator, the fellowship could "mark them which cause divisions and offences contrary to the doctrine which they have learned; and avoid them" (Rom 16:17).

Fourth, pastors – regardless of their position in the church – need to spend more time preaching and holding in-depth seminars on family issues. With this, they might remind congregants they will be held accountable and responsible to the Board and congregation for what occurs in the home. Too often pastors speak on family issues, once or twice a year, with a casual, care free reference to Paul's admonition for each member of the church to be subject one to another, and to honour one another (Rom 13:7). What is needed is the message of submission one to another with a clearly stated addendum that this is done in the honour of God to whom parishioners are already called to be submitted. If the church finds incidences of abuse – child, spousal, animal – the abuser will be disciplined, given opportunity to repent and receive remedial counsel whereby he or she may overcome his abusive conduct. Discipline within the local church has become a forgotten practice. Rod Wilson is correct when he states, "Discipline is at the core of what the church should be about."[38] If abuse is only suspected, the pastoral team may offer the *Twelve Step Program* for abuse recovery offered in many local churches.

At no time, even if the perpetrator is convicted and incarcerated for child abuse, should he or she be abandoned by the local church. Regardless of the sin committed, God does not abandon individuals, and neither should His church. In this time of stress, distress and emotional unrest, the transgressor needs to be assured grace, forgiveness, and restitution to fellowship is available to those who recognize their need for help, and who are willing to receive it. As this is offered, there is a high probability the transgressor will confess his or her wrong, and will receive appropriate counsel towards mental and spiritual well-being.

Fifth, members of the church need to be cautioned by the leadership team against gossiping about the abuser or discrediting him or her to be a reprobate, alienated from God because of his or her action. Instead of giving in to gossip, God's people need to extend grace to the wayward person as the first step of restoring him or her to full fellowship within the church. This action would be the hope of other congregants if they were the transgressor, and it should not be a difficult consideration for them to the abuser. If the offender does not feel a welcome by the fellowship to return to the church, he or she might begin to think and believe the people of God bite and devour one another to destruction (Gal 5:15) instead of caring, serving and loving one another to the glory of God and the edification of the church as the scripture teaches.

Conclusion

Child physical abuse has been becoming more prevalent over the past twenty years due to the voluminous amount of stressors facing the family. Although we empathize with parents, and extend a hand of grace to them in their plight, society at large and the Christian community can never sanction parental child physical abuse under any circumstance. Rather, we affirm that child abuse of any nature is the most reprehensible, despicable, and degrading form of attack on children, and we offer ourselves to be of help to those that would seek out our aid or counsel with regards to this matter so that we can safeguard our children from the plight that does not belong to them!

Chapter 5

Guilt: Understanding and Coping With It!

Some years ago my wife, Martha and I were driving through Brewster, Washington. In our travels we came across several large apple orchards, which, had not yet been harvested. It had been about four and a half hours since we had eaten. Without thinking, I stopped near an orchard, and picked a couple of apples to enjoy as we made our way towards the Canada and US border.

We had driven about half a mile when my wife turned to me and said, "You're really going to eat those apples aren't you? I suppose you won't feel an ounce of guilt about picking them!"

To this painful question, which was intended to probe my moral responsibility for the wrong I may have done, I refused to give a response. I knew I was guilty for picking them without asking permission from the owner but, to protect myself from further complications, I said nothing.

Definitions of Guilt

Guilt may be defined as "the realization that one has violated either a moral or religious principle, with a regretful feeling of lessened personal worth on that account."[1] Guilt usually centers on violating rules on which one places high value, and it always carries a sense of self-punishment. Guilt befalls the transgressor as reproach or hostility "because of a wrong committed, and is strongly imposed on the inward self,"[2] as one "feels regret doing something he or she believes the person should not have done."[3] Guilt "presupposes the option of choice, and the acceptance of consequences when one decides to do wrong when he or she knows he or she ought not to." Guilt is always a result of interpersonal and communal interaction. The closer the offender is to the offended, the stronger the guilt. Through it individuals harm spouses, family, friends, associates, and their fellowman. Roy F. Baumeiter comments:

> Guilt is an interpersonal phenomenon that is functionally and casually linked to communal relationships between people. The origins, functions, and processes of guilt all have important interpersonal aspects. Guilt can be understood in relationship contexts as a factor that strengthens social bonds by elucidating symbolic affirmation of caring.[5]

Inherent in guilt is the sense of responsibility or culpability which means, "It is my fault, or I am to blame" for the offence. It often acts as a sense of pain, telling the person some part of the "psyche is ill, and therapy is necessary if guilt is to be avoided."[6] Paul Gilbert suggests that guilt is not the same as shame. His reasons for distinguishing between the two are:

> In contrast, guilt requires different motives, emotions, competencies to that of shame, such as sensitivity to the feelings or needs of others, motivations for caring or reparative behaviour and sharing.[7]

But neither is guilt remorse. Whereas guilt is an objective realization a wrong has been committed, remorse is "a deep sense of sorrow for what has been done that may lead to compassionate care of the person offended."[8] Guilt is present because a transgression has been enacted. Remorse, however, is displayed in hopes of undoing the psychological damage extended to the offended by the act.

Everyone does not feel guilt when a wrong is committed. Psychopaths, who take joy in causing hurt, pain, and trauma "through antisocial behaviour,"[9] likely will have no guilt. Because of this, they usually continue violating laws, and hurting individuals until they are forced to receive clinical therapy.

There are two "schools" about the cause(s) of guilt, these being, Secular Humanists and the Christian Community. Secular humanists have concluded there are three causes of guilt. First, an "abandoning one's potential, second never fully knowing others, because their capacity to socialize is limited, and third, a separation from being nurtured by upright and ethical friends."[10] The Christian Community expostulates there is one cause for guilt, that being unwholesome and sinful acts. Augustine writes:

> For this purpose man has been made, to be lord and master over other creatures, but through the sin of the first man we have fallen, and have all come into the inheritance of death. We have become lowly mortals, filled with fears and errors. This is the wage of sin. Every man is born with this penalty and guilt.[11]

Types of Guilt

Psychologists agree guilt is o produced when one violates a legal or moral code. But guilt is not always caused by the same influences. Psychologists, therefore, have separated guilt into several, varying types, these being:

- Real Guilt is manifested after a known or recognized commission, or omission of an act that may have resulted in noticeable painful and damaging hurt to others. Real guilt often is at the same intensity of hurt he would have felt if someone had done the same act to him.

- Imagined guilt is present when one omits to do his expected duty, especially if the neglect is damaging to a group setting, not because the task is left incomplete, but because the expectations of the group/society have not been realized.[12]

• Moral Guilt includes "criminal, political and military actions, as well as indifference and passivity and it include a sense of responsibility and guilt for unjust treatments which no criminal or political propitiation can appease."[13]

• Associated Guilt is often felt by police officers, firepersons, and those of the medical profession, when responsibility for another's welfare is directly related to their job.[14] When a person under their care dies, the caretaker is often overwhelmed with guilt even if the person's illness was beyond their ability, because they feel that if they had done just a little more, the outcome might have been different.

• Survivor's Guilt is manifested when one survives an accident, holocaust, or some other horrendous event such as 911, and others die in the same event.[15] People who suffer this guilt often question, "Why did they have to die, and not me?"

• Manipulative Guilt is used by individuals to gain a desired result. An elderly mother may use manipulative guilt on her only daughter by suggesting that if she puts her in a senior's retirement centre, instead of caring for her at home, the home will have to be sold to support her, and the daughter will receive no monetary inheritance.

• Metaphysical Guilt, also known as Collective Guilt, is guilt that is common to all humanity by being part of the human race.[16] Adam, as human kind's representative, sinned in Eden; because of his 'fall' which brought sin into the world, all humans are scarred with sin and suffer guilt that is incurred because of all transgressions. Regardless of the vice committed, guilt is the common denominator.

Impact of Guilt

Guilt is a pervasive, unavoidable consequence of life which may be brought on because of a multiplicity of effectors such as: having an abortion, eating too much, alcoholism, and pornography, just to mention a few. Its negative effects spread to every part of one's life: spiritual, emotional, mental, physical, and social.[17]

Apprehension and fear of being caught and being punished, are the most common, immediate instigators of guilt. It often inhibits one from enjoying life because of mental trauma such as depression, self-condemnation, anger, or a sense of unworthiness. With this, it may also incite physical problems such as, intense migraine headaches, gastral problems, and the inability to sleep, or eat. When guilt is at is "peak," psychologists suggest it may cause social withdrawal such as alienation from family, close friends, and work colleagues as one "goes into hiding" so he or she will not have to personally affirm, or take responsibility for the misdeed.

Release from Guilt

Although knowledge of a transgression can never be fully purged from one's memory, guilt associated with it can be substantially reduced. But, before one attempts to exonerate himself or herself of the "wrong done," he or she must recognize no one can be liberated from guilt until the individual takes responsibility for the act(s). This is a necessary, first step action one must take so he or she may discover peace! Joy Ufema, Death-And-Dying Specialist at Supper Chesapeake Medical Center, comments:

> I've companioned many individuals who did find peace before death, so it's sad to see someone continue to be so troubled at the end of life. But dispensing peace isn't our job. Our job is to continue to offer kindness and support, and hope that our patients, knowing they were worthy of our kindness, can find peace within their own hearts.[18]

When one is plagued with guilt, his or her first immediate response may be to ignore the feelings saying to himself or herself, "Don't worry about it, no one will ever find out!" If, perhaps, the person is found out, his or her next recourse might be to turn to innovative social programs for help. If these fail, he or she might write letters to the offended, do penance, seek friendly, compassionate counsel, or impose on himself or herself severe self-debasing punishment. These acts, however, usually are not sufficient to rid the person of guilt. Therefore, several more favorable and promising steps so one can discover freedom from the frenzies of guilt, are offered.

First, the transgressor must confess he or she has contravened a law, offended a fellowman, or disobeyed God. Once this is honestly, and sincerely done, he or she must take full, personal responsibility for what has transpired, regardless of the self-justification for committing the act. Confession is the watershed that offers healing to the delinquent. Through it, the individual reveals the evil committed, affirms personal responsibility for the wrong, and willingly accepts the consequences imposed on him.[19] Confession, in the past, usually was done before a priest or pastor. In more recent years, however, it has been done to lawyers, doctors, psychologists and the like. Avoidance of this primary, essential step "could intensify the guilt and shame harassing the offender."[20]

Second, the individual must show remorse, or contriteness of soul for the wrong done. Remorse extends beyond "feeling sorrow for what has happened." Rather, it includes feelings of disgust, and self-reproach. In its fullest expression, remorse should motivate the offender to meet the offended so steps towards righting the wrong may be implemented. Remorse calls for an abandonment, by the offender, of any self-justification for the wrong done, and a strong wish to change his present direction in life.

Third, with theft, and other commodity related offences, the evil doer must provide restitution in cash, or by returning the item stolen. Restitution should always be of a greater amount or value than that which has been taken. In an article produced by the Council of State Government/American Probation and Parole Association, under Cooperative Agreement Number 2009-SZ-B9-K001, the committee discovered that an "order for restitution" helps both the victim and the offender. It states:

> Restitution is a court-ordered requirement for a convicted offender to compensate his/ her victim for the financial losses resulting from the crime. The benefits to victims are clear—they receive economic compensation for their losses, they witness the offender being held accountable for his or her criminal actions, and they see the criminal justice system responding to their needs. For offenders, restitution offers the opportunity to comprehend the injury of the offense, and the very real and often financially devastating consequences to the victim. Restitution also provides offenders with the opportunity to take responsibility for the injury and losses they have caused, and to accept accountability to the victim and society for the resulting damage.[21]

Fourth, the person must repent from his or her actions; in other words, he or she must display a purposed inclination to terminate activities which engenders guilt. Repentance must provoke a change of mind, and practice which will prompt an immediate, sincere, and full abandonment of the unwholesome and untoward activities previously manifested.

This change may not occur by one's own initiatives. Therefore, those who may need help in this area, will need to seek a psychologist, pastor, priest or some other person of trust, who will walk with them through this necessary time of healing, which may take one or two years.

Fifth, the offender must make atonement for the misdeed through incarceration or some other form of externally imposed punishment - moral, physical, or merely symbolic. In so doing, both the transgressor and society will realize the offense is more than just a 'faux pas' that can be easily set aside through excuses, compensation or other counterfeit tokens of justification.[22]

Theological Implications of Guilt

A Christian perspective of guilt "suggests a one has committed a willful and purposed rebellion against God through defiance of his rule of order"[23] within the society in which one lives, and is a result of sin. When carried to its fullest extent, rebellion includes disobeying God's direct ordinances or disobeying civil laws which have been legislated by political powers for humanity's good "because they have been ordained of God as a minister of God, and a revenger to execute wrath on evildoers."[24]

That individuals will violate God's laws is a foregone conclusion because of man's depravity which is affirmed through scripture that says, "For [they] all have gone like sheep astray, and every one of them have turned unto their own way."[25] This willful, purposed, and planned turning apart from God is generated because man, at his core, is self-serving. Because of this, man, with little or no regard for his fellowman, or of the consequences of his acts, lives a pleasure-seeking, self-serving life style doing whatever he must to gain his desired end. Guilt, that awaits him when a wrong is done, is of no importance, because, "after all, no one is really supposed to feel guilty; guilt is not the conducive to dignity and self-esteem"[26]

Guilt is like a cancer that incessantly eats away at an individual's dignity by relentlessly haunting the person as it repeatedly brings the transgression before him[27] until some amends for the wrong are made. Regardless of the advice one might receive through secular counseling in order to find liberty from guilt, these, at their best, usually only offer temporary freedom from its grip.

Relief from guilt is best obtained through a personal faith in Jesus Christ (Eph 2:7-10), as one "taps" into the well of grace, mercy, and forgiveness which is freely offered to all those that come to Him as they are with their faults. Scripture assures the troubled, wrongdoer, who is willing to repent, his guilt will removed from him as far as the east is from the west through regeneration offered by Christ, and God will never hold these against that person again (Is 43:25). As one comes to Christ, he or she gains an awakening to virtue. As this happens, the person understands "the eventual disastrous and damaging consequences that may befall him" (Rom 6:23), if he or she does not change his or her ways.

Faith in Christ is a powerful catharsis which delivers the culprit from the harassing guilt that besets him, as it enables the person to believe that God receives and forgives sinners – regardless how bad their sin was – if they repent. This freedom is guaranteed because Christ has promised "If one confesses his sins He is faithful and just to cleanse us from all unrighteousness (1 John 1:9)· Christ's forgiveness does not relieve the offender from the consequences of his sin or her sin . The thief, the murderer, the loan shark or the drug trafficker can expect to be fined or incarcerated for his or her crime. As well, he or she may be required to provide restitution, and reparations to the offended.

Temporal freedom from guilt may be realized, in this life, as the individual studies scripture, submits to the guidance the Holy Spirit, and seeks godly and upright counsel. Unrestricted, full freedom from guilt will be realized by "those that have in this life enjoyed Christ's gift of full salvation" (Rom 8:1),[28] on that day when Christ returns to inaugurate his everlasting rest for those who love and serve Him. Clyde M. Narramore comments:

> Genuine guilt feelings cannot be rationalized and dispelled by the efforts of a counselor alone. They have been implanted by God and can only be removed by Him. This loving guilt must be dealt with by the loving forgiveness of God's Son, Jesus Christ, 'in whom we have forgiveness through his blood', the forgiveness of sins, according to the riches of his grace.' Only through genuine repentance and a life lived in close fellowship with the Lord can true feelings of guilt be overcome.[29]

Christians suffering from guilt need to seek out godly counsel from psychologists, psychiatrists or other trained therapists within the Christian community. Ungodly therapists, because of their untoward attitude towards sin as the root cause of guilt, may suggest seditious and unwholesome solutions to guilt, thereby leaving the seeker in a greater dilemma than he or she was at the beginning. The Christian therapist, understanding the damaging influence of sin, will direct the seeker to know Christ and then, through well thought out and tested righteous therapy, bring the seeker to healthy foundational principles that need to be followed if healing from guilt is to be known.

It is in this context of Christian community a bearing, sharing, and caring support for the "infirmities of the weaker brother" (Rom 15:2), is offered by those who are strong so "the guilty may gain a sense of hope towards forgiveness and restoration"[30] and be "healed." As discipleship, by which one learns to walk uprightly before man and God, is received the former wayward individual will be empowered to lead others in the "way of righteousness so other sinners will be converted to God" (Ps 51:7). This is the way of love, righteousness, and of Christ from which, one having obtained freedom of guilt, will never turn aside, or be turned aside by Christ.

Chapter 6

Proposed Safeguards Against Secularization for Christians

Introduction

Throughout the centuries numerous philosophies such as Greek Gnosticism, Platonic Dialectical Realism, Aristotelian Categorical Logic, and Augustinian Scholasticism have been espoused as truth. Philosophical, propositional truth is never static. It continuously shapes social and cultural worldviews. These, therefore, cannot be overlooked. In this paper it is my intention to examine secularization and to propose reasons why Christians need to safeguard themselves from being "ruined through the vain deceit" (Col 2:8) it offers. Secularism, which is boastfully promulgated in the west "as the accepted foundation for living," finds its genesis in the "secularization theory" of the seventeenth century. Although there have been many attempts to define the term, there still remains little collective agreement as to what it means, or how it should be used. Secularization comes from the Latin, *saeculum,* meaning "age". Throughout the Middle Ages it represented anything that was removed from religious serve to be used for the secular. Os Guinness defines the term as:

> The process by which, starting at the centre, and moving outwards, successive sectors of society have been freed from the decisive influences of religious ideas and institutions. In other words, secularization is the process by which we have neutralized the social significance of religion in the central areas of modern society such as science, technology, bureaucracy and so on, making religious ideas less meaningful and religious institutions more marginal.[1]

The first use of the term, "secularization" was made by G. J. Holyoake in 1885 in *The Reasoner,* when he provided the following explanation for the term:

> Secularization, as a primary pursuit, inculcates the practical sufficiency of natural apart from Atheism, Theism, or the Bible, and selects, as its method of procedure the promotion of human improvement by material means alone.[2]

Tenants of Secularism

Secularization's goal is not to totally remove God from the consciousness of humanity. Rather, its intent is to minimize God as the sovereign, *prima facie* director of human affairs. When this is fully engineered, humankind, and not God, will become the centre of meaning in this world. As Leslie Newbigin suggests, this will "Empower humans to be liberated from all religious tensions.[3] Secularization, furthermore, is not anti-God or antireligious. It, on the other hand, sanctions both as being valid as long as they are contained in the private domain where they cannot influence national policies nor have a privileged position in education. It was hoped, as secularization became more widely espoused, public religious influence would be so profusely decried God would be allocated to the "wings" of humanity and be called on only for the worst of human crisis. Pope Benedict XVI, fearing this possibility, contends the neutralization of religious faith has potential, serious consequences for humanity. During a recent speech in Germany (2000) he commented:

> Put simply, we are no longer able to hear God – there are too many frequencies in our ears. What is said about God strikes us to be pre-scientific, and no longer suitable for our age. I know in our pluralistic society it is not an easy thing, in our schools, to bring up the subject of faith. But, it is hardly enough for our children and young people to learn technical knowledge and skills alone, and not the criteria which gives skill and knowledge for their direction and learning. Encourage your children and students not only to raise questions about particular things, but also to ask about the why and the wherefore of life as a whole. Help them to realize that answers that do not finally lead to God are not sufficient.[4]

Secularization is intensely anthropocentric[5] and prompts humans to feverishly elevate themselves above the Divine. This charge takes place "through a shift from a religious framework of thinking, whose foundations lie outside the world, to this-world framework, asking only this-world questions and looking only for this-world answers in a human framework of thinking."[6] To Auguste Comte, secularization was the zenith of personal liberation from God – or other gods – for through it humans would find liberation from religious dogmas which robbed them of uninhibited self-actualization and fulfillment. Regarding Compote's statement, Rodney Stark comments:

> Compete vigorously contended for a secularized society. If secularization were given enough time, human society would outgrow the "theological age" of social evolution, and a "new age" would dawn in which the science of sociology would replace religion as the basis of moral judgment.[7]

Regardless how ardently the Church presents religious faith, and devotion to Yahweh as a viable alternative to secularization, its efforts will be considered contentious. The reason, the slightest reference to God curtails humanity from having an "absolutely humanly willed reality."[8] Mankind, therefore, has no choice but to forcibly buffet against God and religion of any nature. Kenneth Crag adds:

> Secular alertness to the difficulties of having God rule over society may propose a self-reliant solution. Let the corporate will undertake its own value system, supply from within its own sanctions, and contrive psychic well-being and social peace by its own energies. Enthrone the "sovereignty of the good" and be self-subjected to a subjective self. The Kingdom of God is so far within you, that it remains no longer God, but has become yours. As self-generating creatures, mankind is both empowered and authorized to create the world which will best accommodate his needs.[9]

The irony of secularization is it aggrandizes man as self-directed creator of this world, while it incapacitates him from answering the deep questions of life pertaining to "from where did humans come, why are they here, and what is their ultimate end?" Realistically, when examined under the "glass of reason and rational thinking," secularization is a whimsical fantasy whose end is emptiness, futility and vanity.

Historical Progression of Secularization

Throughout the Biblical Patristic Period belief in a personal, sovereign, authoritative, and benevolent God was commonplace. This conviction extended up to, and including the Greco-Roman period when the world was still "haunted" with the presence of Jehovah who was regarded as "the Creator and Sustainer of all things" (Col 1:16), and who humanity willingly worshipped.

Since the second century, however, the progression towards secularization – which elevates man above God – has strongly influenced humanity to dump religion as being important for knowing the purpose and meaning of life. The probable catalyst for the increase of secularization, especially throughout the third and fourth centuries, was Aristotelian Dialecticism, "which explained the metaphysical in terms of reason and science."[10] With this, it also postulated reality is discovered through self-directed investigations which would – after a sufficient time – yield empirical evidence as the sole validator of truth. Gnosticism – closely aligned to Aristotelian Dialecticism – suggested there was a "secret wisdom which could be known only to a select, chosen few, and which depreciated the Jewish

God from being the supreme authority in human history."[11] The continued teaching of this dynamic in secular universities contributed largely to the rise of secularism which was widely accepted by the fourteenth century. By the beginning of the Reformation, most individuals – including prominent religious educators – were accepting a "two-fold worldview" which consisted of the divine, and the natural. Man, because he was natural, was also vulgar. Being vulgar, he was limited in understanding only what he could reason out. Since God could not be "reasoned out and fully understood," man had no need for Him.

From this basic meaning humanity began believing the world "is an autonomous, separate kingdom over which it had full, unrestrained and unrestricted control for its benefit."[12] Building on this premise, the necessity of believing in a metaphysical, supreme and all powerful God became secondary. Instead of recognizing Him, humankind centered its affections on "reason and rationalism by which it could disprove God's existence, and the claim that He, alone created the world and all that is in it."[13] Knowledge, Aquinas argued, was what humankind needed to explore. Through it the "door of experience" would be opened, and humanity would be provided understanding about all that needs to be known.

Although Augustine esteemed the "revealed knowledge of God through scripture" highly, he nevertheless proposed God's revealed plan for humankind could best be understood through human relationships in the Church. For him, the Holy Spirit instructed pastors about the "knowledge of God which they were commissioned to teach to "strangers of the kingdom" (Eph 2:1-13). As this teaching was offered regularly week after week, humankind would receive insight how it, through self-designed schemes, "could make the world a better place."[14] Augustine never discredited God from co-partnering with humanity in "constructing this new world." However, he minimized God's importance, suggesting He empowered humankind to turn to Reason, and the community for insight how this new and better world could be established.

During the Monastic Period, the Church ruled with autocratic, authoritarian power. Parishioners unreservedly submitted to its dictates as if they were submitting to God, Himself. However, during the twelfth and thirteenth centuries, as the Agrarian Age ended, countless individuals moved to the cities. As this happened, a new social strata of "free thinkers"[16] arose which questioned the legitimacy of the Church's teachings. When the Church could no longer explain God in understandable and appreciative terms, parishioners turned to philosophers and their teachings to gain an understanding of the important questions of life. Because of this, everything became a transcendent and subjective reality beyond the explanation of human understanding. Humans desire to know reality, but they cannot know it if it remains purely subjective and hidden. To resolve this problem – subjective knowledge of the world – Descartes postulated the world – physical matter – is objective and can be known[17] while God, on the other hand is spiritual and hidden and can "never be known by man." With this, Decartes also suggested God created humans with a physical body in which they are to enjoy their world – even if it be limited. In compliance with "God's will," humans have no choice but to be consumed with the physical, real world in which they dwell. Religion and contemplation of a metaphysical God would be of no value because this is hidden.

In exchange for the metaphysical, hidden, and unknown God, Grotus and Hegel immediately introduced man as being the creator of a new, just and prosperous world. If man could create the world of meaning, he could dispense with the metaphysical God. Now released from the Tao[18] humankind would become the subjects of chance and follow after whimsical choices which it hoped would result in rational, wholesome and welcome benefits. Glasner adds:

> Now, based on a rationalistic interpretation which elevated man to be his own thinker, they (secular society) concluded that the immediate present functioning or progress of the state was more important than the transcendent. No longer were the theological claims of the Church valid, unless they took into account the shifting, local variation of human insight.[19]

While most seventeenth century philosophies continued to reference God and the Church as valid contributors for moral and social attitudes, eighteenth century philosophers were resolute on eliminating religious consciousness within society. The most powerful voice against public, religious affection at this time was Auguste Comte (1798-1852). Through his writings about Positivism, Comte gave religion and humanity equal significance "because the only way of knowing either is the unifying factor of human knowledge."[20] By equating faith and human experience, Comte detached God from being the authoritative voice in human history. By doing this, he empowered humankind to transform itself into "god" so it could decide and do whatever it deemed best for itself, while creating a new society. Whereas prior to Comte's teachings humans would say, "We will look to the hills from whence comes our help; our help comes from the Lord who made heaven and earth" (Ps 121:1-2), they now would say, "We will look to ourselves, and our scholars from whom we will gain knowledge to create everything we deem best for our existence."

The arrival of Kant, Hegel, Schleiermacher and Weber and the introduction of the Enlightenment exponentially increased humankind's detachment from God as a needed "helper."[21] Through this new tenet, espoused through public lectures and books, humankind quickly learned and accepted the human mind, alone, was the paramount faculty by which humans can know reality. For those who readily accepted this new teaching, there was no limit to what they could do to create a new world which would harmonize with their moral, educational and spiritual quest.[22] The voice that would give humans direction "would no longer be the voice of God who is above humanity, but the voice of Reason."[23]With this being widely promulgated as unquestioned truth, Max Weber could emphatically conclude "religion was paralyzed in the West, and humankind had no alternative but to guide his or her actions according to the dictates of knowledge."

With reason and rational thinking now front and centre, over against religious faith, the impetus for human self-sufficiency and creativity could not be curtailed. By the middle of the twentieth century Western Society, now disenchanted with religion called by any name, and consumed with it creative genius, no longer mused about God, or remembered Him as Sovereign Creator and Sustainer of the cosmos, for to it the God of Genesis was now "dead"[24] indeed!

From the foregoing assessment of secularization it might be concluded religious consciousness and faith has been annihilated and "a new age has dawned in which the science of sociology has replaced religion as the basis for moral judgement."[25] Regardless how strongly secularism might propose itself as the new "authority for human meaning and knowledge," Christ's Church must never entertain this proposition. Rather, under the Lordship of Christ, the empowerment of the Holy Spirit, and the instruction of scripture, the church needs to become bold and counteract the tenets of secularism and there protect humankind from its untruthful, pernicious and damning lies.

Biblical Wardship against Secularization

Although unregenerate humanity may be willing to readily adopt the propositions conjectured by secularization, Christians need to be cautioned about entertaining its teachings. Secularism – regardless who teaches it, or what benefits it promises humankind – is nothing more than a prideful and vulgar twisting of the truth. With this it demeans Jehovah to having no valued place in the welfare of humankind and elevates humankind, to be the epitome of creative intelligence.[26] In light of the lies presented by secularism, the following suggestions are presented by which believers may protect themselves against being swept away by its teachings that are nothing more than lies.

First, secularization has fraudulently misrepresented God by suggesting "He is dead," and therefore, religion no longer has a valued connection with society. This conclusion may be construed as truth because church attendance and growth has decreased over the past sixty years. Secularism's success in promoting this untruth could be accepted as fact because Christians have not analyzed or challenged the data secularism offers.

Contrary to what secularism states, the Christian church, and other religious faiths are not facing obliteration as is demonstrated by credible statistics offered around the world. In the USA there are

224,457,000 Christians, in Brazil 189.000,000, in Mexico 86,120,000, in the Philippines 63,470,000 and in Nigeria 38,180,000.[27] And in other parts of the world – South Africa, China, Taiwan, and Cuba – Christianity is on the increase. Such evidence clearly indicates personal faith in the supernatural, sovereign God has not ceased. Tom Small adds:

> However, God is not so easily disposed of as the secularists imagine and teach. Many who reject theology embrace spirituality, betraying the fact they long for something that will take them out of themselves, and beyond themselves to a reality that will provide for them what they, in and of themselves, cannot find. That reality can be located in naïve superstitions about the stars that control and reveal their future, or in the great world religions in which the "god question" is still recognized and faced, and answers however diverse, are offered to it.[28]

Second, secularism is abject atheism because it does not "give Yahweh recognition as being the only True, Supreme God in the world."[29] Secularists will quickly respond to this charge stating "it has not totally discarded God from the affairs of humanity. It, on the other hand, has put Him and religion "*out in the wings of society,* and He is welcome to do whatever He wants in the private affairs of humanity."[30] Regardless of the civility intended by this "welcome to God," secularism can be charged as being militant atheism because it willingly, defiantly and "conveniently" places God in a secondary, subjective role to satisfy humanity's whimsical need of power, instead of elevating Him to the exalted role as Creator and Sustainer of creation. This forthright and flagrant berating of God to this low position can be regarded as society's highest disdain and haughtiness towards the Almighty. No other term except "atheism" adequately describes the situation.

Third, secularization is unmitigated idolatry in that it elevates humankind above God, thereby setting its mind, its will, and its affection on self and other things as it primary focus. This prejudice to self-actualization and fulfillment lessens within humanity the God consciousness given at conception, and replaces this with vanity, distrust, disbelief and incorrigibleness toward God."[31] Because of this overriding need honour self, than God humanity has been "drugged" with narcissistic vanity. Because of this it strides about with contemptuous conceit because it has forgotten that God, and not mankind, created the earth, flung the stars in space, and keeps the world in its orbit. Society's pretentious attempts to accrue accolades of praise are slanderous before God, and humans would do well to remember God gave dominion "over this world to humanity" to be protectorates over what He created for their pleasure and use (Gen 1:28).

The catalyst for secular humanism is unrestrained, insidious pride "which intensifies humankind's worth as it affirms humans as the sole architect of this world, void of any assistance from God."[32] When the verdict of humankind's pretentious view of self and its accomplishments is honestly and rationally considered, it demonstrates humanism and secularism provides nothing but loneliness, confusion, corruption and unwholesome inter personal rivalry for power, prestige and position. This pitiful and shameful judgement on humanity could be radically lessened if humans would remember that the "chief end of man is to glorify God, and enjoy Him forever," instead of competing with God for notoriety, position and authority.

Moses clearly understood the detrimental and perilous effect human success could have on people as they "feasted at the trough of self-accommodation and prosperity." Whenever the Children of Israel fell into the trap of self-praise, because of victory over enemies, the gain of wealth, or the abundance of crops, Moses implored them to remember "it was the Lord, their God, who gave them the power to attain it", and not the works of their hands (Deut 18:17-18).

Fourth, secularism inculcates the love of stuff, and the quest for immediate self-aggrandizement within humans as it places inexorable emphasis on the temporal cosmos, at the full exclusion of God's eternal kingdom. As this dynamic is emphasized people start believing "they can make it on their own," "the only way to make it to the top is to look after number one," and "he or she that has the most toys wins." Inherently worldliness shackles humanity to this present, rational, known world as it placates individuals to believe a "new and just world" is possible as humankind becomes more enlightened to its creative potential. Ferd L. Wagner recognizes that humankind has a desire to do good towards its fellowman, and often is successful in accomplishing. But, unless it cooperates with God, his attempts will be mediocre and produce little, if any, lasting profitable results. He writes:

> All human need can be traced back to our human pride, greed, deceit, and neglect. But more fundamentally all that is wrong is our separation from the will and the Word of God. It cannot be denied that many caring people, organizations and activities are responding to worldwide to help others. People who liberally care, share, love, sacrifice, and give of their substance, and their lives are to be thanked. There are times and circumstances where a selfless act on behalf of another fleetingly allows us a glimpse of what God intended for humanity. But interposed between every selfless act, below the surface, there is an underlying tension between God and man, and man himself. There can be no peace between man and God, with others or the inner man, until God's justice prevails. There can be no true justice unless there is universal common goodwill grounded in obedience to God's will and Word. There can be no common ground goodwill until one allows the Holy Spirit to intercede, lead and purify the inner man to faithfully serve God. Because man is incapable of willing himself to be something he is not, he will always be at war with God, in some capacity at odds with others, and at war within himself.[33]

Scripture cautions believers to be on guard regarding the "many voices" (1 Cor 14:10) that "bid for their attention." Secularism is one of them. Although Christians have no alternative to live in this world, and be "tainted by some of its influences," they are strongly entreated by John, the Beloved, not to be intoxicated with this world's philosophies because, "All that is in this world, the lust of the flesh, the lust of the eyes, and the pride of life is not of the Father (1 John 2:16). Possessing this knowledge, believers are mandated to give no place to Satan (Eph 4:27), and the diabolic philosophies that come with worldliness. Leslie Newbigin adds:

> There are good grounds for saying that the secularization theory has been accepted by Christians to justify a social institution. The idea of a secular society has been attractive to Christians because it seems to hold out the hope of peaceful coexistence between the religious and nonreligious worldviews. It promises a society in which public affairs are governed by beliefs which are shared by all "enlightened" people, and in which there would be free for individuals to profess and practice their religious or nonreligious beliefs. Beyond this, it also promises deliverance from the tyranny of dogma and peaceful existence in the economy of shared rationality. But just because secularization offers these ideologies, there still remains the failure of the theories to produce them.[34]

Secularized people will postulate, and intimidate Christians by suggesting only "weak and irrational" individuals need to believe and trust in a metaphysical, unknown and unexplainable God. Rational people, who recognize the full potential of human enlightenment, will eventually discover what can be accomplished through intelligent, collaborative and coherent discussions. And to support this thesis, they present the accomplishments of Socrates, The Wright Brothers, Pasteur, Einstein, Newton, and other who have improved humanity's plight through their creative genius. But what secularists often leave out of their argument is the declaration by many creative geniuses – Robert Grosseteste, Albert Magnus, Otto Brunfels, and Francis Bacon – that God gave them the insight and ability to complete their work. Scripture is true, "unless God builds the house, they that labour, labour in vain" (Ps 127:1).

Fifth, secularization credits humankind with unlimited creative intelligence and potential design. Eventually, if enough rational thinking is done and adequate experiments are completed, this world will become utopia for humanity. The problem with this postulate is humanists are constantly on guard against shaming their "intelligence" by being forced to admit many of their self-generated schemes failed, while many others – unexpectedly – created immense, unwelcome crisis for humanity. Examples that could be cited to support this claim include, the Thalidomide Pill of the 1960's that became a medical tragedy for many as it affected people in Canada and worldwide, genetic engineering of food, which has caused ecological imbalances in South America's rain forests to such an extent many of the trees, common to the area, no longer grow there.[35]

Sixth, secularism contends the only reality humankind can know "for sure" is material reality, because it is restricted of knowing anything beyond this by being encased in a physical body. But the truth of the matter is humans are constantly seeking, finding, and "enjoying" the metaphysical daily. To validate this claim one need only talk to a newly engaged couple who will pleasingly discuss "how much they love one another" and anticipate the "joy of living together." Stand beside a refugee from Iran, Iraq or Syria and within minutes one will hear them speak about the need for peace in their country. And stand beside the grave of a dearly departed husband or wife, and hear the surviving spouse confidently speak of the hope the departed has for eternity because he or she knew Christ as Lord and Savior! Although humanists believe humankind is the sum of all possible knowledge and meaning, very few, if any humanists, will decry another's hope for a better, more peaceful, and welcome world where generous acceptance of one another, and hospitality towards one another, is shown. This hope – consciously announced, or subconsciously hidden – discredits the secularist claim that humans can only know the physical, real world. Drawn to its furthest conclusion, it also discredits their view that mankind cannot possess a desire to know God.

Seventh, although Christians are obligated to concur with secularists human knowledge and skill has created numerous medical and social improvements for humanity, it must not succumb to secularism's suggestion that it is the source of all creative design. It is not, as can be shown by the following examples. Secularism cannot explain the variant languages spoken throughout the world (Gen 5), it cannot explain how the sun rises in the east and sets in the west (Is 45:6), the rainbow that appears after a heavy rain (Gen 9:14-16), and it cannot explain how a seed, regardless in which direction it may be planted, always grows upward in soil. These limitations clearly demonstrate that despite humankind's claim to possessing a great genius and creative ability, it – over the past six to nine thousand years – has not been able to explain how these aforementioned things came about.

If secularism is to retain credibility of any level, it must honestly examine the evidence and admit it does not possess all power in heaven and earth. In light of this, there is a possibility – a great possibility – there is a "higher power," extant and beyond humankind's control who maintains control and equilibrium over the cosmos. This "power" is God – metaphysical in nature, but personal in relationship with humankind through Christ – who "by the power of His word sustains all things (Col 1:17).

Eighth, secularism dehumanizes individuals as it replaces their human worth and dignity with material gain. In that secularization is intently and intensely concerned with the advancements procured through science and technology, it is – of necessity – primarily concerned with what mankind can do, instead of who he is as a creature. In light of this, secularism avoids investigating the questions, "Who is man, why is he here, what is his purpose in life, and what is his eternal destiny?" With human worth being minimized, mankind is delegated to being nothing more than a "nail."[36] Consequently, he experiences the "death of his soul"[37] and becomes a "moral anonymity."[38] Instead of seeking and knowing God – in whose image humanity was created (Gen 1:26-27) – humans seek intensified productivity whereby they may gain increased notoriety and wealth for no longer does one's personal worth matter. Humanity's value is connected to what one does, or to what one possesses. Because of this Americans, especially, "have begun to conceive it as their birthright to experience a full range of 'self-fulfillment,' even though this leads to endless and debilitating frustration."[39]

Secularism may further dehumanize individuals because it teaches humanity what should and could be done to create a better world, but it often side steps holding humans responsibly accountable for the injustices they do year after year. Because of this oversight, many have escaped judgements for unfair market practices, pyramid schemes, fraud, money laundering, murder, and other serious criminal offenses. This inequality in judging the unrighteous could lie in the fact that secularism holds no objective, common ground rule – the Ten Commandments – by which it might bring individuals to accountability.

The Believer's Response to Secularism

In order for believers to remain unscathed by secularism and secularization, there are a number of factors they must remember.

First, Christians like the ungodly live within a real world that is encourages self-aggrandizement and fulfillment as one of its foundational axioms for meaning in life. To safeguard oneself by being overcome by this dynamic, believers must continuously remember that they are "in the world, but they are not to be of the world" (John 17:14-15). In its fullest meaning, this delegates believers as foreigners in this world who have their affections and hopes founded on a new worldview that empowers them to see God as an inseparable part in their thoughts and activities so He, and not they, receives the glory for their accomplishments (Eph 1:15). Further, this also privileges believers with the certainty that a better, just world – fully designed and created by God – awaits them beyond this life. As this hope if continuously refined, believers see personal worth through developed, godly relationships as being more important than personal accomplishment. It should be of no amazement to believers that when they gather for dinners, games, and like fellowship, conversations often centre on their fulfilled life in Christ than around their self-created accomplishments

Second, believers need to remember they are created in God's image. Because of this, the inner spirit constantly yearns or desires to know God personally. This desire – conscious or unconscious – cannot be easily disposed of by humankind, for regardless where they go, the knowledge of God exists (Ps 139:8). Blaise Pascal recognized this in stating:

> What else does this craving, and this helplessness, proclaim but that there was once in man a true happiness, of which all that now remains is the empty print and trace? This, he tries in vain to fill with everything around him, seeking in things that are not there the help he cannot find in those that are, though none can help, since this infinite abyss can be filled

> only with an infinite and immutable object; in other words, by God Himself.[40]

And Augustine, similarly, suggests humans have an insatiable, innate desire to know God as Lord. He writes:

> What place is there in me to which my God can come, what place that can receive the God who made heaven and earth? Does this mean, O Lord my God, that there is in me something fit to contain you? Or, since nothing that exists could exist with you, does this mean that whatever exists does, in this sense, contain you? If this is so, since I too exist, why do I ask you to come into me? For I should not be there at all unless, in this way, you were already present within me.[41]

Whenever secularists, therefore, contend humankind cannot know God, who is metaphysical, they either are lying forthrightly, or they are seriously – but vainly – attempting to quash an inner feeling which they do not know how to handle. The path for the secularists to resolve their inner need to know God necessitates they recognize His position as Lord and Creator, and then receive Him as Savior and Redeemer Friend. Believers – unlike the ungodly – are readily able to recognize God as an inseparable part of their world because God, through Christ and the Holy Spirit, has quickened their mind to understand the glorious gospel of truth which reveals His power and good will for humanity to them. Secularists, until they receive this revelation, have no choice but to "buy into philosophies" that exclude, or minimize God's activities amongst humankind.

To be effective in evangelism, Christians need to be sensitive to times when secularists discuss spiritual matters, and address their concern as part of God's plan for them to know Him personally. This caring, sharing bearing of their fellowman's problems may be the first step to leading their friends or associates to Christ so they, too, might become a coworker with Him in kingdom business.

Third, believers need to remember they are not of themselves; they have been purchased through the blood of Christ. Because of this "redemption" they are Christ's bond-slaves who honour and glorify Him in everything they do. No longer, as the secularists may, do they seek recognition for what they might be, regardless how "deserving" the accolades of praise might be, or how good these might make the person feel. The reason believers shun self-aggrandizement is they accept that whatever they do "in word, thought or deed is done unto the Lord as they give thanks unto him for the intelligence, insight and invigoration for the task (Col 1:17).

Fourth, believers need to return to an intense study of scripture so they might gain instruction regarding the ungodly teachings and practices of secularists, and be ready to counteract their teaching with godly principles. Contending with, and overcoming secularism is not an academic exploit. Rather, it is spiritual warfare into which believers can enter and defeat secularism as they are "thoroughly furnished unto every good work, so they can rightly divide *and speak* the word of truth (2 Tim 3:16-17). Allister McGrath submits this helpful observation regarding the significance of believers knowing the scripture when contending with secularism and post-modernity.

> As the reformers affirmed so strenuously, we are under obligation constantly to reexamine our ideas and values against scripture, and avoid the complacency of laziness of thinking that the parrot-like repetition of the past ensures orthodoxy. As J. I. Packer pointed out in a careful and wise study of the role of tradition with evangelicalism, we must be prepared to submit all our ideas to the court of scripture, and verify them on its basis. N. T. Wright further challenges us to ensure that our views represent a biblical perspective. Evangelicalism is principally about being biblical, not about the uncritical repetition of past evangelical beliefs and doctrine.[42]

Fifth, believers need to know how to deliver a reasoned and rational apologetic, or defense, for the "reason of the hope that lies within them" (1 Peter 3:15), that is based on scripture and objective evidence so the lies and confusion promulgated by secularism can be effectively thwarted. Whenever this defense for the faith is offered, is must be offered with compassion, and it must give opponents to Christianity a valid call for examining the fallacy of their beliefs without being intimidated. John Stackhouse writes:

> So let us consider all the reasons we find Christianity to be true, good and beautiful. Let us enjoy listing the blessings we have received in following Christ. Let us work to articulate the virtues of our religion in accurate and winsome speech, and to embody lives of integrity. We present a generous God, and we need to be generous, especially in offering our friends everything we can offer to help them along their particular paths. At the same time, let us offer the warrants we have with appropriate circumspection so that we, by our intensity, do not move them to greater disapproval of the God they already shun.[43]

Finally, believers must reaffirm constantly within themselves and to other fellow believers their purpose on earth is to represent and announce the kingdom of God to all peoples, in all places, at all times, through all means available to them. As this "grips" them, they will attend seminars, take college courses, and discuss with other believers how they might be better lights to those who unwisely have accepted secularism as the "norm" for life. Individuals, "drugged by secularism," may hold to its principles simply because they are unaware of alternate teachings provided through scripture and the church. A wise and prudent follower of Christ is constantly looking for opportunities to grow in the knowledge of Christ, and in defending the faith. Training in this area can be gained by reading scholarly books, watching scholarly documentaries, and by reading journal articles on the topic. The author suggests George Holyoake and J. H. Rutherford's book, *Christianity Versus Secularism* and D. A. Carson's book, *The Intolerance of Tolerance* as first readings for those who desire training in counteracting the views of secularism.

Chapter 7

Age Integrated Church Worship: Instilling "Family Connectedness" Within Christ's Church

Introduction

Ask most Christians what the local church represents and they would likely respond, "It is the coming together of the elect of God as the family of God for worship." From a quick assessment of the definition, one would agree with the conclusion. The church, from its start on the Day of Pentecost, consisted of believers who assembled in unity for fellowship, for instruction in the apostle's doctrine, for breaking of bread, and for prayers (Acts 2:42). This should not be considered strange when one remembers those who comprised the Early Church understood the need for unity, because Christ encouraged this despite their varied ages, occupations, personalities, and skills. That the gathering of God's people should be regarded as an "integrated, intergenerational, unified family" is congruent with biblical teaching found in the Old and New Testaments. Although numerous examples could be appealed to, four examples from both books are provided to support this claim.

Age Integration throughout Scripture

First, God's call to Moses to speak to Israel during its first Jubilee, after its successful, God directed escape from Egypt. In giving Moses instruction, God tells him to, "Gather the people together, men and women, and children, and the stranger that is within thy gates that they may hear, and that they may learn, and fear the LORD your God, and observe to do all the words of this law" (Deuteronomy 31:12-13). Second, the occasion of Ezra's prayer as he confessed Israel's transgression of marrying foreign women. During this event, he assembled with him "out of Israel a very great congregation of men and women and children: for the people wept very sore" (Ezra 10:1-5). Third, when Ezra reads the Law to Israel (Nehemiah 8:1-3), facing the Water Gate on the first day of the seventh month. During this event Ezra ensures the men, women and children were present as a collective audience and all the "ears of those present were attentive to the book of the law." Fourth, when Moses provides Hebrew parents direction about teaching the Decalogue to their children, he delegates the event as an intergenerational practice by telling them to teach the Word of God "to their children, speaking of them when they sit in their house, and when they walked by the way, when they lied down, and when they woke up" (Deuteronomy 11:19).

From Christ's teaching in the New Testament, one also discovers this principle being advocated in the following examples. First, Jesus suggests those who are regenerated through the "new birth" have been brought into the family of God with Jehovah being their "Father." Because of this "family connectedness," they are to pray, "Our Father who art in heaven" (Matthew 6:11), knowing, with unshakable confidence, He will hear and respond to their petitions. Second, while speaking to a large crowd near Jerusalem, Jesus discovered some of His followers had promoted themselves above others as teachers following the prideful pattern of the Pharisees. Quickly, He reproves them for their arrogance, reminding them of their family status stating, "But do not call yourself Rabbi: for one is your Master, even Christ; and all you are brethren" (Matthew 23:8). Third Jesus offers a commendation to children as an integral part of His following by placing them on His lap and blessing them. The disciples were disgusted with the children's interruption, so they implored Christ to send them away. Jesus, trying to teach the disciples the need of an age-integrated community of worship, responds to their requests, "Allow the little children to be part of my gathering for such are also included in the Kingdom of heaven" (Mark 10:14). Worthy of notice here is the disciple's lack of response to Christ's rebuke, which might signal their remorse for excluding children as valued members of the kingdom. Fourth Christ willingly accepted and blessed two loaves and five fishes a lad brought for his lunch, and multiplied it so he could feed thousands attending the function (Matthew 14:16-21). He did not send him away, even though he was young and had only a small gift, because He recognized the significance of this boy's contribution that could be used for the good of others.

If these examples are not sufficient to confirm the claim Christ desired His people to be an integrated, intergenerational fellowship, the author offers this example. As Christ fed the five thousand by Galilee, which consisted of men, women and children of all ages, He directed His disciples to sit the crowd in mixed groups of fifty. If He approved of age discrimination, He would have told them to separate the children into groups of fifty, those under the age of thirty into groups of fifty, those in middle-age into groups of fifty and those in their senior years into groups of fifty. But He did not, because He valued the inclusive nature of worship and learning for those gathered.

Paul also contends the church should be an intergenerational integrated family throughout his writings. In Galatians 4, he reminds the Christians that before the "new birth" they were slaves, alienated from God and from one another. On stating this, he further reminds them that through repentance and regeneration, they were adopted as the "sons of God" (Gal 4:1-7, cf. John 1:12 & 13; Rom 8:14-17; 1 Peter 1:14-17), and were made one with Christ, and with those who were regenerated through faith. In other passages, he affirms the church is a unified, integrated family by using terms, "brethren" (Philippians 3:17; Colossians 4:5; 1 Thess 1:4), and "sisters" (1 Timothy 5:2), as descriptors of the close, inseparable spiritual, and "family" connectedness members have because of salvation. Because of this unique, God endowed relationship; Paul cautions them against all segregation or isolation of believers from each other. His reason, everyone in the "spiritual body" is essential for the progressive health, edification, and endorsement of the others, even as every part of the physical body is needed for its health (Rom 12:3-11). Paul encourages unity because this will preserve brotherly love within the church, and safeguard it against disruption of the fellowship it enjoys. This is what the church should be as a coming together of the family of God as a unified host of saints loving and edifying one another to grow in the knowledge of the Lord Jesus Christ.

From Paul's letters to the Ephesians and to the Colossians, it is clear men, women and children met regularly together for worship. Notable in Ephesians 6:1-4, and Colossians 3:16 is Paul's instruction about wholesome, godly relationships between husbands and wives, fathers and children, and masters and slaves. If the members cited were to hear the counsel offered, it is likely they were all present in an unsegregated gathering. Paul reinforces age integrated gatherings when he counsels Timothy how to "treat an older man," "older women" and "younger men" all in the same context. Howard Vanderwell adds:

> From what we discover in the New Testament Church, "it seems that in the early New Testament-era believer lived with the assumption, that of course, each generations needed each other. This was an urgent concern among their relatives in the Old Testament era, and we could expect it to carry over to the new generations. So when Paul says to the Colossians, "Let the word of Christ dwell in you richly; teach and admonish one another in wisdom" we can assume he pictures young and old in relationship with one another, for later, in the chapter, we find him specifically referring to wives and husbands, children and parents, and slaves and masters.[1]

Problems with Age Segregation in the Church

Unfortunately, in the twenty-first century, most local churches are not following the New Testament pattern of intergenerational worship. Instead of reflecting biblical member integrated worship, they have embraced an age segregated and isolated philosophy by which parishioners are set aside into specialized ministry groups, such as Children's, Youth , College and Career, and Seniors Ministries. Rarely do these groups have interactive, intergenerational worship together. Even though these groups are regarded as "essential parts of the church in name," there often is little or no connectedness between the groups spiritually or socially except during "collective family events" such as Sunday school picnics, Christmas banquets, mission conferences and the like. If Christ, or any of the apostles, were to visit churches that have adopted this format, they would be shocked and dismayed with the promoted disconnect within the local fellowship. Assessing the present isolation of members in the age segregated church, the Family Integrated Church Movement suggest age segregation is an apostasy because it "is the product of humanistic philosophers, educators, and sociologists, who espouse the need for meeting individual, immediate needs, rather than caring for the community by following what is taught in scripture.[2] Often the result is minimal intergenerational identity, minimal encouragement for spiritual growth one member to the other, and minimal mentoring by the aged to the youth by providing "correction, reproof and instruction in righteousness" (2 Tim 3:16).

Despite the anomaly age segregated worship has when compared to the teachings in scripture, few pastors appear to be concerned with the ill effect this is having on the local church. When one objectively assesses families in which every member – regardless of his or her age – is invited to share his or her abilities, talents and opinions there usually is a strong sense of valued acceptance noted. In most families, a middle-aged mother cooks supper for her teenage and young children, and they sit together enjoying the meal while they discuss the events of the day. Rarely does a teenager take his or her meal to the bedroom, and eat it isolated from the rest of the family because he or she needs special, private separation. Consider also, secular college and university education. In the over seventeen years of formal education, at secular and religious colleges, the author has never come across age, generational, cultural, or sexual segregation. Students, despite their age, sexual preference, learning ability and the like are included in the "mix of academics," and study collectively for personal growth and the growth of others.

If social institutions – schools, universities and the like – find value with intergenerational learning and employment, the author questions why the local church readily adopts age segregation for its variant ministries. As it has earlier been stated, scripture, the accepted guideline for doctrine and church practice among believers, nowhere encourages segregation of any nature within the local church. It, on the other hand, strongly infers worship as a collective coming together for the good of everyone attending. Because age segregation is contrary to biblical teaching, parishioners should be asking, "If the Bible does not teach this practice, how did this infiltrate the church?"

Answering this question, Brandon Dauphinais suggests age segregated church worship started in 1960s, when congregations, "abandoned multileader shepherd directed, worship in exchange for a secular counterpart where the pastor became the CEO of the Church, with divisional managers providing "faith products" for each segregated group."[3] Reb Bradley, Pastor of Hope Chapel Family Ministries, Sheridan, California, suggests when this became the "norm for congregational gathering," several serious problems arose within the local church. He comments:

> First, it deprives the youngest of ministry God desires them to receive from the older, and seniors receiving ministry from the younger. Second, it often reinforces the immaturity spiritually of the younger because of simplified teaching received from untrained youth leaders. Third, it creates an unhealthy and unnatural age gap with independence which is not seen in regular life, where interdependence of all ages is common. Fourth, it centres a new, nonbiblical self-centred view of church as biblical. And fifth, it limits the vision for outreach, because each segregated group is interested in inviting new comers to specialized program each group may offer.[4]

Under the biblical, foundational format by which the church began ministry, it gathered as the integrated, unified family of God to worship Him, and to edify one other irrespective of their age, or specialized skills. Under the secular, present-day format God's people gather to have their particular needs gratified. Because different ages have different needs, if the new church of the '60s were to be effective in ministry, it would need to have specialized leaders trained to meet these specialized desires. Once the biblical, theocratic format was dispensed with, new, isolated and independent divisions within the church became commonplace. Now the gospel became "marketed" to meet the age needs instead of being proclaimed as the welcome sustaining power of God for all people, regardless of age, race, culture and the like. Because of this "swing" to the exclusionary age programing within the church, one often hears parents state, "We have had to move to a new church because there are no teenagers for my children to interact with," or "we need to move to a new church because there are no programs which will maintain my children's interest." From a biblical view of worship, every Christian's priority for attending services should be "to meet God, to worship Him in Spirit and truth, and to grow in the knowledge of the Lord Jesus Christ as the Holy Spirit speaks through the Word" (Eph 1:1-17), as the church comes together regularly as family "even as the day of the Lord approaches" (Heb10:25). Satisfying one's need for programs or for personal identity and comfort – although these may be psychologically and socially welcome – must never become a primary focus for God's children gathering with others.

One of the benefits of the age-segregated, needs specialized church is it ensures growth in numbers as seekers choose the ambience of worship that best fills their need. But, despite this, this new approach is leaving many "as babes in Christ" deprived of a biblical understanding of the real purpose for the church. With this, other concerns may be cited. First, there appears to be a lack of responsible accountability between groups, because of their independence one from the other. Second, there appears to be a disconnect that fosters alienation of one group from the other. Third, it may foster a primary focus on accommodating a group's passions, rather than focusing on its needed spiritual formation. Fourth, it distorts the biblical principle of covenant in which the whole people of God walk together to edify, educate, encourage, endorse and then empower the church for the mission of announcing the Kingdom of God. Fifth, it may discredit scripture (Deut 6:6-9; Ps 78:1-8), from being the primary source of spiritual formation, as it makes being part of the group" more significant than being part of the collective family. Sixth, there could be engendered among the groups a spirit of competition about the effectiveness of the program, based on the number attending in each group, as opposed to creating a spirit of cooperative edification and blessing for everyone who attends, all to the praise of God's glory.

Recommendation for Age Integrated Ministry

Despite the gloom and doom that appears to be present within the church about age segregation and independence within the local church, there are corrective measures that can be implemented to protect the church from further division. The author suggests the following steps:

First, pastors and elders need to go back to scripture and meditate on the Boss' desire[5] for His people to be the "called out" who come together as His age-integrated and gift integrated family for worship. Second, local churches need to maximize times of collective gathering, if they do not want to dispense with age segregation they have adopted. This may be attained by having "family Sunday Worship services" during which entire families sit together, by having "family festival events" during which families jointly sing special numbers, put on skits, tell their family faith history and the like, or have family progressive suppers where the entire family is encouraged to partake as a godly unit.

Third, churches could seek older people, who have special talents, and group these people with younger individuals so they be mentored in the skills, the ministry and faith the older members possess. Paul mentored Timothy, Tabitha mentored the younger women in the church, and Barnabas mentored John Mark. Fourth, younger men could be trained to help the elderly by mowing lawns, painting their homes, and doing other meaningful ministry work that could connect the generations together. Fifth, churches could hold a "My Story Sunday" where a younger member of the church and an elderly person of the church shares how they came to faith in Christ. With this, a younger member, with an older member, could share their appreciation of the local church and their hopes for it. Six, older people – especially those who love reading – could be connected with younger children (5 – 8 years) and be readers to them and help them learn to be more effective in their reading skills. Sixth, intergenerational bimonthly banquets could be held during which the older and younger members of the church sing a song, play an instrumental, or tell a story, and edify the body. Seventh, the church, bi-yearly, could hold a craft exchange night. During this time anyone within the church could bring their craft with the provision a youth would be willing to exchange his or hers with an adult, and an adult would be willing to exchange his or hers with one of the youths. Eighth, adult to youth or conversely pen pals could be established with letters of encouragement being sent one to the other ever two to three weeks. And ninth, young married couples could be asked to be volunteer drivers to take the elderly on grocery shopping trips and to medical appointments, or on special outings when time permits.

The list could go on based on the inventiveness and the insight of the local church leaders as they moves from having one group insulated and isolated from the other, so the church can become a warm, welcome community of faith in which everyone is recognized and cared for as an integral part of the family. The church has a choice. It can choose to be age and generation segregated, or connected. From God's perspective, the latter is what is desired. In light of this, the author hopes the local church will soon discover the error of its way in adopting the generational segregated philosophy. When this is accomplished, a new sense of "belonging to the family" will be inculcated within the local fellowship, and everyone – children, youth, middle aged and seniors – will feel welcome to use their gifts, talents, and abilities as a unified, integrated force for the good of the collective body, instead of having these hidden among segmented, isolated smaller groups.

Chapter 8

Authorship of the Fourth Gospel: Examining Its Authenticity

The Gospel According to John

For years the authorship of the Gospel of John has been seriously questioned. It, like other books[1] of the Canon, lacks substantive qualifiers about who the author is. Because of this, scholars of various academic proficiencies have been examining both the internal and external evidence available to discover if they can accurately conclude who wrote this, the Fourth Gospel. Newbigin has rightly concluded, "the question of authorship of the gospel is one on which the argument is voluminous, fascinating, and inconclusive."[2] But this should not troublesome to those who want to know whether John wrote this gospel, for there is no indisputable proof William Shakespeare wrote all the literary works accredited to him.

Two major schools of thought about the authorship of John exists, these being the Conservatives and Liberals. Conservative scholars[3] proposition John, the son of Zebedee, also known as the *disciple whom Jesus loved,* is the author of the book. The Liberals, on the other hand,[4] suggest Lazarus, Thomas, called Didymus, a second John - known as John, the Presbyter - or a group of mature Christian disciples, known as amaneuenses[5] wrote it.

There is not, presently, substantial evidence whereby one might dogmatically conjecture who the author of John might be. Therefore, the investigation must continue with a sincere hope that shortly, early fragments that have also been translated from Greek[6] will be found, and bring the contention over this matter to an end. Until then, if scholars desire to know for certain who the author of John is, they will need to continue examining the issue from a scholastic approach, and "weigh" all the evidence offered objectively.

After reading several acclaimed academics who have diligently researched the matter under consideration, and who present reasonable arguments for and against John as author, the author of this paper, based on preponderance of the available evidence, accepts John, the son of Zebedee, as the author of this book!

Disputations about the Authorship of John

When one makes the assertion John, the son of Zebedee is the author he or she must be prepared to respond to the charges that could disqualify him from being the author of the Fourth Gospel. These may include the following points of contention.

First, John was nothing more than an unlearned, uneducated, and undignified Palestinian fisherman. Because of his well-known, low social status, he could never have authored the work. Someone who possessed more social grace and status than he exhibited had to be the author of the book. But, such a conclusion is an oversimplification of first century Palestinian society. Most individuals, especially those living in Jerusalem, Jericho or Galilee, were educated at the Synagogues by well-educated Rabbi who taught them to read and write Hebrew and Aramaic. With this, most first century Palestinians – John included – also received education in the Greco-Roman education system[7] through which they learned Greek, the common language of the day. John's father was a very wealthy fisherman (Luke 5:3), who had several employees. Therefore, it may be possible that through one of these educational facilities he received a formal education which gave him the skill to document and write this book.

If, perhaps John had missed the opportunity to receive this formal, academic training he still should not be disqualified as the author of John. Documents indicate he could have learned to read and write while he travelled as an itinerant preacher for twenty-seven years[8] throughout Asia, or while living in Ephesus, during his early retirement. During both stages of his life, he could have encountered the educated elite, who would have gladly aided him to gain the essential skills to write this gospel in Greek, "the simple and beautiful language of the common people."[9]

Second, John's economic status did not provide him timely opportunities to meet, associate or communicate with the Jerusalem High Priests. This conjecture is absurd. John came from Tiberias, one of Israel's wealthier cities and, was raised by a prosperous fisherman. Because of John's father's prestigious status in the marketplace, it is likely John regularly visited Jerusalem, and sold fish in the public and temple markets. Such being the case, he would have had no difficulty encountering Caiaphas[10] and other priestly court agents.

John may have had the opportunity to meet with Caiaphas personally because of direct family connections. Craig Blomberg, in his book, *The Historical Reliability of John's Gospel,* suggests Mary, the mother of James and John of Zebedee, and Elizabeth, the wife of a Jerusalem priest, were sisters.[11] If this an accurate conclusion, it is not improbable that John, during various stages of his life, would have had direct contact with Caiaphas. Such contact with Caiaphas would have given John opportunity to gain extensive knowledge and insight about the High Priestly practices, and the Jewish religious festivals about which he proficiently writes (John 13:23-26, 19:25-27, 20:1-10, 21:1-14, 21:20-24).

Third, John's arrogant claim he is the *disciple whom Jesus loved* establishes reason to discredit him as author of John. Even if John was "in the inner circle," and possessed a special relational attachment to Christ, which was separate and apart from the other disciples, it is not appropriate Christian grace to boast one's position by using such a lofty title. Rather, in humility, he should have waited for others to assign him this title.

But John's claim is not arrogant! Rather, being "labeled" with this title signifies the deep and meaningful spiritual oneness John enjoyed with Christ, the living God Incarnate, through the day-to-day contacts he had with Him. Furthermore, the term is one of inclusion. When used contextually to show one's devotion to Christ as Lord, it verifies to other believers the greater the commitment one has to Christ, the deeper his or her love for Christ should become. John does not want to alienate himself from the rest of his associates through the spirit of elitism. He wants his colleagues to know how he understands, and appreciates his relationship to Christ. D.A. Carson comments:

> Perhaps the most frequently advanced reason for denying that the beloved disciple is the Evangelist lies in the expression "beloved disciple" itself. It is argued that no Christian would want to call himself 'the disciple whom Jesus loved.' The expression is strong, and is better thought of as someone else saying this about another disciple, than as something any believer would say about himself. Similarly, the person who wrote that Jesus was in the bosom of the Father would be loath to say of *himself* that he reclined in the bosom of Jesus. But these arguments should be abandoned. When a New Testament writer thinks of himself as someone whom Jesus loves, it is never to *suggest* that other believers *are not loved* or somewhat loved less than others.[12]

And B. F. Westcott adds:

> The words 'the disciple whom Jesus loved' express the grateful and devout acknowledgment of something received, and contain no assumption of a distinction above others. Christ loved all; St. John felt, and confesses, that Christ loved him, and showed His love in this single matter. But it does not make him more accepted than any of the other twelve.[13]

Fourth, much of the information covered in this gospel does not coincide with the materials presented in the Synoptic Gospels. Opponents to John's authorship arduously suggest if John "bore witness" to the same Christ Matthew, Mark and Luke did, the accounts of His miracles presented in John should be similar to that presented in the Synoptics.

This accusation may not have been fully thought out. John, like Matthew, Mark and Luke, documents similar activities of Christ's life. Whereas John does not script the same overview of Christ's miracles as do the other writers, he supplements[14] their accounts by adding greater, in-depth detail by which clarity to their works is added. And if this is not his purpose in writing from a different perspective than Matthew, Mark, and Luke, he may have nothing more in mind than adding materials the Synoptic writers may have omitted. It must be remembered John is documenting the life of Christ from a vastly different perspective from the Synoptic writers, as two witnesses to a car accident might provide the same evidence from different perspectives.

Whereas the Synoptic writers analyze Christ's earthy ministry in light of his genealogy and humanity, John examines it from Christ's relationship to the Father, and His purpose for coming to earth. The four Gospels are corroborating the same activities of the life of Christ, but from different views, and with different emphasis. No wonder then, the accounts look different, and contradictory to each other. Joseph S. Exell adds:

> In the polished, and thousand-faced diamond there shines one and the same light in a multiform blending of colours; and should we expect the case to be different in an infinitely higher sphere - the spiritual and the Divine? If a drawing is made of a city first from the east side, then from the west, though in both cases the tallest and the most striking towers and edifices are presented, yet in all other respects the two sketches not only can, but must differ widely. And yet both are faithful copies of the original.[15]

The book of John and the Synoptics may look conspicuously different one from the other because of the sharp contrasting audiences to whom the authors are writing. The Synoptic writers address their works predominantly to Jews, located within Jerusalem and the surrounding areas. John, however, because the book is written while he is living in Ephesus,[16] in all probability, is addressing Jews within Israel, Hellenistic Jews visiting Jerusalem, and Jews scattered abroad throughout Asia. This would necessitate a sharp, immediately recognizable difference in the content of the four Gospels.

Fifth, John never names himself directly as the author, and no one else within – or beyond the text - infers he is the author of the book. But, because one does not draw attention to himself or herself, this does not mean he or she could not have invented something or authored a writing. History demonstrates no one, during the inventing of the Atomic Bomb, knew the name of the director overseeing the project. But, not knowing his name does not nullify the indisputable fact Robert Oppenheimer[17] brought the project to its completion.

John could have intentionally avoided identifying himself as the author because he felt the title *the disciple whom Jesus loved* would readily betray who the author is. Those who had strong connection with John and Christ[18] and others, who closely followed their activities, knew to whom this title referred. Therefore, no further explanation was required.

From the Synoptics (Jn 1:35-51), it may be inferred Peter knew John, to whom this title referred for he, and John, had an inseparable close friendship as Christ's disciples. Because of this, it would not be presumptuous for one to conclude the *disciple whom Jesus loved* referred to another individual than John who, "testifies of these things, and wrote these things" now retained for us in the fourth gospel. Lacoste Munn contributes the following:

> It is clear from other passages in scripture the 'beloved disciple' occupied a place exceptionally close to Jesus at a most crucial moment. It is also clear from other passages of scripture that this same 'disciple' was continuously connected with Simon Peter. In the Synoptic gospel and in John they are often mentioned together. This close connection between the 'beloved disciple' and Simon Peter is enough to create the suspicion the unnamed person is the Apostle, John.[19]

John may also purposely be using the title, *the disciple whom Jesus loved* as a pseudonym because such a practice may have been culturally accepted. In the three passages in which John mentions Thomas, he is never identified strictly by his first name. Rather, he is referred to as "Thomas, called Didymus" (John 11:16, 20:24; 21:2 cf. Mark 3:17)[20] without grave concern to others about the use of an additional title. The term "Didymus" qualifies which Thomas is being spoken of. Likewise, with John, the term *the disciple whom Jesus loved* qualifies which John is being spoken of that being, John, the son of Zebedee. Craig Keener comments:

> To suggest that the author cannot be John because he is not named negates tradition. If internal evidence leads us to conclude that this disciple was most likely the Apostle John of the Synoptics tradition, this suggests that John is either the author in some sense or the book is pseudepigraphic. Ancients recognized that forgery of letters occurred and sometime suspect it, but literary pseudepigraphy was more common than forgery for literary works; pseudonymity was an established and acceptable literary practice of the day, both in broader Greco-Roman and in some Jewish circles.[21]

Sixth, there remains the strong possibility that another John, John the Presbyter[22] also regarded as the "unnamed disciple" of John 21:24, wrote this book. According to those who suggest this John, like his brother James, had been martyred shortly after Christ's death while John was in Ephesus. This 'unnamed disciple' refers to one of John's disciples who, while associated with John, had received detailed copies of John's messages. After hearing John had been martyred, this disciple compiled John's notes in a gospel.[23] He, however, did not claim authorship of the work because he feared incarceration, or some other serious consequence might befall him if he were to be found out. F. F. Bruce comments regarding this "other John:"

> As far as the ascription of this Gospel to John can be traced back, it is regularly assumed that the John in question was John, the son of Zebedee, one of the twelve. There is indeed positive evidence for another 'disciple of the Lord' called 'John' living in the Roman province of Asia, to which John, the son of Zebedee, (according to tradition) migrated from Palestine in the later part of the first century; but no one in antiquity, as far as we can tell, ascribed the Fourth Gospel to the other John, rather than to the son of Zebedee.[24]

By interacting with the common arguments which attempt to obviate John, the son of Zebedee as being the author of the fourth gospel, and by presenting alternative responses to them, it should be clear why dismissing John as the author of the Gospel of John, would be a grievous mistake. To add further support and validity to the claim that John, the son of Zebedee, is the author I also add both external and internal evidence.

Internal Evidence

Internal evidence gleaned from the primary text provides several substantive clues supporting John, the son of Zebedee being the author of this book.

First, the author is an eyewitness to the events reported. On completing the prologue of this book, John states, "We beheld his glory, the glory of the Father, full of grace and truth" (Jn 1:14). With this, John faithfully provides a clear account, as a full time and believable witness, "of all those things that Christ began to both do and teach" (Luke 1:1 & Acts 1:1). In considering John's usage of the term, "we," two possibilities exist. First, it could being used as an inclusive by which John suggests he and others - presumably his fellow disciples - beheld God's glory. But, second it could also be used as the "royal we," by which John means himself, individually. If it is used in the second manner, this would affirm John was Christ's continuous associate and was cognizant of His activities. From the narratives John gives, one may conclude John was present at the marriage celebration in Galilee (Jn 2), Last Supper as one of the twelve (Jn 13), at the crucifixion (Jn 19:32), at the tomb after Christ's resurrection (Jn 20:5),[25] at the home where Jesus presents himself in his glorified body (Jn 20:7), and at the final "fellowship breakfast" Christ prepared for his disciples by the Sea of Galilee (Jn 21:7-14).

John may also be affirmed as most probable author of the book because his writings demonstrate he was familiar with the Judean life-style, with the Israel's topography (Jn 4:3),[26] with the yearly Jewish festivals (Jn 2:13, 23, 6:4, 13:1, 18:28), with the Jewish law which necessitated burial of the dead before the Sabbath (Jn 11:38, 44, 19:40), and with the Old Testament teachings[27] provided in his accounts with which first century Palestinian Jews would have association.

When the Chief Priests decide to arrest Christ, and have him crucified for His claims, John is not surprised for, as a Jew, he knew that according to the Law, anyone who blasphemes God must be put to death (Lev 24:16). The details of the place of Christ's arrest (Jn 18:1),[28] the group that was involved in the arrest (Jn 18:5),[29] and the unbecoming activity of Peter (Jn 18:10)[30] towards Malchus, one of the High Priests servants, unquestionably qualifies John as the witness to what has occurred.

Based on this evidence, any suggestion someone, other than John the son of Zebedee, wrote this gospel could be regarded as a gross overstatement. A secondary redactor may have been able to document the generalities of Christ's activities, but it would take an eyewitness to retain, and present such a detailed and orderly account of Christ's life as one finds in John. The eyewitness, and the writer, because of this necessity, can be no other than John, the son of Zebedee.

It has also been conjectured John did not personally write this gospel, but enabled it to be written by hiring affiliate scribes to document the information while he dictated it to them from memory. This conjecture should not be given much consideration for two reasons. First, the term Greek term "graphew" accurately describes the primary connotation of the verb, "to write down". Second, nowhere in this document, or in other external writings, is there a mention John had others write his manuscripts. But, even if John used scribes as his agents, it remains he possessed the original material, and provided it for their writing. In the truest sense of the word, John "wrote the book." Howard M. Jackson states:

> This passage is meant to mean exactly what it was written to say, the *beloved disciple* was, himself, the author of the Gospel of John. It is use-less, in this light - and it is philologically questionable as well - to propose, as some have done that gray as might be causative (mean 'had someone else') write the text. To suggest that someone else was caused to write the text would give a secondary, unnatural reading to it, and would also provide the necessity for unprecedented anonymity of to whom the work is ascribed. If it were a

pseudo author, his identity probably would not be questioned as early as the pseudonymity of a person usually outlasts his true identity.[31]

The language of the Fourth Gospel, when compared to the that of The Revelation – which John, the son of Zebedee is also purported to have written – it is quickly concluded there is similarity in the structure, the content, and the purpose of both books. A further, stronger witness to John's authorship of both books is the parallel structure of the prologues (Jn 1:1-14 cf. Rev 1:1-7)[32] in which John openly claims to be the authentic, first-hand witness of what he is writing. If there is no contention who wrote Revelation, there should be no debate who wrote John because of these similarities.

External Evidence

With this internal evidence affirming John, the son of Zebedee's authorship of this book, there also exists extensive external evidence that strongly supports this claim.

The earliest, external witness affirming John's authorship is taken from Ignatius.[33] While writing to the church at Ephesus, he makes no mention of John's authorship, but neither does he question the legitimacy of it. The apparent reason for the purposeful oversight is "he unwaveringly assumes and accepts John is the author."[34]

The most significant and convincing testimony to John's authorship comes from Irenaeus, "who lived in the second half of the second century, and who was the first churchman in Gaul to achieve prominence."[35] In a letter written during this time he describes all four canonical gospels. Regarding John specifically, he writes, "John, the disciple of our Lord, who had leaned on his breast, did himself publish a book, during his residence in Asia." It is believed that Irenaeus gained this knowledge from Polycarp, a former student of John[36] who had either heard him preach, or share stories about his personal encounters with the Lord, Christ.

Eusebius,[37] (c 342), a fellow student with Arius, who had great influence at court, and believed Polycarp's record was accurate, recounts that John wrote the gospel after he had asked his colleagues to give themselves to fasting and prayer so he would know what to do with the information he possessed. C. Hill provides the commentary on John's request:

> On the same night that John made the request, it was revealed to Andrew, [one] of the Apostles, that with all of them reviewing [it], John should describe all things in his own name. And so, although different, beginnings might be taught in the separate books of the Gospels, nevertheless, it makes no difference to the faith of believers since all things in [all of them] are declared by one Sovereign Spirit.[38]

Papias of Hierapolis,[39] (c 60-130), a possible disciple of John, and a companion of Polycarp, strongly contends there were two Johns living in Ephesus near the end of the first century, and one of them "put down into writing the things he had encountered while being with Christ, and his report was believed by many." It is believed John, the beloved disciple, may well have been in Ephesus during this time. If so, Papias' record cannot be overlooked, for in it may be hidden the strongest evidence for John, the son of Zebedee, being the author of the fourth gospel.

Most recent discoveries at Qumran will be an immeasurable aid in closing the chasm between what is truth and what is speculation about the authorship of John. In recent digs, documents have been discovered that demonstrate "affinity between Palestinian secular writing and Johannine writings"[40] in the use of opposing concepts such as good/evil, light/darkness, life/death, and in the use of such terms "the sons of light", "the way, the truth, and the life", and "the works of God."

The value of the information is twofold. It provides a better approximation when the document was written, and it provides substantive proof that the language of the fourth gospel is comparatively similar to that used by others of this era. From this evidence one can conclude John, the son of Zebedee, who was also alive at this time, was very familiar, and used the common language to document the time he spent with Christ as *the disciple whom Jesus loved.* With such reliable documentation available, there should be no doubt that John wrote the gospel in question.

Implications for the Faith

Extensive evidence, both internal and external, substantively qualifies John, the son of Zebedee, as the author of the fourth gospel. This somewhat conclusive evidence has a number of formative implications for the Christian faith.

It demonstrates the information about Christ is credible, and can be trusted. Because the author is an eye witness to everything he documents, there is no reason to conjecture or to second guess what he must write to support his claims. Rather, in a straight forward, non-fabricated narrative, he unapologetically declares Christ is fully human while being, at the same time, fully divine, and then provides reasonable evidence upon which he basis these claims. In a court of law John's eye witness testimony would be accepted as reliable. Such being the case, for followers of Christ, is there any common sense reason why the witness of John should be refuted as being genuinely true?

John provides humanity with a logically developed, easily understood declaration of Christ which no other writer has expounded it logically and clearly. In this gospel Christ's church has a powerful tool for evangelism. If the message of redemption were presented with the same clarity, and same commitment as John does, little else, if anything, would be necessary for faith in Christ to be stirred and realized in the spiritually sensitive heart.

John's authorship demonstrates God uses ordinary, common individuals to announce His coming kingdom. Jesus chose twelve unlearned and untrained people, and mentored them to faith so they, after being empowered by the Holy Spirit, would be effective, spontaneous and powerful witnesses of His kingdom. John was a fisherman, willing to abandon everything, and to be taught of Christ. Because of this, John, *the beloved,* was used by God as an oracle presenting the truths of Christ, His love, and His redemption.

The church needs to revel in this thought. God implores His people to bear witness "He is the lamb of God who takes away the sins of the world." He does not ask them to bring the kingdom to earth; He will do that as the witness is faithfully declared. Knowing this, the church needs to shake off the regressive lethargy that has critically negated its effectiveness as "salt and light in the world," and begin, afresh, to point humanity to salvation through Christ. John, the son of Zebedee, was God's choice for first century Palestine, and he fulfilled his calling. Who knows who will be Christ's choice as His witness for this century? The question, however, is will that person be ready to fulfill the calling regardless of the "cup of suffering he might have to drink?"

John's authorship provides believers with the hope of everlasting life with the Father as the gift of God. Other religions offer karma, reincarnation, or some other form of eternal bliss in the afterlife, but none offer this together with God. John presents Christ making this irreversible promise, and validates the promise by Christ declaring He, Himself, will come and receive His followers unto Himself so they can be one with Him and Father forever.

Other religions offer eternal bliss, but this is usually contingent on good works, and is an elusive goal to which very few can attain. But Christianity - as related reliably by John - offers everlasting life to all who believe in Christ. Because no other religion can fulfill this promise, Christianity stands exclusively separate and apart from them. Hope, such as this, enhances the believer's immediate faith, but it also enables them to face death with little or no anxiety, for they know they will awaken to enjoy unending, everlasting life with the Father and the saints who have died before.

John's authorship, sanctions the veracity of other parts of scripture, which he augments by clarifying materials previously expounded by Matthew, Mark and Luke. Liberal scholars suggest John does not "line up" with the Synoptics because his writing leaves out information discussed within them. But John does not contradict the Synoptics, or any part of the Old Testament. Rather, he often clarifies, and qualifies the truth presented by others. For believers this provides confidence God's Word, in its entirety, is true and believable.

John may not be accounting exactly the same narrative other authors documented, but the materials he delivers are parallel to them. When believers read John, they may not encounter everything Jesus said and did, but they gain an unmistakable, clear pronouncement He is the Christ, the Son of the Living God, and on this they can "hang their eternal future" with confidence that their end destiny is good. John given has us no good reason to doubt his witness regarding Christ and His promises, and therefore, like the other disciples; we accept these, through faith, wholeheartedly as truth.

Personal Persuasion and Conclusion

There is no indisputable proof affirming John, the son of Zebedee's authorship. And, at this time, there does not appear to be any forthcoming archaeological evidence that will provide the proof many desire or need to support this claim.

The author readily admits there are newer 'tools' of scholarly investigation that eventually may provide more detailed evidence to dissuade this author John, the disciple Christ loved, is the author of this book. This conclusion is based on the internal and external evidence that strongly affirms my speculation on this matter may be accurate" while the claims of others may be wrong. It remains the responsibility of those that oppose John, the son of Zebedee being the author of the Fourth Book to provide uncontestable, and convincing evidence would disproves the claim and cause the author, with others, to change his/their opinion regarding this matter.

Chapter 9

Christ's Missional Church: Actively Announcing the Kingdom of God

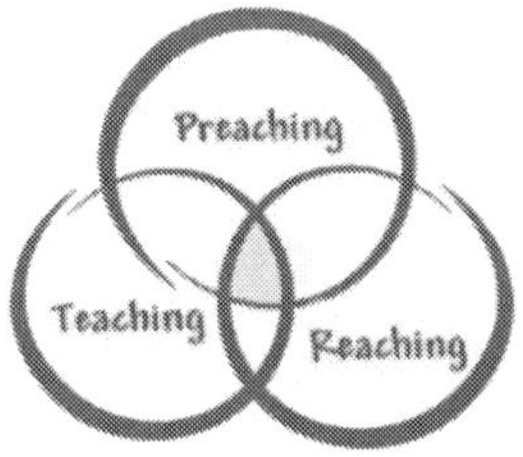

Today the relevancy of the local church is being questioned by many inside and outside its walls. Recent reports suggest that less than two percent of Canadians attend Sunday worship, and less are having Christian weddings or funerals. This decrease in church attendance is caused by several factors. These include, the church cannot provide answers to the questions posed by postmodernity, it has lost its warm, compassionate, welcoming spirit, and it has lost connection with the social needs of humanity. Because of these problems, many evangelical congregations have limited their outreach and have redirected ministry to caregiving of the church members, or overseas missions ventures. For the moment such action might be profitable, but in the long run, they may have serious results for they may be a signal these churches are abdicating their God-given call to kingdom mission.

Regardless what the ungodly might assume about the church's relevancy, the Trinitarian God reckons it as an essential agent whereby people can be redirected to fellowship with Him. The church has received a God-given mandate (Matthew 28:16-20), as His "sent ones" (John 20:25). Understanding the significance of this commission, the church needs to move beyond its "holy huddle" into the world, and prophetically announce the salvific truths of the gospel in the boldness and the authority God has given it.

Since the supreme desire of God is continued, unhindered fellowship with humanity, missional churches are urged to preach the gospel through which it can expresses God's love, and offer eternal hope to those who desperately need to be liberated from self, sin and Satan . An understanding of this mandate is essential if the church is to actively, and meaningfully participate with God in seeing His kingdom come on earth as it is in heaven (Matt 6:9-16). Moltmann adds:

> Where the theological perception of history is concerned, there will be a modern discovery of Trinitarian thinking when there, is at the same time, some fundamental change in modern reason - a change from lordship to fellowship, from conquest to participation, from production to receptivity. The new theological penetration ought also to free the reason that has been made operational - free it for receptive perception of its other, free it for participation in that other. Trinitarian thinking should prepare the way for a liberating and healing concern for the reality that has been destroyed.[1]

But before the church can fulfill its mandate as a 'missional church', there are a several first place, essential commitments it must restate and implement as co-workers with Christ.

First, it must refresh its understanding of what God's plan for humanity is. From scripture (Genesis 1:27), it is clear God's primary purpose for creation is a relational communion with Him whereby humankind may know God and enjoy Him forever. Immediately, after creating Adam and Eve, God came daily to walk and fellowship with them in the coolness of the evening. And, even when Adam and Eve willingly and openly defied God's command not to eat of the Fruit of the Tree of Life, God returned to find and walk with them as friend (Gen 2). In so doing, He clearly demonstrated His heart's affection would always be for good toward His creation. And then, to show this to humanity – as an eternal covenant – He selected Abraham's lineage through which Christ would be born, and eventually suffer and die so the breach of fellowship between God and man, because of sin, could be removed.

Second, the church must regain an appreciation of the message it is to preach, that being, "the kingdom of God is at hand, make straight the way of the Lord" (Matt 3:14). "Preaching the kingdom calls humanity to recognize God's rightful authority to rule as Sovereign Lord over His creation."[2] Both John, the Baptist (Matt 3:2), and Christ (Luke 13:3-5), preached the kingdom of God" as their central message. Both were "charged" with the positive and powerful change news of the kingdom would bring to humanity. Nothing else mattered to them and, therefore, they published this good news everywhere they went. Mortimer Arias comments:

> Jesus' evangelization, then, was kingdom evangelization. Matthew not only confirms Jesus' evangelization was centered "in the good news of the kingdom," but it describes Jesus' holistic method: teaching, preaching, and healing. The "good news of the kingdom" is for the whole person – physically (healing), intellectually (teaching), and spiritually (preaching).[3]

God's intended end of the kingdom is His shalom as He endows humanity with the same compassionate love, grace and mercy He, Himself, enjoys. God's kingdom is not earthly and limited to a few, selected individuals. Rather, it is spiritual and it is extended to all those who will come to Him by faith, repent of their sin, and obediently follow Him as Savior and Lord. The kingdom news God gave to Christ is the same news Christ imparted to His church when He commissioned it saying, "And as you go, preach, saying, 'the kingdom of God is at hand'" (Mark 10:7). In light of this, the church's heart is to pulsate with the same kingdom message of redemptive grace for, "The church is nothing less than Christ's corporate replacement on earth through whom Christ continues His incarnation by dwelling in it."[4]

Unless the church becomes refocused on this message, it may become sidetracked by other ventures, commendable though these might be, which could blind it from its primary purpose. Like Christ, the church must possess tunnel vision, so it can remain faithful, fulfilling the will of the Father as it witnesses to the reality of the kingdom of God. Once this is done, its effects in missional outreach will increase dramatically.

Third, the church must reconsider its source of empowerment. Many North American churches have been seduced into believing signs and miracles, leadership charisma, or an ethereal, heavenly inspired testimony might motivate and empower it to become more proactive in reaching the unregenerate. But such is not the case! If Christ's church is to effectively fulfill its commission as Christ's witness, it needs more than personal insight. It needs the empowerment of the Holy Spirit! The church can passionately tell people about salvation in Jesus Christ, "but only the Holy Spirit can draw individuals to a personal faith in Him."[5]

Jesus affirmed this reality. During His last dialogue with the disciples, before His ascension to the Father, Christ resolutely affirmed its need of the Holy Spirit for effective ministry saying, "But you shall receive power after the Holy Spirit is come upon you and you shall be my witness" (Acts 1:8). This empowerment would make the kingdom message significant to the disciples, give them boldness to live Christ-like, give them favour before their fellowman, and endow them with wisdom to make godly decisions when these were unpopular or when the Spirit-led path seemingly ran counter to common sense."[6] By providing the Holy Spirit, Christ was unveiling a new paradigm by which the disciples – and the Church – would work. Before receiving the Holy Spirit, they rejoiced as they saw miracles occur. But now, after they received the Holy Spirit (John 20:22), they would rejoice because their names – and hundreds of others – were written in the Book of Life (Phil 4:3), and they had a glorious eternal hope that would never end!

The church that is ready to delve into kingdom announcement must rely solely on the Holy Spirit to bring about change, for spiritual formation "comes not by might, no by power, but by God's Spirit says the Lord of hosts" (Zechariah 4:6). Charles Van Engen adds:

> We have found the most effective missionary congregations are incarnational - that is, they reflect the presence of Jesus Christ, and embody the Holy Spirit within their communities.

> Therefore, Spirit-led administration is an requirement at all levels - sending church, missionary agency, and receiving congregation. Only with the Holy Spirit's understanding and empowerment can a church balance the task of contextualizing the church's witness to the culture, and also calling the culture to repent and to confirm to the unchanging demands of scripture. Without the Holy Spirit, none of this is possible.[7]

The Holy Spirit plays a second role in kingdom extension (Jn 16:8)[8] as He woos individual's to seek Him by arranging circumstances in a person's life so the individual will seek Him for redemption (Lk 19; Jn 3; 1 Tim 1:11-13). The church needs to work with the Holy Spirit, by raising curiosity about redemption through the preaching of the Word faithfully, so all the Father has given Christ will come to Him (John 17:22). Regarding this co-partnering C. Sumner Wemp comments:

> The people of God must live a Spirit-filled life. Individuals cannot manipulate people into getting saved. The Holy Spirit alone can convict and convert unregenerate humanity. Someone has figured it takes a thousand laymen, and six preachers to win one soul per year. No – a thousand times no! It just takes Spirit-filled Christians faithfully sowing the seed for hundreds to come to Christ day after day.[9]

Any church that lacks appreciation of the Holy Spirit's work needs to reread the book of Acts. Here it will rediscover how the people of God copartners with the Holy Spirit so He, once again, will have unrestrained liberty to change the "world" over which the church has influence.

Fourth, missional churches must affirm the priority of evangelism. I am not inferring worship, fellowship, prayer and hospitality should be neglected - these are all valued ministries of the church. But the church needs to move beyond "caregiving" to "career building" by encouraging its people to "see the fields are white unto harvest" and pray that He will send forth workers – from its people – to cause others to know Christ as Lord (John 4:35). Once this is realized, the people of God will move beyond the sanctuary walls, and proclaim the message of the kingdom. Christ knew the joy of fellowshipping with His disciples, but His commission to them, from the beginning was, "follow me, and I will make you fishers of men" (Matt 4:19).

Because the disciples prioritized evangelism, the church, after the Day of Pentecost, grew rapidly as the Lord added "daily those who should be saved" (Acts 2:47). As an extension of the disciple's fervency in sharing the gospel, thousands of Christians today also have experience the salvific grace of Christ. God could have chosen angels or other means by which His kingdom message could have been declared among the heathen. But He chose to use His church – men and women who have experienced His grace, love, and mercy and who are dedicated to His work to accomplish the task. Missional churches need to reaffirm their call, and commitment to Christ's commission, shake off their lethargy, and begin calling men and women to "taste of the Lord and see that He is good" (Psalm 34:8). If Christ went everywhere preaching the kingdom of God, should not His church, as it submits to Him in unwavering obedience, be doing likewise?

Fifth, missional churches need to recognize the whole community of believers as coworkers in kingdom ministry (2 Cor 6:1). Regardless how insignificant an individual and his or her gift might appear to be, he or she is essential to kingdom ministry, because a church can never accomplish its God-given mission unless the whole body enthusiastically is working towards the same end. Missional churches, therefore, need to "invite the whole congregation to make a contribution to the life and direction of the church."[10]

In recent days (1990-2015) the employment and deployment of the laity's gifts in missional work has been ignored. Therefore, many Christians felt disqualified to contribute anything to missional outreach. But, this must change! Missional churches are to be "safe places"[11] where the people of God explore new ideas, and use their gifts so the body can function holistically in the ministry to which it has been appointed. Christ delegated the whole church to evangelism, not just a select, isolated few. George G. Hunter adds:

> The recovery of the apostolic ministry of the clergy, and all the people of God, to peoples who do not yet believe is, perhaps, the most significant movement in the world church. The church in many lands is rediscovering God entrusts evangelism, church planting, and cross-cultural mission to all disciples - (not only the professionals). When the vision of apostolic ministry is recovered, it begins communicating the gospel, raises up some converts, forms them into a congregation, equips the congregation for its mission, grounds the people in its beliefs, life-style and vision that informs and energizes the mission, and eventually compels some of its members to become apostles to other nations. This is the true end of God's great commission for kingdom advancement in our generation.[12]

The Early Church knew the value of every believer engaging in Christian witness, and so "day-by-day, in the temple courts and from house-to-house, they went about teaching and proclaiming Jesus is the Christ" (Acts 4:42). Only as a fully gift integrated witnessing community can the church effectively portray the mystery of Christ's redemptive love in all its power and fullness. R. Paul Stevens adds:

> With the lordship of Christ, the outpouring of the Holy Spirit, and the dawning of the end/last days (Acts 2:7), the whole church, according to scripture, is the true ministerium, a community of prophets, priest or princesses, serving God seven days a week. All are clergy in the sense of being appointed by God to service as His dignified inheritance. All have a share in the power of the Spirit. All are laity in the sense of having their identity rooted in the people of God. All give ministry.[13]

The church preaches full collective body ministry. Now, however, it's time to commission the whole congregation for witness so Sunday's spiritual counsel "will have some relevance for living a life of faith in the real world"[14] Monday to Saturday. The New Testament is filled with accounts of ordinary people telling, and retelling, what

what we should do with the message of the kingdom presented in the gospel, is there any reason why we should neglect doing this?

Implications for Missional Churches

In light of scripture, and the aforementioned 'theology of the missional church', Christ's church must critically re-examine its present approach to evangelizing unregenerate humanity so that it will maximize its potential as an effective witness to Christ's kingdom. Five areas of re-examination may be necessary.

First, any programs, outreach endeavours, or evangelistic crusades that do not intentionally align with God's original manifest of kingdom advancement need to be revamped, and be brought in sync with it. Christ sent out His church preaching the gospel of repentance. Two thousand years later, this still remains the foundational purpose for the church's existence. If missional outreach fulfils anything but Christ's original commission, it would be better the church did not exist, then to be wasting human talent, and time on misguided, and unprofitable ventures.

Second, the church needs to immediately begin listening to the narrative of the laity, encourage them their narrative is significant, and then commission it to share it with associates in the market place. Empowering the laity will provide impetus for it to do more than just live its faith out for twenty-four hours on Sunday. Rather, it will motivate it to prepare themselves as conduits for kingdom grace every time it gives an answer "in love for the hope that lies within itself" (1 Pet 5:18).

As the laity present their narratives, churches need to note individuals who gifted as evangelists (Eph 4:11-17), and then link them with mature, energized and focused mentors so they will become effective "kingdom seed planters." If missional churches fail in this one area, it is very likely the laity, also Christ's chosen ambassadors, will believe only church delegated ministries are special. Then they will, tragically, abandon any effort to share their faith with the needy. Charles Ringma adds:

> The tragic implication of the church ignoring the laity in kingdom ministry is the church operates an agenda that pushes the multitudinous expressions of the people's love to the margin. Only the church's formal expressions of service

are now considered to be legitimate. The people's work as the 'scattered' church is not supported and remains unacknowledged and becomes alienated from any meaningful ministry of the church.[24]

Whatever needs to be done, missional churches need to begin empowering the laity so they, as Christ's ambassadors, will confidently represent His kingdom wherever they go! The stronger and more enthused a church is in commissioning the laity, the stronger its maturity and outreach potential will become.

Third, missional churches must "shake off" any delusion that kingdom outreach can be accomplished through man-centered initiatives, for the "kingdom of God is not meat nor drink, but righteousness in the Holy Ghost" (Romans 4:17). The church, by human persuasion, will never turn humanity to the righteousness God demands. To accomplish this, His church desperately needs Holy Spirit empowering so it may persuade humanity to repent, and turn from its sin. Unless God's Holy Spirit permeates, and empowers the church, it will be nothing more than another social entity, offering moralistic programs that cause humanity to accept as expected its present ungodly plight. God help the church if it should ever slip into this state of affairs! Such an action, undoubtedly, would grieve the Holy Spirit!

Fourth, missional churches must see the urgency of the hour. Christ warned His disciples not to procrastinate doing kingdom ministry because the "fields are white unto harvest." Christ's church, like the disciples, needs to perceive, and honestly assess the severity of the situation (John 4:35), and then, "pray the Lord of the harvest to send forth labourers into the fields" (Matthew 9:38), so all the Father has given Christ may come to Him.

Christ's missional church needs to see humanity as more than intellectuals on a temporary, earthly pilgrimage. It needs to see humanity as being spiritual entities with an eternal destiny, and begin refocusing its ministry so those who need Christ will find the new birth as a discovery worth finding. God's desire for humanity, from the very beginning, has been "that no one should perish, but all should come unto repentance" (John 3:16). With this intent, He gifted His church with the ministry of reconciliation (2 Cor 5:18). Being conscious about the lateness of the hour, and the apathy of individuals dying as aliens of the kingdom, missional churches have no justification for doing anything less than the Father's business. Christ's heart pulsates with God's kingdom desire. If His heart pulsates with this, and so should His church's heart so as a corporate body it will be compelled to reach out as they touch the least, the last, and the lost with kingdom grace.

Fifth, missional churches must use all resources at their disposal to disseminate kingdom knowledge among the ungodly. This could happen as God's kingdom message is interwoven in special dramas, concerts, or feasts when the community is invited to gather with the church in community functions. Neighbourhood bar-b-cues, evening video presentations, women's morning coffee fellowships, family weekend fishing or skiing outings, and the like should also be marked as opportunities during which Christ's caring love could be extended to family, colleagues and associates who do not yet know Christ. Church leaders might also teach members how to use gospel tracts, the Roman Road coin, or the Evange-Cube as effective personal witness aids. Paul said, "I am made all things to all men, so by all means I might save some" (1 Cor 9:22). All resources can be effective for outreach if they are blessed by Christ, and empowered by the Holy Spirit. God has provided the resources; now it's time to fulfill Christ's mission by implementing them so the church may do kingdom work in this time for this generation.

Chapter 10

Eternal Security: Is It Biblical?

Some years ago a friend and I were discussing our childhood experiences while attending church. As the conversation advanced he interrupted, "Well, at least we don't have to worry about how many times a day we've lost our salvation." Our childhood, spiritual adventure had been overridden with fear that somehow we had "accidentally" sinned in word, thought or deed and thereby, we had lost our salvation because we had lost favour with God. Each night, before retiring we would earnestly seek God in prayer, and plead for forgiveness from every sin we might have committed lest, during the night we should die and, because of unforgiven sin, be cast into the lake of fire.

This relentless fear haunted me for years. I was always on guard about what I might say and do. I just couldn't take the chance of losing my salvation. The consequence would be dangerous! In this devastating state of mind, I tried to secure my salvation through good works, instead of resting confident in God's promise it had been procured for me through Christ, once and for all, on Calvary.

This changed in 1968 when, through diligently searching scripture, I discovered salvation is the free, unending gift of God extended to all who would come to Him by faith, and not the temporary, fleeting work of man. My doubts regarding the security of my salvation in Christ "evaporated." Immediately I received peace and assurance that if I loved, honoured, obeyed and followed God in accordance with the teachings of scripture, I would be "sheltered under the wings of the Almighty," and no one could pluck me out of His hand (John 10:29).

The Context of Eternal Security

There are two predominant, evangelical schools regarding the believer's security in salvation these being, Arminianism and Calvinism.

Arminianism teaches one's salvation depends largely on an individual's acceptance or rejection of God's offer of redemption as the Holy Spirit speaks to him or her, regarding this matter, through the preaching of the Word. Arminius writes:

> Evangelical faith is an assent of the mind, produced by the Holy Spirit, through the Gospel, in sinners, who, through the law, know and acknowledge their sins, and are penitent on account of them, by which they are not only fully persuaded that Jesus Christ has been constituted by God the author of salvation to those who obey him, and that he is their own savior if they have believed in him as such, and through him on God as the benevolent Father in him, to the salvation of believers and to the glory of Christ and God. The form of this assent is confirmed and increased by the daily exercise of prayers and mortification of the flesh, and by the practice of good works. Knowledge is antecedent to faith; for the Son of God is beheld before a sinner believes on him. But trust or confidence is subsequent to it; for, through faith, confidence is placed in Christ and through him in God.[1]

Since humankind is responsible for coming to God through faith, it is also responsible for maintaining his "connection" to it. Accepting this proposition insinuates one's salvation depends on what he or she does or does not do. A "falling-out of grace" is possible for the believer immediately if he or she – knowingly or unknowingly, willingly or unwillingly - violates any commandment of God! This places the person in a precarious dilemma when the matter of his salvation is considered.[2]

Even if the believer repented and was "reinstated into the faith," that individual's assurance of salvation would be temporal and fleeting, because by committing the next sin, his or her salvation, once again, would be jeopardized. And, if he or she should die without having opportunity to confess his or her sin, he or she, most certainly, would be damned to everlasting torment in hell.

Calvinism, contrary to Arminianism, teaches salvation is the gracious gift of a kind and benevolent God, who seeks lost and unregenerate humankind. Through the work of the Holy Spirit, unregenerate humans are made aware of their sin (John 16:15), drawn to Christ's redemptive grace, and are redeemed. Once redemption – justification – has been finalized by God, the individual is adopted into the family of God, and permanently sealed unto the day of redemption (Eph 1:13). All this is completed by Yahweh who, sovereignly, according to His will, predestines those who should be saved. Humankind never initiates salvation because "it is dead in its trespasses and sins" (Eph 2). Until God's love (John 3:16) permeates one's heart, and convicts the individual of his or her need for Christ's salvific grace, the person can do nothing to know or gain everlasting life (John 3:1-5).

God, Initiator of Redemption

That man, of his own desire and initiative, cannot believe in Christ as Savior is certain according to scripture. Apart from God, man is "dead in his trespasses and sin" (Eph 2:1). In this deplorable, detestable, and desperate state, he is estranged from fellowship with God. There is nothing he or she can do to find release from the bondage of sin. In this sordid state he is a slave to Satan, and "continuously does the works of his or her father who is a liar from the beginning" (John 8:44). To find release from sin and Satan, humankind needs a quickening of the heart, mind and will towards godliness and righteousness. Because one cannot do this himself or herself, he or she must rest on the mercy, and calling of God who is "willing to seek and to save all those that will come to Him by Christ"

(John 3:17). Scripture concludes no one can come to the Father except the Spirit draws him or her (John 6:44). Anyone, who would attempt to take credit for his salvation contradicts scripture, and is an affront to the Almighty, who, before the foundations of the world, of His own will and design, inaugurated salvation. Calvin emphasizes Christ's supreme role in wooing one to salvation stating:

> As all humankind are, in the sight of God, lost sinners, we hold that Christ is their only righteousness, since, by His obedience, He has wiped off our transgressions; by His sacrifice, appeased the divine anger; by His blood, washed away our stains; by His cross, borne our curse; and by His death, made satisfaction for us. We maintain that in this way man is reconciled in Christ to God, the Father, by no merit of his own, by no value of works, but by gratuitous mercy. When we embrace Christ by faith, and come as it were in communion with Him, this we term, after the manner of scripture, the righteousness of faith.[3]

God, the Holy Spirit, draws or woos humans to redemptive grace, and everlasting life. Without this drawing, John Flavel contends, there is nothing one can do to merit, earn or receive salvation. He comments:

> Surely, for any poor soul to venture itself forever upon Jesus Christ whom it never saw, nay, upon Christ whose very existence its own unbelief calls in question whether he be or no: and that when it is even weighed down to the dust, with the burdensome sense of its own vileness and total unworthiness, leaving nothing in itself except shame and misery, the working of death and fears of wrath; go to Christ, of whose pardoning grace and mercy it never had any the least experience, nor can find any ground of hope in itself that it should be accepted; this is as much above the power of nature, as it is for a stone to rise from the earth, and fix itself among the stars. Well might the apostle ascribe it to that Almighty Power which raised Christ up from the dead (Eph

1:19-20). If the Lord draws not the soul and that omnipotently, it can never, from itself, come to Christ.[4]

The Preservation of the Saints

Even as humans have no privileged position of inaugurating forgiveness of sin or salvation, they are not capacitated – in and out of themselves – to keep an accepted, welcome, honourable and sure standing as the "children of God" (Gal 4:4-7). This remains God's self-imposed, willing responsibility because of His unwavering, unshakable and unending covenant of love which He established before the foundations of the world were laid (Ps 103:17). Theologically, this is known as Preservation of the Saints.

Preservation may be defined as, "God's power intervening in the lives of the saints to keep believers in a state of grace until the end."[5] Robert L. Reymond enlarges this definition:

> Every true child of God, that is every person whom the Father has chosen in Christ before the foundation of the world, and for whom Christ died, will never come into condemnation. That person can never be lost, but is eternally secure. By the nature of God's saving grace he/she will be finally and certainly saved."[6]

The "preservation of the saints" is possible because the Holy Spirit seals God's ownership and security on the believer's life, guaranteeing his or her redemption until the Day of Jesus Christ (Eph 1:11-17). The following scriptural affirmations about God's character, and His love towards the saints invigorate believers to hold an unthreatened and unceasing confidence in God's preserving power.

First, God's nature. Scripture states "God is the Alpha and Omega, the Beginning and the End" (Rev 1:8). There has never been a time when God has not existed, and there will never be a time He will not exist. With God there is "no variableness, neither shadow of turning" (James 1:17). Because of this promise, saints – regardless how long they have enjoyed redemption by God – can be assured, their position in Him will remain firmly established, "for faithful is He that calleth, who also will do it" (1 Thess 5:24).

Second, God's creative power. God created, and now maintains "all things by the word of His might" (Heb 1:3), totally independent of man. At no time has there ever been the slightest interruption to His plan. Because of this unchallenged and unwavering power, the believer preserves a strong confidence that nothing, absolutely nothing, will interrupt, shake or destroy God's protective custody of his or her soul, or his or her everlasting salvation regardless of the sin that besets the person, for "where sin abounded, grace did much more abound" (Rom 5:20).

Third, Christ's personal testimony about His persevering power over the saints. Out of His own accord, for the sanctity of the beloved, He covenants with those who know His voice and follow Him, "He will give them everlasting life, and they shall never perish, neither shall any man pluck them out of my hand" (John 10:28). Augustine comments:

> Concerning those who are His sheep by virtue of the Father's election and effectual summons, Jesus declares: 'my sheep hear my voice and I know them, and they follow me', (John 10:27), that is, as their shepherd He knows them, and as His sheep, they hear Him and follow Him as a matter of course. And of those who are His sheep Jesus says that they shall never perish, and that no one will or can catch them out of his and the Father's hand. Here Jesus affirms the saint's eternal security in terms of that precious Shepherd-sheep relationship which eternally prevails between Him and His own.[7]

Fourth, testimonials of like-minded believers. Paul states, "for I know in whom I have believed, and I am persuaded "He is able to keep that which I have committed to Him against that day" (2 Tim 1:12). Paul is giving more than mental ascent to the possibility that his salvation is safe in God's hand. Rather, he is stating, in the strongest terms possible, he is unreservedly convinced and certain that God is able to keep, hold, protect, and insure his salvation during his present life, and into eternity. And then, as if this claim needed reinforcing, he asks, "What shall separate us from the love of God" (Rom 8:34-36)? His conclusion; "nothing shall ever separate the believer from it" (Rom 8:37-39).

The most notable example of God's preservation of His chosen people can be found by examining King David's life. David's sins of adultery and murder demonstrate the low, degrading level to which one may fall when he or she disobeys God's rule of righteousness. From a human perspective, David should have been cut off from God's favour. But, God did not do this. Instead, because of His preserving love and care for David, He accepted David's plea for forgiveness, and restored unto him the joy of his salvation (Ps 51:12). Through this example of forgiveness, true believers can be confident their salvation is secure in the Christ, regardless to what level of perverseness they might sink, if they seek God's forgiveness which He willingly gives to the repentant heart.

Fifth, the definition of salvation. It is called "eternal life" (John 10:28), "everlasting life" (John 3:16), and "life everlasting (Matt 25:4; John 17:3). Everlasting life, in its simplest form, means salvation has no beginning nor ending with God, and can never be terminated. Everlasting life can be given only by Christ, who is from everlasting to everlasting (Ps 90:2). Since faith, regeneration and salvation are in God – who is from everlasting to everlasting – it remains for the redeemed everlasting, "for it cannot be possessed by men apart from a living union with Christ, in and through whom that everlasting life is available to men."[8] If salvation were anything less, it would have discredited Christ's promise to His disciples at the Last Supper, "Whoso eateth my flesh, and drinketh my blood, hath eternal life" (John 6:54). If Christ's offer were not genuine, and reliable He would have told His disciples to seek for something more. He did not. Obviously, He was offering those that came to Him the fullness of meaning and life that is available because of His love!

Sixth, the High Priestly and Intercessory work of Christ. Believers are instructed that they "are to mortify the works of the flesh" (Col 3:5) so they will not fall into diverse sins, and John, the Beloved counsels them directly that they should "sin not" (1 John 2:1). John, in spite of his counsel, knows believers will sin because, "the spirit is willing, but the flesh is weak" (Matt 27:46). He, however, does not despair, and neither should believers, for they possess, he states, freedom from all condemnation because they have "an advocate, even Jesus Christ, the Righteous" (1 John 2:1), pleading their case before the Father, and obtaining full forgiveness of sins on their behalf.

This, then, is the glorious certainty believers possess; He that has begun a good work in them is well able to perform it unto the day of Jesus Christ (Phil 1:6). Now the believer has tranquility of spirit because he is persuaded Christ – as the believer's faithful security – will guard his standing before the Father. With this he or she also has serenity of mind because of the assurance that he or she cannot lose his salvation.

The Assurance of the Saints

By 'assurance' we mean "the joyous, unwavering confidence of an intelligent trust, the security of a fear less trust,"[9] which guarantees for the believer that he is in Christ and Christ is in him (Gal 2:20-21). The Westminster Confession of Faith defines the term to mean:

> That those who truly love Christ with sincerity endeavouring to walk with all good conscience towards Him, may in this life be certainly assured that they are in a state of grace, and may rejoice in the hope of God, which hope shall never make them ashamed (WCF 18:1).[10]

The believer's assurance does not rest on any good work he or she does because of salvation; rather, it is established on the co-witness of the Holy Spirit, Who, "bears witness with the believer's spirit he or she, indeed is a child of God" (Rom 8:20). From the moment one receives Christ as Lord and Savior, he or she has confidence before the Lord, as Redeemer Friend and guardian of his soul, his or her salvation can never be dissolved or removed. Such confidence is not a secondary, afterthought of faith. It, on the other hand, is the integral and inseparable element by which "assurance of God's love, peace and conscience, (Romans 5:1-2), joy in the Holy Ghost, (Romans 14:7), increase of grace, (Proverbs 4:18), and perseverance to the end, (I John 5:13), are the natural result of the believer's commitment to faith in Christ."[11]

Paul, the Apostle, had the assurance of a living an unending faith in Jesus Christ. He unreservedly affirmed "He had been translated from death unto life" (Eph 2:4-12), he had received "adoption as the child of God" (Rom 8:15), and he had "received the seal of the Holy Spirit of Promise to everlasting life" (Eph 1:12-15). Paul's assurance of salvation was founded solely on knowing Christ, "Whom to know is life eternal" (John 8:46). When he says, "I know in whom I have believed (2 Tim 2:12), Paul uses the Greek term oida which, "most often refers to knowing only the crucified Christ,"[12]as against knowing other gods. But Paul's assurance is corroborated when he states "he is persuaded that God is able to keep that which he has committed to him against that day in Jesus Christ" (Phil 1:6). The term, peiqw which Paul uses represents, "Christian confidence in the faith through an increase of knowledge and understanding, which leads to trust and obedience to His commands. It is "in the Lord" (Gal. 5:10; Phil. 2:24), the author of his faith, (Phil. 1:6; cf. Heb. 2:13; Mt. 27:43) to which Paul has been won over, and which can never be destroyed!"[13]

Satan, the archenemy of the faith, may attack the believer, he may seduce him to sin, and he might then cause him or her to doubt his or her salvation. Despite such attempts and beguiling accusations, the believer needs to remains unshakably assured of his salvation for he knows, "that the completion of salvation is in the hands of the omnipotent Lord,"[14] who is the "author and finisher of his or her faith" (Heb 12:2).

In light of this tenacious assurance, it should be of concern to children of faith when fellow believers harbour fear, and despair about certainty of their salvation. They cannot, they must not allow such ungodly, satanic thoughts to influence their thinking for God, "will never allow any believer to fall away from grace; he will never be entirely left without any token of God's favour; and with the fruit of faith remaining, his assurance of salvation in due time may be revived."[15]

An individual, possessing unrestrained assurance he or she has been redeemed by Christ, and his or her salvation is forever secured, becomes embellished with immeasurable confidence that causes him or her to heartily sing, "Blessed assurance, Jesus is mine; Oh, what a foretaste of glory divine,"[16]for, nothing in this world, should be more earnestly desired by Christians "than to be well assured and satisfied of the love of Jesus Christ to their souls."[17]

Perseverance of the Saints

The believer's assurance, under no circumstances, gives one an "open door" to antinomianism or licentiousness (Rom 6:15). Rather, as a testimony of gratitude, love, and willing servitude to God, in light of the glorious salvation received, the believer is called to demonstrate a life of good works grounded in righteousness. Assurance yields obedience to the Christ's commands, and incites "works meet for repentance" (Matt 3:8) the person can be "a pattern to them which should hereafter believe on him to life everlasting" (1 Tim 1:16) . Nothing short of this will do!

When Paul tells the Philippian saints to "work out their salvation with fear and trembling, for it is God who is continuously doing His good will and pleasure" (Phil 2:12) – meta fobou kai tromou ten eauton soterian katepgazesthe [18] – he implies a needed response to something God has already started in their hearts, i.e. a turning away from iniquity, unto righteousness because of salvation. By using the term katergarzesqe – 2 person plural present imperfect[19] – Paul is emphatically enjoining fellow believers to determinately enact righteous works that will be a lasting witness to Christ's radical, life changing power as demonstrated in salvation, to both the brethren and the ungodly. Perseverance is a life long, tedious task in which the believer is called to continuously "mortify the deeds of the flesh" (Col 3:5), so he or she will not be in bondage to the flesh, but he or she will be able to enjoy the abundant life which comes from the Spirit of God (John 10:9).

Perseverance is a joint effort between God and the redeemed. God, by the Holy Spirit, empowers the believer to know righteousness, and live by it (Rom 8:14). The believer, then, responds to this empowerment by discharging conduct that is pleasing before God, and commendable to His glory. This "living out of righteousness" is only possible as believers have a renewing of the mind towards godliness, and then seek out what is the "good, the perfect, and the acceptable will of God (Rom 12:1-2).The World Council of Churches states perseverance is an ethical matter for the believer by which he or she is constrained to seek the will of God once he or she has "tasted the goodness" of God's redemptive grace.

> Within a fellowship of witness and service, believers discover the significance of the one baptism as the one gift of God to all of God's people. Likewise, they acknowledge that baptism, a baptism into Christ's death, has ethical implications, which not only call for personal sanctification, but also motivate Christians to strive for the will of God in all realms of life, (Romans 6:9 ff; Gal. 3:27-28; 1 Peter 2:21-4:6).[20]

Perseverance is not an arbitrary, whimsical behaviour for believers. Rather, it is the expected mark of obedience for all those who "are a chosen generation, a royal priesthood, a holy nation, *and* a peculiar people unto God" *so* "they would shew forth the praises of him who hath called *them* out of darkness into his marvelous light "(1 Pet 2:9). Joel R. Beeke comments:

> Being in Christ may be known, first, if we live openly Christ-like lives as children of the King; second, if we feel a holy comfort and joy in our heart from the presence of Christ; and third, if we grieve when His presence is not felt. Means to gain this form of assurance include: (1) the reception of God's ordinances; (2) the exercising of faith, hope, and love; and (3) an upright running in the way of Christ's commandments.[21]

Paul emphatically instructs believers to have a new deportment in righteousness since they have come into the faith. He, in Ephesians writes:

> This I say therefore, and testify in the Lord, that ye henceforth walk not as other Gentiles walk, in the vanity of their mind, having the understanding darkened, being alienated from the life of God through the ignorance that is in them, because of the blindness of their heart: Who being past feeling have given themselves over unto lasciviousness, to work all uncleanness with greediness. But ye have not so learned Christ; if so be that ye have heard him, and have been taught by him, as the truth is in Jesus: That ye put off concerning the former conversation the old man, which is corrupt according to the deceitful lusts; And be renewed in the spirit of your mind; And that ye put on the new man, which after God is created in righteousness and true holiness" (Eph 4:17-24).

Concerning the significance and importance of perseverance – or a godly, good and upright worldview and conduct by believers - Polycarp writes:

> Stand fast, therefore, in these things and follow the example of the Lord, firm and immoveable in faith, loving the brotherhood, cherishing each other, united in the truth, giving way to each other in the gentleness of the Lord, despising no one. When you are able to do good, do not put it off because charity delivers from death. All of you be subject one to the other and maintain an irreproachable standard of conduct among the Gentiles, so that you may be praised and the Lord may not be blasphemed because of you. But woe unto them through whom the

name of the Lord is blasphemed. Therefore, teach all the self-control by which you yourselves live."[22]

And on the same matter, Spurgeon comments:

> it seems to me if a man is a Christian, Christianity ought to eat him right up. It ought to go right through him, and he should be known first and foremost as a Christian man. Let him be all the rest on equality with his fellow man, and I think he may even be superior to them in business act and capacity. I believe that religion will sharpen his intellect and that often communication with God in prayer will give him a calm frame of mind which will enable him to do business the better."[23]

Conclusion

Although scripture does not directly mention eternal security, it is replete with references to this subject. God's plan, before the foundation of the world was laid, was to have uninterrupted, unending fellowship with man who He had created in His own image and for His own glory.

The 'fall' in Eden temporarily decimated this hope and dream; for a short time it looked as if man and God would be eternally separated. In the wisdom of God, however, Christ was sent to earth to be the Suffering Savior and bridge the huge chasm which separated man from God. His sacrifice was well pleasing to the Father; the sacrifice has been made and now there needs to be no further propitiation for sin for a pattern to them which should hereafter believe on him to life everlasting.

The "bridge by which man comes back to God" has three support pillars; preservation, assurance and perseverance. Jointly these supports excite the believer about his faith by providing them tranquility in spirit because of God's saving and keeping power, serenity of mind because of the assurance they have as pertaining to their salvation, and motivation of spirit because of the gratitude they show in Christian service by acts of righteousness.

And that's what faith should be, a confident working relationship, and fellowship with one's God.

Chapter 11

Francis of Assisi: A Directed and Devoted Disciple

Introduction

Mention the name Francis of Assisi in most settings and the immediate association with the name most likely will be with the well-known and often recited Francis of Assisi, "Peace Prayer". But association with Francis of Assisi should extend beyond this, for he, by many, is also regarded as the "mirror of Christ."[1] This title has been bestowed on him because, through self-emptying and unwavering devotion and servitude to Christ, he brought about reform within the Catholic Church that motivated thousands to become poor materially, so they could become rich spiritually as they increased their knowledge of Christ as Lord. Before a discussion about how Francis "mirrored Christ," a history of Assisi is in order.

Background

Francis was born in 1181 or 1182[2] in Assisi, Italy to Pietro Bernardino.[3] He was a wealthy clothing merchant in the city who strongly desired his son to be active in the Catholic Church. At birth Francis was given the name Giovanni.[4] However, while his father was on a trip purchasing clothing for the business, his mother Picca[5] had him baptized as Francesco – which meant "little Frenchman." This she did in honour of her French heritage, and because Francis' father avidly traded with France.[6] This name stayed with him until his death on October 13, 1226.

During his childhood, Francis was a happy, well-adjusted boy who received a good education, and often helped his father in the clothing business. It was his father's hope that after Francis had received adequate religious training as a Friar he would take on the responsibilities of the business. Francis, however, had other aspirations for life. Instead of loving business and profit, he preferred the life of partying and enjoying the "good life" with his friends.

Around eighteen or nineteen Francis became enamored with the troubadours[7] who often went to battle in nearby countries. As soon as it was possible he enrolled in the military, "for to Francis the military was the best place to gain prestige, and it was prestige that he longed for."[8] Shortly thereafter, Francis went to battle in one of the petty wars between Perugia – a neighbouring city – and Assisi. His military life, however, was short lived. Within a month of enlisting, he was injured and taken captive by the Perugian Army.[9] After a year of imprisonment he was released. It is presumed this happened because a large ransom may have been paid by his father.[10]

After his release, Francis returned home to recover from an illness with which he had been inflicted while in prison. During a year of recuperation he rested, worked in his father's store, and contemplated the true meaning and value of life. Because he was still smitten with the glory of the military, on the request of the Duke of Apulia[11] he re-enlisted in the army. As he travelled to join the battalion, Francis encountered a radical, life changing experience which would later be referred to as the beginning of his conversion. This, unlike the conversion of the Apostle Paul, would be a gradual learning process by which he would gain an understanding of Christ's grace which he would mirror throughout his life. Regarding this dramatic conversion, Kenneth S. Latourette comments:

> The conversion of Francis to the life of religion was not a sudden dedication, but came as the result of a spiritual pilgrimage of many months which began in his adolescence. It was partly induced by illness and disappointments and was

influenced by painful and intense struggles of the spirit and in its earlier stages by relapses in the former way of living.[11]

Conversion

Francis' conversion was to be as unique and as varied as his life-style. One night, while waiting for commissioning for battle, he had a vision of a "fair and great palace, and an array of war implements that were marked with a cross." Being completely stunned, he yelled out, "To whom do these things belong?" The answer was immediate and simple – "To you and your soldiers."[12] Immediately Francis accepted the vision as a confirmation God would enable his brigade to win the next upcoming battle. The next day, with full confidence of a victory, Francis once again headed out to battle. After continuing for only a short distance, he heard the same voice speak to him a second time saying, "Return home, for that which you have seen means something will be accomplished spiritually. This is to be fulfilled in you, not by human counsel, but by the Divine."[13]

As Francis considered the messages he had received, he became consumed with the need to discover their meanings. Within a few days he returned to Assisi, and found some abandoned caves in which he lived as a hermit while he waited for God to show him his true calling and purpose for life.

The Triune Calling

For almost a year (1201-1202), Francis' life was an endless adventure of seeking God's direction for spiritual fulfillment. Hours were spent reading and meditating on scripture. When he was not meditating, Francis rode his horse throughout the nearby countryside, enjoying nature which he believed God had created perfect, "as one of the sacraments for His Church."[14] During one of these occasions he was confronted by a leper who was begging for alms. At first sight he was repulsed by the individual's smell, and uncomely appearance. To rid himself of the beggar's presence, he quickly satisfied the man's need by handing him a coin or two. But, as he was about to depart, something supernatural constrained him to have pity on the man for he, like the birds and the flowers which Francis worshipped, was also a part of God's creative power and should be honoured.[15] Immediately Francis jumped off his horse, embraced and kissed the leper, for he saw standing in the man Christ, manifested as a leper. This incident sealed Francis' unwavering commitment of servitude to Christ to all people, in all things.

Sometime later (1205), Francis would encounter his second life-changing experience, while visiting the church of San Damiano,[16] which was pastored by a poor, dejected priest. While in the church meditating, Francis was impressed to look on the crucifix which hung directly over the altar. As he obeyed his impulse, he heard the crucifix say, "Fix My Church." The church, at this time, was in a dilapidated and deplorable condition structurally. Francis was a builder. Immediately "he sold his horse, and many bales of his father's cloth, making the sign of the cross over them to indicate their pious and charitable destination."[17] With the money he received, he purchased materials to repair the church.

After hearing about Francis' stealing the bales of cloth, his father brought him before the Church, and charged him with theft. When the Church ordered Francis to repay his father, he became incensed with his father's arrogance, and separated himself from his family completely. G. K. Chesterton describes the event:

> There was a new air about Francis. He was no longer crushed, still less crawling, so far as his father was concerned: yet his words do not, I think, indicate either just indignation or wanton insult, or anything in the nature of a mere continuation of the quarrel. They are rather remotely akin to mysterious utterances of his great model, 'What have I to do with thee?' or even the terrible, 'Touch me not'. He stood up before them all and said, 'Up to this time I have called Pietro Bernardino father, but now I am the servant of God. Not only the money, but everything else that can be called his, I will restore to my father, even the very clothes he has given me.' And he rent off all his garments except one; and they saw that was a hair-shirt.[18]

Now fully separated unto God, Francis set out on a lifelong venture of "fixing Christ's Church." However, this time it was not physical disrepair he would tackle. It, on the other hand, was spiritual reformation through preaching the Kingdom of God, calling fellow church members to repentance, and demonstrating the compassion of Christ wherever he went.

In 1208, Francis had his third and most profound life-changing encounter with the supernatural. It happened while worshipping at the church in Portincula, some two miles below Assisi.[19] As he sat thinking about God's direction in earlier days, he was directed to Matthew 10:7-19, which called Christ's disciples to abandon earthly riches for servitude to God. For some time Francis knew God had been calling him to a special, selfless servanthood. How he would fulfill this calling, he was not sure. The passage from Matthew answered his question. He was to become poor in earthly matters, and of himself so, through this poverty, he could become rich in Christ as he imaged the Christ-like life "with a deep sense of humility and compassion to others he met."[20]

Immediately he submitted himself to the "call" by discarding or selling all his earthly possessions, and living among the poor. When his friends heard Francis was exhibiting this abhorrent and unbecoming behaviour, they thought he had gone mad. In response to their concerns, Francis had one reply, "He had married 'Lady Poverty' who was "the noblest, the richest, and the most beautiful woman ever seen,"[21] and he was ecstatic. Henry H. Milman adds:

> Francis was now wedded to Poverty; but he would love it in its basic form – mendicancy. He wandered abroad, was ill used by robbers, on his escape he received from an old friend at Gubbio a hermit's attire, a short tunic, a leathern girdle, a staff and slippers. He begged at the gates of monasteries; he discharged the most menial offices. With even more profound devotion he dedicated himself to service at the hospital at Gubbio to that unhappy race of beings that even Christianity was constrained to banish from the social pale - the lepers.[22]

Whereas Francis could have lived the "good life" enjoying his father's wealth, he cast it aside so he could preach the gospel as he lived among the poor in relentless, compassionate servitude, for "his attentive care for others was rooted in Jesus Christ."[23] On first consideration one might think he was "swept away" by a social gospel which attended only to the temporary ills of society. Such, however, was not the case. By marrying 'Lady Poverty,' Francis wanted to touch individuals in their need, and motivate them to seek Christ as the final and full source of meaning in life. Frederick Sontag states:

> The treasure of eternal life is what Francis sought to convey to those in want, not necessarily a socio-economic program, although in his own case, the renunciation of possessions was his road to success. He speaks of 'holy poverty' so we must be sure to distinguish poverty connected to spiritual intent from a simple economic state. We remember the stories surrounding Francis's relation to birds and animals as we consider his own rejection of wealth, and service to the poor. His sympathy with the animal kingdom is a sign of his simplicity as much so as his poverty, and the two virtues are distinct. Francis was 'confirmed in Grace and in the sure sense of Salvation'. This is what he wanted to convey to the poor, although he needed to be pure himself in order to serve as a vehicle, not in that poverty is itself a virtue.[24]

Francis and the Three Orders

Being certain of his calling, Francis, with steadfast resolve, set himself to "mirroring Christ" through a life of self-debasing devotion wherever he went. Within a year of beginning his public ministry, he drafted a set of "rules" by which he would govern his life. At twenty-two, with twelve of his companions who were also consumed by the same devotion to Christ, he went to Rome to seek papal approval from Pope Innocent III for starting a new Order.[25] On first consideration of the request, Innocent was hesitant to grant Francis his desire, stating Francis could easily join either the Benedictine or the Augustinian Monks.[26] On November 19, 1223,[27] when Francis vehemently opposed the suggestion because he did not agree with Orders owning wealth, and when Cardinal Giovanni di San Paolo pleaded before a council on Francis' behalf,[28] Innocent III gave his approval for the Order. And with this, Francis started his work known as "Little Brothers," "Friars Minors," or the "Franciscan Order of Monks."[29] This, throughout the following centuries, would grow and become a powerful force in spreading the gospel to the least, the last, and the lost throughout the world.

Having received authority to establish the Order, Francis spent the next few years travelling throughout Europe preaching the gospel, while seriously living the life of poverty in devotion to Christ, which he had adopted many years earlier. Within a short time the Order grew in numbers as "thousands – coming from all classes of society: knights and peasants, priests and laymen, scholars and illiterate – joined it."[30]

As the Order grew, Francis recognized a set of "Rules," which would clearly delineate the conduct of the friars, was necessary. Therefore, between 1221 to 1223[31] three sets of "Rules," which were based on his personal Regula Prima of 1209, were written. Each rule included the stipulation that "those who would follow after the Holy Order of Christ, namely the Friars Minor, are to observe the teachings of Christ by living in obedience, without anything of his own, and in chastity.[32] Although emphasis in the Regulae is on the friar's commitment to poverty, each also set forth the need for friars to fast and pray, work, abstain from accepting money, do penance when they sinned, abstain from visiting nuns, and preach the gospel. Francis delineated the "Rules" as follows:

> Let the friars appropriate nothing for themselves, neither house nor place, nor any thing. And as pilgrims and exiles in this age let them go about for alms confidently, as one serving the Lord in poverty and humility, nor is it proper to be ashamed . . . cleaving totally to this, most beloved Friars, may you want to have nothing under heaven in perpetuity, for the sake of the name of Our Lord Jesus Christ.[33]

Two other orders were also founded because of Francis' ardent commitment to Christ. The first was known as the "Order of Poor Ladies" or "Poor Clares," and was comprised of women living in nunneries. This Order was approved by Innocent IV in 1253. The second Order was known the "Brothers and Sisters of Penance." It consisted of individuals who lived a life of poverty within the community as instructed by Innocent IV in 1289.[34]

For Francis, leaving a legacy of his life was not important. Regardless what he did, he desired strongly that God, who called him to servitude in poverty, would be glorified only and always.

The Death of Francis

Two years prior to his death Francis began to feel severe physical tiredness. During prayers one day, he felt strangely impressed he should separate himself to a high place where he would fast. For the next forty days he sought the Lord, and earnestly implored Christ to allow him to share in His sufferings. Unexpectedly, Francis was visited by seraphim having six wings. As the seraphim ministered to him, he touched him, and then placed in his body the marks of the nails and the lance wound that Christ had received as He died on the cross. This identity with Christ later became known as Francis' Stigmata.[35]

Francis died on October 3, 1226, in Portincula, the birthplace of the Franciscan Order of Monks, rejoicing in his Lord, for he was equally content with either life or death.[36] His death did not diminish the spirit of his work. Rather his life engulfed by the "richness of true poverty, and the unmistakable brightness of a soul consumed by the love of God,"[37] drew countless thousands to follow the path that leads to hope in this life, and in the life to come. By 1521 it was estimated that over fifty thousand Franciscan Monks were in Europe. Today many thousands still do the work Francis started over seven hundred years ago, as they live in poverty as related to this life, but with riches as pertaining to godliness.

Francis, "Mirror Of Christ"

To equate Francis of Assisi to Christ would be nigh unto blasphemy. But to suggest he "mirrored his Christ" would be a welcome conclusion in light of the manner in which he lived as the "reflection of the One he loved and served." Even as the moon has no light of its own,[38] but reflects the light of the sun, so Francis, who had no life of his own, reflected the life of the Son, Christ Jesus.

How, then, does Francis of Assisi "mirror Christ?" The author suggests the following examples:

First, Francis, like Christ, was determined to know and live the will of God. Francis had exceptional opportunities to live life to the fullest and make a name for himself. He had been raised by a godly family; he had received a good education; he, twice, had attempted to gain his valued prestige by joining the military; and he had a certain future of wealth awaiting him in his father's clothing business. But all this brought emptiness to Francis; life, although it looked glamorous and fulfilling, was totally destitute of meaning and purpose.

Once converted, absolutely nothing captivated Francis than knowing and doing the will of God regardless of the cost entailed. Like Christ, Francis, after his conversion, would often pray, "Father, not my will, but thine be done" (Luke 22:42), and as friends would approach him regarding his activities, he would respond, "Do you not know that I must be about my Father's business" (Luke 2:49)?

Second, Francis, like Christ (Matthew 8:20 & Luke 9), emptied himself of personal prestige, power and position, and lived among the despised of this world, so through his poverty, others could become rich in this life, and toward eternal life. In Assisi, his father had a home and business which, unquestionably would have afforded Francis the comforts and luxury of the good life. But Francis willingly abandoned all of it, and he could rightly say, "The foxes have holes, and the birds of the air have nests; but Francis has no place of his own in which to lay his head" (John 15:19). Christ set aside heaven's glory for the joy of humankind being reinstated to a righteous relationship with the Creator. This, too, was the sole purpose of Francis' life.

Third, Francis, like Christ, was a servant to God. At no time do we hear Francis elevating himself to a position of authority in light of the ecstatic visions he had. Neither do we see him becoming an indignant overlord once the Franciscan Order was approved. Rather, Francis was a servant regardless how demeaning the task was. In "fixing the church" at San Damiano, in servitude, he sold everything he had, purchased the materials needed for the repair, and then gracefully applied himself to the task with no ambition of self-glory. And, when through the Spirit, he was charged with reconciling the Church to Christ by the preaching the gospel, Francis, as a servant, went everywhere preaching the Kingdom of God, calling men to repentance. As servant, Francis willingly ministered to the lepers at

Gubbio – not for fame and recognition – but, like Christ, for the glory of the Father. Regardless of how we know Francis, he would remind us to remember him as the individual, "who came not to be served, but to serve"[42] for Francis knew "he that would be the greatest in the kingdom of God must be the servant of all" (John 15:20).

Fourth, Francis, like Christ, started his earthly ministry with twelve followers – disciples – who were intent on seeing a work of compassionate evangelism and Christian purity spread throughout the world. Who, exactly, these men were, we are not told. However, each one, like the disciples of Christ, willingly submitted themselves to the Regula Prima which existed when Francis and the group appeared before Innocent III. They, like Christ, also wanted God's Kingdom to be established on earth in which "everyone would be equal in the fraternity as brothers and sisters, and would hold all possessions in common trust,"[39] so no one would lack any good thing as they worked together to bring about God's kingdom on earth. Francis' desire for those who followed him was that they would be one as family, with God being their Father.

Fifth, Francis, like Christ, suffered abuse, ridicule, alienation and unrighteous treatment at the hands of friends for "going about and doing nothing but good" (Acts 10:38). When his youthful friends saw Francis living among the poor, and giving his alms to them as aid, they mocked him, and then they abandoned him. When Francis sold his horse and bales of his father's clothes to raise money for repair of the church at San Damiano, his father charged him with theft and brought him before the Pope to be tried as a criminal. Even more caustic than this was the reaction of Innocent III to Francis's request to start an Order through which both the Church and the world would be brought to full life through God's grace. Instead of granting the Order directly, Innocent called a counsel to verify the veracity of the request.

Sixth, Francis, like Christ, was led into a secret place for forty days of prayer, and fasting so he could receive a revelation of the purpose for his suffering, which was to bring mankind knowledge of the Kingdom through personal deprivation, ill treatment and death.[40] Francis's stigmata, unquestionably, verified for him that his life's endeavours would not be in vain, but in his death an example would be left of his life's good works which would draw many into obedience, and servitude to the God of eternity.

Seventh, Francis, like Christ, commissioned ambassadors of faith to "go into the entire world and preach the gospel to every creature" (Mark 16:20). Through the three Orders that were established by Francis, most of the then known world was evangelized. The work of Franciscan worldwide missions, following the vow of poverty, remains a viable, godly ministry today. The Franciscan Mission Board reports the following:

> Franciscans have been involved in missionary activities since the very beginning of the Order. Pope Innocent III orally approved the Rule of the Order of Friars Minor in 1210, and by 1217 five friars were sent to preach to the Moors in the Kingdom of Granada. By 1263 there were 22 friars in the Holy Land, and six Poor Clare monasteries. The first mission to China started in 1245 when Brother John of Pian Carpino left for Manchuria. The first saint born in the Americas was a Franciscan, Brother Felipe de Jesus of Mexico, martyred in Nagasaki, Japan in 1597. Today the Franciscans have 5,400 missionaries and 800 missions throughout the world. They serve the poor on every continent, following in the steps of St. Francis of Assisi.[41]

Who knows how many redeemed individuals will grace heaven's portals because of the obedient servitude of Francis of Assisi, who, through his human life, mirrored the Divine Life of Christ?

Conclusion

Undoubtedly there have been many others who, through deep devotion and obedience to Christ's will, have radically changed the world in which they lived for time and eternity. However, through evaluating his Assisi's as "the mirror of Christ," one recognizes that being a Christian is more than saying that he's a Christian; it demands living a life in unwavering servitude and obedience so Christ's kingdom can be done "in heaven and in earth" (Matt 6:10).

Chapter 12

The Pietists: Spiritual Awakening in the 16th Century Lutheran Church

Introduction

Within most religions there often arises a desire by the faithful to discover and follow a gratifying and edifying form of worship which will satisfy both the mind and soul. Throughout many religions, when segments of the church become dissatisfied with the populace view of faith, and no longer see any meaning or purpose in worship, a split within the sect occurs, and a new group is formed. This occurred in the German Lutheran Church around the middle of the seventeenth century when a new group, The Pietists, started under the leadership of Jakob Spener.

The Origin of Pietism

The catalyst for establishing Pietism was found in the contemptuous spiritual condition of Germany after the Thirty Year's War. This struggle between Catholics and Protestants, which ended in the Peace of Westphalia in 1648, could be described partly as economic, partly political, and partly religious. Germany, spiritually, was in a chaotic condition. Within the Lutheran Church, there was no spiritual direction or stability. The noble and the rich occupied important places within the Church, and they almost controlled the depth of worship offered by their pastors. The deep, devoted personal commitment to Christ and His Church had been minimized. In its place came structured liturgy which stressed the study of dogmatic.[1] Unfortunately, this new direction taken by the Church strongly promoted the notion Christianity was nothing more than a matter of intellectual assent to correct doctrine.

Luther's central teaching of "justification by faith" was being taught in the Lutheran congregations, but without a complementary, and balanced emphasis on the work of God in spiritual regeneration of the soul. Apathy to reading scripture, praying and godly care one for the other was commonplace. Nothing would change until a new call for the laity to display their faith through interpersonal, Christ motivated care, was preached. F. Stoeffler comments:

> Lutheran orthodoxy did not only succeed in theologizing the Christian faith, but in so doing often distorted it. Examples are numerous. While it paid lip service, for instance, to the authority of the Bible, the real authority was lodged in the orthodox perspective upon the Bible. Devotion from that perspective, and its accepted forms of expression was considered a deviation from scripture and, hence, heresy.[2]

This polemic condition in the church was heightened through a pronounced lack of Christian service by the laity because of "ethical insensitivity."[3] From the clergy to the commoner in the pew, troublesome problems existed in the church because few, if any, knew their ministry gifts or were given opportunity to use them for the good of the body. Instead of endorsing everyone's ministry gifts, competition for ministry opportunity, based on favoritism, was widespread in Lutheran Churches. Spener, recognizing this unwholesome and ungodly situation existed, states:

> Distressing as conditions in the political estate are, we preachers in the ecclesiastic estate cannot deny our estate is also thoroughly corrupt . . . when you see the people are undisciplined you must realize, no doubt the priests are not holy. We must confess not only men are to be found here and

> there in our estate who are guilty of open scandals, but also there are fewer than may appear who do not understand and practice true Christianity, (which consists of more than avoiding manifest vices and living an outwardly moral life). Although, according to the common estimate of men as seen through eyes captivated by the fashion of the world, they may seem to be blameless, yet their lives reflect (subtly, to be sure, nonetheless plainly), a worldly spirit, marked by carnal pleasure, lust of the eye, and arrogant behaviour, and so it is evident they have never taken even the first practical principle of Christianity seriously, namely, self-denial.[4]

Clearly recognizing that a situation such as this did not honour God, and did not build the body to the fulness of Jesus Christ, Spener launched his campaign for spiritual renewal within the Lutheran Church. His emphasis – regardless what other pastors might think – was to teach a Pauline commitment of spiritual renewal by which parishioners – young and old – would comprehend the basis of salvation, in and through Jesus Christ, and then would live it out through expressions of kind, godly good works daily.

Background to Spener

Jakob Spener, who was born on January 23, 1635 in Rappotsweiler, Upper Alsace, Germany, is credited with starting Pietism.[5] He was the son of a well-to-do merchant of the community, and because of his father's status, he often had contact with the wealthy and influential people of the area.

From his earliest childhood Spener was prepared for service, within the Lutheran Church, by his devout parents. During his early years in school, he spent much time reading religious, scholarly books. Because of this, he was greatly influenced by John Arndt's, *True Christianity,* and by the English Puritan author, Richard Baxter. In 1651, at sixteen, he attended the University of Strasbourg[6] for religious education. After gaining a comprehensive knowledge of scripture, he concluded there was more to being a Christian than the Lutheran Church had been teaching. Being disappointed the Church had not been teaching "the full gospel," he started investing his time in reading John Calvin's writings. Much to his delight he discovered

Calvin taught much of what he believed about the need for the laity being instructed to exemplify Christ by doing good works. Immediately he resolved he would study Calvin's writings more in-depth and see what changes might be brought within the Lutheran Church. In the middle of his third year of studies at Strasbourg, Spener started speaking publicly about the radical, God inspired changes that needed to take place within the Lutheran Church if it were to provide effective ministry in Germany.

In 1659, shortly after completing his studies at Strasbourg, Spener spent the following two years travelling throughout Europe visiting Lutheran Churches which, he concluded, "were far from what God had intended them to be." In 1661 he arrived at Geneva. After residing here for five months, he started studying the teachings of Jean de Labadie. Labadie was a Jesuit who, some months before Spener's arrival at Geneva, had met a popular Reformed Church preacher who had left the Reformed Church to establish "Separatist House Churches"[7] in which parishioners were taught how to live out Christ by doing good works. Probably, it was from Labadie Spener got his idea for the "cell groups," which he later established and called, "Conventicles."

In 1666, after a time of preaching in Strasbourg, Spener accepted a "call" to be senior minister in Frankfurt Am Main. So impressed were the people with his preaching, they asked him to be the president of all the churches in the region. Although only thirty-one, he had responsibilities in the city's main principle church, as well as over a dozen or more pastors. Throughout his ministry Spener was convinced Christians needed to intensify their appreciation of salvation by gaining a deeper understanding of scripture. Therefore, he published his *Collegia Pietatus*. These were devotionals by which he instilled within Lutheran parishioners the fundamentals of personal piety. He also took steps to improve the instructional atmosphere of the children, and to review the Lutheran "Rite of Confirmation" which had fallen into disuse.[8] In 1669 he "planted the idea" of spiritual renewal for believers by suggesting:

> How much good it would do if good friends would come together on a Sunday, and instead of getting out glasses, cards, or dice would take up a book and read it for the

edification of all, or would review something of the sermons that were heard. If, they should they not be quite able to find their way through, they would ask a preacher to clarify the matter. We preachers cannot instruct the people from our pulpits as much as is needful unless other persons from the congregation, who by God's grace, have a superior knowledge of Christianity, take the pains by the virtue of their universal priesthood, to work with and under us to correct and reform as much in their neighbours as they are able, according to the measure of their gifts and their simplicity.[9]

The impact of this message on the people of Frankfurt Am Main was outstanding. Many parishioners started to meet as Spener had directed. But the reform the Lutheran Church so badly needed, and desired did not take place as fast as Spener had hoped. Therefore, in 1675 he published his *Pia Desideria* in which he set out the spiritual condition of the Lutheran Church, and suggested six proposals by which the Lutheran Church could be renewed spiritually from within the ranks. The writings were reservedly accepted, and the foundation for reform was established. Within a few months, after the book's publication, hundreds of "cell groups" were established. A spiritual rebirth was now awakened within the Church.

Spener died in 1705. But by this time, the movement had been firmly founded. A coworker, Hermann Francke took up the "torch of truth." Through his strong preaching of the Word, and consistent mentoring of new converts, the movement grew rapidly. Positive, marked reform in the Church, as a whole, took place throughout Germany.

Tenants of Pietism

The Lutheran Church was in an appalling, and shameful spiritual condition. Although church attendance was large, devotion to, and understanding of the gospel was weak. Spener was driven with an insatiable desire to correct the reprehensible problems which included, "both the laxity of the clergy, and the shortcomings of the established church system."[10]

In starting the Pietists, Spener was looking to establish an authentic life-style expression of faith within believers which would reform, and possibly, replace the then present superficial practice of worship which he had found in it. The cause for Spener was simple; reform at any cost, but reform that would last and touch people within and without! At the onset of his reform attempts for spiritual renewal in the Church, he gathered small numbers of people in his home with the sole aim, "to reestablish the old apostolic pattern of church meetings as St. Paul prescribed in 1 Corinthians 14."[11]

The first meetings were held twice a week on Sunday and Wednesday. Attendance at the meetings was voluntary. No one was excluded, yet no one was forced to attend. Both men and women attended the gatherings, although they were seated separately and women were forbidden to speak. In the sessions conducted scriptures were read, and a short message was preached by the minister who was in attendance. After the message was concluded, informal discussions on the material covered were held. After this, great lengths of intercessory prayer were conducted so the attendees might come to a greater awareness of their faith, and of their God. In some meetings, times were set aside for the asking of questions, and for confessionals when the people so felt laid by the Spirit.

The intense desire for a spiritual awakening was based on Spener's conviction "a better tomorrow" was possible. To inaugurate this "better tomorrow," Spener postulated six reforms that needed to be implemented within the Lutheran Church immediately. These were:

> More extensive Bible study, with personal spiritual growth as the aim; restoration of the principle of the priesthood of all believers; emphasis on practical Christianity, including the practice of Christian love; charity in religious controversy; reorganization of theological studies and the establishing of higher spiritual standards amongst professors and students; and reform of preaching with a view to edification of the hearers."[12]

Personal salvation was inseparable to the pious and devoted life of believers. Many within the Lutheran Church regarded themselves as being "saved" because they attended church regularly, and lived a relatively good life. But to Spener "believing" one's self as being born-again was not good enough. The people should "know they're saved" by repenting, and then by living an intensified, spiritual life demonstrated by works of righteousness."[13]

Spener could see the parishioners were not exemplifying the life of Christ in their behaviour. He noted, with much shame, Lutherans were offending Christ's grace by their drunkenness, taking their brother to court, being fraudulent in business practices and by presuming upon the grace of Christ. The reason for this reprehensible, ungodly behaviour is the Lutherans either were not saved, or they did not understand the salvation they had received from Christ. About this sad state of affairs in the Church, Spener writes:

> How many there are who live such a manifestly unchristian life. They themselves cannot deny the law is broken at every point, they have no intention of mending their ways in the future, and yet they pretend to be firmly convinced that they will be saved in spite of all this! If one asks on what they base their expectation, one will discover, as they themselves confess, they are sure of this because it is of course not possible to be saved on account of one's life, but they believe in Christ and put all their trust in him, this cannot fail, and they will surely be saved by such faith. Accordingly they have a fleshly illusion of faith (for godly faith does not exist without the Holy Spirit, nor can such faith continue when deliberate sins prevail) in place of the faith that saves."[14]

Salvation, or spiritual regeneration, by the Holy Spirit, therefore, had to be personalized as it was initiated "through deep sorrow over past sins and an experience of repentance."[15] Through this personal relationship with Christ, a deep devotion to Christ is expected. Personal gain, notoriety, and self-love would be set aside so the parishioners would "love the Lord their God with all their heart, soul and mind," and so grace of redemption would instill an uninhibited and unreserved love, and servitude of the saints to their Christ and Savior. Nothing short of this would be acceptable to Spener, and the Pietists whom he led. But this could never be fully understood until the parishioners, within the Lutheran Church, fully understood the teachings of scripture they, up to this time, had vainly been trying to follow.

Spener understood the people presumed they were saved regardless of how they lived, even if their lifestyle was not in accordance with scripture, because they had no "hands on," individual understanding of its teachings. Recognizing this, Spener determined his followers needed to come under regular reading and exposition of the gospel. By providing this for them, godly instruction would permeate their heart and mind. Over a period of time, Spener hoped this would change them into devoted followers of Christ who, "through seeking eagerly and diligently in the book of life for their joy, would see their spiritual life wonderfully strengthened so they could gather Sunday after Sunday as altogether different people."[16] The home meetings were a call to interaction with the scripture so the Holy Spirit could bring about, and finalize "justification by faith," which would be demonstrated by good works of love and kindness in social good among the brethren of the church.

With in-depth exposition of scripture, Spener also taught a "practical theology" to the congregants by "which they were encouraged to show, through a sanctified life, the fruit of the Spirit wherever Christians lived."[17] Professing children of God were encouraged to read the Bible, and memorize scriptural passages weekly so "their faith may not be founded upon the reputation and faith of a man, but upon divine truth so they would understand how to worship "God in spirit and in truth" (Jn 4:23-24) as He had commanded them. To Spener this was imperative so believers would be empowered with boldness to live the life of righteousness in obedience to God their Father, which Christ had imparted to them.[18] All forms of worldliness were to be avoided by devout Pietists. They were not "to give any room to the devil," lest their commitment to the faith be eroded, and they err in the way. Joyce Irwin comments:

> In accordance with the centrality of regeneration in Pietist Theology, Vockerodt's view of the profession a Christian musician stresses Christian commitment over musical competence. He notes with disapproval that many musicians have reversed the priorities or even have disregarded altogether Christian commitment, with the result music has

become a profession in its own right the central location of religious activity for him is not in congregational worship, but communion in the heart with God. Externals, such as frivolous people or frivolous music are a distraction; to avoid these one would do better to build a little church in one's house."[19]

Reform of the clergy was also mandatory to Spener, if a true reflection of Christ's grace and goodness was to be demonstrated in good works. The pulpits of all Lutheran Churches need to be filled with pastors, "who above all, are themselves true Christians and, then, have the divine wisdom to guide others carefully on the way of the Lord." This calling of "true Christians," to ministry starts at the schools and universities where proper instruction in godliness, needs to be taught and re-enforced. Spener comments:

> However, if such suitable persons are to be called to the ministry, they must be available, and hence they must be trained in our schools and universities. May God graciously grant everything thereunto may be diligently observed by the professors of theology and that they may assist in seeing to it that the unchristian academic life, which prevails among students of all faculties and which has been sorrowfully lamented not only by the sainted John Matthew Meyfart, but also by other pious persons before and after him, may by vigorous measures be suppressed and reformed. Then the schools would, as they ought, really be recognized from the outward life of the students to be nurseries of the church for all estates and as workshops of the Holy Spirit rather than as places of worldliness and indeed of the devils of ambition, tippling, carousing and brawling.[20]

With a dramatic change in the pastor's behaviour, and preaching Spener knew the parishioner's conduct would also change. Once the Holy Spirit interacted with the pastors, their pulpits would no longer be a place "for an ostentatious display of one's skill." Rather, it would become "the place to preach the Word of the Lord plainly, but powerfully and be the divine means to save the people."[21]

Within the Lutheran Church most of the parishioners were distant from their faith. They had little, if any understanding of the scripture. With this, they did not actively participate in any ministry functions during body public worship. Like Catholic Church Priests, the Lutheran Church clergy held tight control over the people, and kept them in ignorance and submission to their dictates. Spener was much disconcerted with the slothfulness, ignorance and the alienation the people had from their church. Therefore, he called for the immediate reinstatement within the Church of the "priesthood of all believers." By reintroducing this, the believer's internalized faith would find access to open expression within the body. As the people were encouraged to practice their faith openly, they became "intently motivated to perform-spiritual priestly acts"[22] towards the brethren, and their fellowman - both friend and foe.

> This high priestly calling of the saints could easily be demonstrated by having parishioners offer up both their body and souls unto God, as sincere sacrifices to God for his use within the church. This offering, according to Spener, should take place "always, through our whole life. For although we surrender and offer ourselves to God with body and soul once for all when we first yield our hearts to his service, nevertheless this purpose should be repeated, and sacrifices of this kind should be brought by us to God the Lord daily and even hourly.[23]

By acknowledging all believers are priests appointed by God for ministry to one another, a deeper awareness of their calling would be birthed in the church. With this awareness Spener hoped the congregants, and not only the clergy, would be empowered to take better care of themselves, and apply their gifts for edification of their fellowman. With this, they would also have a greater influence and impact in reaching the ungodly for Christ. He comments further:

They must become accustomed not to lose sight of any opportunity in which they can render their neighbour a service of love, and yet while performing it they must diligently search their hearts to discover whether they are acting in truelove or out of other motives . . . in fact, they should diligently seek opportunities to do good to their enemies. Such self-control may hurt the old Adam, who is otherwise inclined to vengeance, and at the same time so love may have been more deeply implanted in their hearts."[24]

What good is faith if it is bottled up within the person and never expressed? What value is there in calling Christ Lord if one does not follow His commandments, and work out his salvation with fear and trembling? And what growth could the Church possibly realize from within and without if the people were never given opportunity to express, and use the gifts God had given them as priests unto him and unto one another? In all of these questions, Spener undoubtedly responded there is no value, whatsoever to the Church. In so concluding, he would be absolutely right.

The Pietists emphasized the importance of soul winning. The spiritual edification, and instruction which was received during the cell group meetings, was not to lie dormant. Rather, it was to be openly and actively shared with others, within and without the Lutheran Church, so they might find the joy of salvation presently being experienced by the Pietists.

Expression of the faith in word and deed within society was also inherent to the Pietists as a duty.[25] Arguing and disputing over the faith does not bring people to Christ. This, however, is accomplished by believers reflecting the love of Christ through works of charity, which clearly show believers have interest about social concerns and needs. The scripture, "Love your neighbour as yourself"[26] was taken literally, and no one within Pietism was exempt from fulfilling its injunction.

When any member was overtaken with burdensome difficulties, others from the group quickly came to his or her aid by providing relief and scriptural encouragement. Besides helping one another, they were also encouraged to assist the poor beyond the church. By doing these acts of grace, others would also be motivated to do similar acts of kindness. Beyond this, the ungodly would be drawn to the light of the gospel, and know salvation which is the church's primary purpose for existing. Stoeffler comments:

> There was never a question as to whether the Christian is to be involved in the concerns of the world. While the Pietists did not intend to bring about major changes in the political situation, they did, in fact, intend to change the entire world, including the political realm, through the conversion of all people, including those in the ruling class."[27]

Although Spener encouraged the Pietists to care about, and provide social needs wherever possible, this practice became more widely followed during the leadership of John Francke. He, in a more pronounced way than Spener, was empathetic about everyone's problems."[28] Because of this, he encouraged congregants to demonstrate their faith practically by giving financial aid to the poor, feeding the needy, inviting their neighbours to fellowship Bible studies, and by doing whatever is called on them, as if they were doing it only to God.[29]

Meeting the needs of one's fellowman was an inherent obligation of all saints. Anyone who considered this an option obviously, according to Francke, did not fully understand his or her calling to faith in Christ. John Francke, by establishing the orphanage at Halle, demonstrated "practical Christianity" so intensely that German Pietism, though not practiced today, has indelibly marked the social milieu of the land. It was through this institution orphans by the hundreds were cared for. Eventually, under the careful management of Francke and others, a training centre for the clergy was established at Halle. Through Francke's investment in the lives of thousands at Halle, evangelistic endeavours touching Europe, Africa and the United States were started.

Francke's great foundation at Halle, now known as the *Franckesche Stiftungen*, was founded in 1698. Suspended during the GDR period, the Foundation was revived in 1990. Originally consisting of only an orphanage for the poor children of his parish, Francke added a range of charitable and evangelizing institutions including schools, a teaching training college, a Bible translation institute, a library, a printing house and book shop, a farm, a pharmacy, and even a cabinet of curiosities. The Foundation is now again flourishing, although the work of restoring all the original buildings after some fifty years of neglect, will take many years. 1998 marked the reopening of the historic library. Francke's disciples worked extensively abroad, reaching the North American colonies, Russia and even South India. They were active in London from an early date, establishing close links with the Society for Promoting Christian Knowledge. The influence of Pietism in early eighteenth century England can hardly be overestimated."[30] Through the endeavours of Francke, and other committed Pietists, countless lives were touched and changed.

Conclusion

Pietism was not without its problems. It erred by dispensing with the important offices of the church, it relied much on experiential knowledge of scripture at the expense of intellectual knowledge, it emphasized works an adjunct to salvation, and it shunned all forms of worldliness which gave way to a new form of justification by abstinence.

But the contributions towards personal understanding of the faith, and active personal involvement in it through conversion, scripture reading and comprehension, ministry one to the other and eventually to the world at large, far out way any problems it might have possessed.

Although Pietism, as a movement, only lasted for sixty years, the effects it had upon Christianity cannot be measured. Through the Pietist movement people learned that participating in faith could be more than just hearing about it; they could live it out, and see results which would change them, and also change the world.

Chapter 13

Liberation Theology: Its Influence on South American Christianity

Introduction

Before 1960 little, if anything was heard in North America about Liberation Theology that was gaining growth in Latin America. For the major part North American Christians considered Latin America as a "third world mission field" which desperately needed its evangelistic message so the uneducated, poor and unregenerate could know redemption in Christ. Undoubtedly, this desire was commendable for believers in North America. But, despite what they planned and what they did, God had a new, fresh, Holy Spirit rebirth of faith for Protestants and Catholics alike whereby thousands of poor, disenfranchised and forgotten poor, would come to faith in Christ and a more welcome socio-economic standing.

Since 1970 Liberation Theology has become a prominent theology practiced in many parts of the world, including Latin South America, Asia, and Africa. Therefore, an understanding of it no longer remains an option for North American believers, if they are to understand the 'fight' for socioeconomic, political and religious freedoms faced by the disenfranchised so they can enjoy unrestrained dignity as humans. Although it is not the author's goal to minimize the significance of Liberation Theology in other communities, his focus will centre on the effect Liberation Theology has had in Latin America.

A Brief Historical Overview of Latin America

South America was discovered by Columbus in 1492. In 1495, by the Treaty of Tordesillas, Pope Alexander VI allotted colonization of the 'new world' between Spain and Portugal. With this order in place, immediate settlement of South America by Europeans began. From the onset the Church's primary goal was evangelization of the Aztecs of Mexico and Incas of Peru through commendable peaceful pronouncements of the gospel. But, shortly after their arrival, and the acquisition of large landmasses, the clerics became sidetracked and reverted to violence to control the natives who questioned their misdirected activities. As cleric, autocratic power increased within the Church questioning of their authority, by the natives, was repelled through inhumane punishment or segregation of the natives into the isolated and rural areas of the country.

During the sixteenth century, when colonization was well on its way, and excessive profits could be realized from exports of South America products, class distinction and class segregation became ramped. Because the Church clerics held unrestrained authority and had no tolerance to the inquiries posed by the natives, the natives became "isolated to a subordinate status because of the imposition of social, economic and religious groups carried out during this time."[2] Already, by this time, natives were deprived, by the Church, of food, clothing, and education, even though it offered them religious instruction providing they submitted to the Church's authority. If Christ or Paul were to have visited Latin America at this time, neither would have detected the Church's commitment to Christ's teaching of Matthew 25, "whosoever doeth these things does them unto me."[3]

By the middle of the nineteenth century, as the wealth of the Church increased, national officials began openly attacking the Church about the inconsistency between its financial holdings compared with that of the grass-roots population in Latin America. Despite this, however, the Church made no efforts to correct the disparity. Instead of offering relief, the Church alienated and 'crushed' the people more, so within a short time they became regarded as "nonpersons".[4]

In the twentieth century Latin America gained independence from Spain and Portugal. Having grasped this, hope for improvement in the now deplorable conditions of the poor was induced. But, despite this and later "economic development programs"[5] started by Britain and the United States, no immediate notable change in the welfare of the oppressed, and isolated natives would be realized "because only those at the top of the 'social ladder' received the benefits offered, while the natives were left powerless with no recourse to address their continuing plight of exploitation, and abuse."[6] Equating the conditions in Latin America to those of Africa, Dianne Stinton, considers the economic efforts of multinational corporations hypocritical as they poured wealth into nations for cultural reform, while forgetting to reach out, and meet the needs of the impoverished. She writes:

> Can a nation develop culturally while being politically oppressed and economically exploited to such a horrifying degree, while its people, faced with starvation and many other catastrophes, struggle for survival? Social concern and theology cannot exist if these take a one-sided interest in culture while not being directly concerned with the people of God being liberated from their deplorable misery.[7]

As far as the poor were concerned there was no immediate remedy for their despicable plight. But knowing of the works of such people as Francis of Assisi, who had "married poverty,"[8] John of the Cross, and others who had also identified with the plight of the poor, the natives accepted their present status and hoped, beyond hope, their plight would eventually be changed.

Ground Work for Liberation Theology

Because of the church's quest for riches without having concern for the disenfranchised, the plight of Latin America's poor looked dismal and irreversible. However, during the middle of the twentieth century, 'seeds of redress' were to be planted when, in 1955, Pope Pius XII attended the Council of Latin American

Episcopacy. During his visit he pleaded with the clerics to "reexamine and return to the true message of Christ which was to bring liberty to the poor."[9] Although there was no immediate, radical provisional relief offered to the poor, this meeting aroused many clerics to review the Church's prejudiced and unorthodox practices that were extended to the poor.

A second, more pronounced, incentive for change within the Church, came during Vatican II (1962-1965). During these sessions Pope John XXII challenged the Church to "integrate doctrine with pastoral care and practices which would influence for change on the despicable, harsh, and inhumane life-styles of the poor around the world."[10] For the greater part the clerics departed Vatican II with an intense realization that they needed to move the gospel beyond the sanctuary to the streets where people lived if they were to be effective in ministry. For the first time in Latin America the Church began to see and empathize with the poor who they previously had regarded as nonpersons.

The most profound influence on the church to reevaluate its attitude towards the poor came in 1968 at Medellin, Colombia. During the General Conference of Latin American Episcopate, the clerics discussed the political attitude of faith, and began working for social justice among the poor. Their approach was to be distinctly contrary to what had been practiced earlier. Sherron George provides the following:

> Seeking to apply the edicts of Vatican II, the bishops introduced a new hermeneutic to the Roman Catholic Church by integrating scripture 'from below,' from the perspective of the people of God. The 'liberation narrative' in Exodus, and the emphasis on poverty and wealth in Luke, *especially Luke 14:18-19,* opened a fresh chapter on interpretation for both scholars and oppressed people. From these, and other biblical accounts in both the Old and New Testaments, they discovered that collective identity and solidarity with the poor was the central theme of the biblical ethic.[11]

Through this conference the Church was reawakened to what it believed, and should have been practicing, that being the contending for social, economic, political and religious liberation for the poor. With this new appreciation of faith projected as practice, the Church collectively would "find itself moving its traditions and ministry beyond the confessional walls as it joined others in the common struggle for a just and sustainable world for everyone, including the poor, who, for so long, had been ignored."[12]

Definition of Liberation Theology

Although Liberation Theology is practiced in many parts of the world, no homologous definition for the term has been reached. Generally, however, "all genuine Liberation Theology finds its motivation in fighting against all forms of oppression, be it sexism, heterosexism, homophobia, racism, classicism, or cultural and religious discrimination with effective solidarity."[13] The hermeneutic for Liberation Theology was unveiled as clerics reread the scriptures and discovered that God displays both preferential love and concern for the poor.

Holding this understanding, proponents of Liberation Theology began openly declaring all of God's creation is essentially good because it possesses dignity as the *imageo dei,* which should not be abused regardless of one's socioeconomic, educational, political or religious standing. This affirmation incited Liberation Theologians to align themselves with the poor, and contend that change for the poor, must rise from the "bottom up" - from the marginalized 'nonpersons' who are afflicted with appalling living conditions, malnutrition, inadequate health care - as they recognize they have inalienable human rights. The result will be love in action, moving all believers to participate with each and God, in a collective struggle for radical, positive improvements socially for the poor. As this happens, a nonviolent and radical revolution will be spurred on by love and respect one for the other. Eventually social, economic, political, and religious change, for the better of everyone – will be realized. Such a change would allow everyone access – without discrimination – to land, political offices, as and all essential goods for a dignified and healthy life-style. This would not happen automatically because of government incited social reform. This entraps citizens to greater dependency on government.[14]

Gustavo Gutierrez, a Peruvian Priest, and possibly the Father of Latin American Liberation Theology, in his book, *A Theology of Liberation Theology,* delineates three kinds of "violent" poverty recognized in the oppressed and marginalized poor, because women, blacks, the uneducated, and the impoverished are delegated as second-level creatures. These are cited as follows:

> First, there is the overt, immediately recognizable material which is scandalous, and must be fought against. Second there a spiritual poverty of those who have made themselves available to God as little children. But, Gutierrez goes on to elaborate a third meaning, which is known because of the circumstance in Latin America: "Christian poverty," - an expression of love, is solidarity with the poor and is protest against poverty. Christian poverty in Latin America is solidarity and protest.[15]

Four integral steps or "rubics", as provided by the Ecumenical Association of Third World Theologians (EATWOT 1979), were necessary before Liberation Theology could be started. Reuben Rodriguez describes them as follows:

> First, the church's commitment to undertake scientific analysis of social, economic, political reality; second, the church's mission defined as liberative evangelization; the church's commitment to a program of liberation construction of a just society; and fourth, a doctrinal reflection on the church's preferential option for the poor.[16]

Without this collective agreement and directive, Liberation Theology could never have a viable platform from which it could successfully elevate the poor from its deplorable conditions to one of justice and hope! The timing for this foundational attempt was well thought out, and most of the advocates for a change in valuing the poor and disenfranchised, hoped something good would occur within a year of the plan being adopted.

The conviction and determination the poor should be liberated from their insidious plight was not a self-initiated accomplishment. Rather, it was advocated by Thomas Hanks and others. Its purpose was twofold. First, to develop a "detailed assessment of the plight of the poor,[17] and gain the clearest understand of God's plan for humanity so a practical means of action to resolve these problems will be in keeping with God's original plan."[18] The resolve of Liberation Theology includes unreserved release from social, economic, political, and religious oppression as the church and the state is transformed by the grace of God to be what He has always intended them to be. Dialogue to accomplish this may be necessary, but liberation must happen – and it will happen – because hope will drive these entities to it even as it caused the first century church to turn its world "upside down" (Acts 17:6).

Although not appealed to today as strongly as it had been in the early 1970s, the Exodus Narrative is regularly chosen as the example Liberation Theology must follow if justice for the poor is to be implemented. According to the Avant-Gard, who promoted Liberation Theology, God has always wanted liberation from oppression. Although He tolerated it for a season, He eventually intervened, and crushed it by commissioning an avenger – Moses – to activate a unified community with freedom as its primary focus. The Exodus motif provided the stimulant for Liberation Theology, because its proponents saw that the Hebrew Children believed God was working directly with them. Even though their freedom was not immediately gained, God eventually provided it. This motif creates a cooperative solidarity towards a common goal that no amount of oppression can extinguish. Once adopted, it inspired the oppressed to pacifistic, revolutionary action that resonated with unwavering determination to see their freedom regardless of the difficulties incurred.[19]

Many Liberation Theologians have appealed to Isaiah 61:1-3 and Luke 4:18, as further authentication that God empathizes with the poor, and fights with them in their deplorable circumstances. They affirm with David, God's faithfulness in their distress (Ps 18:6). Because of this, they continually collectively pray, study, and work towards correcting the injustices that have been afflicted on to them through the past centuries. For those that hear Christ's teaching in Luke 4:18, and hear the distressful cries of the poor, "it is unquestionably clear Christ congratulates believers who go beyond recognizing the exploitation of the poor, and embrace their destitution by helping them find release from it."[20]

Although the aforementioned have provided inspiration for the marginalized in the "fight for liberation from poverty," St. Francis of Assisi, by "marrying poverty"[21] may be regarded as the greatest mentor in this area. Reflection on Assisi's Franciscan Order at Medellin may have been motivation for the clerics to extend pastoral care beyond the pulpit to the poor for, through His example, they were drawn to scripture to investigate how Christ taught His followers how to relate to the poor, and "demonstrate they had come to a personal relationship with Him."[22]

Despite not being well-known beyond Latin America, Bartolome de la Casa, a sixteenth century Catholic Priest, also provides impetus for believers to contend for social change among the poor. He, during the period when the church was amassing large land holdings, managed several slaves. One day, while reading Paul's claim, "There is neither Jew nor Greek, there is neither bond nor free, there is neither male nor female: for ye are all one in Christ Jesus" (Gal 3:28), he immediately became distressed with his ungodly control over other humans, and their despicable, impoverishment.[23] Early the next morning, without consulting other clerics, he released the slaves, met with the Bishop, and told them he had freed all the slaves for God had spoken to him saying, "Let my people go!" It is believed as clerics throughout the twentieth century rehearsed this narrative, they also were convicted about their deplorable conduct, and heard God say, "Let my people go!"

Though not commendable as a model for Christian deportment, Liberation Theology also borrowed extensively from Marxism. This construes, "the worker, the poor, and the marginalized are thrown into the 'cash-nexus' of capitalism which overrides him like a tyrannical and oppressive force. With this, it further holds he cannot gain liberty from this web, unless human nature resists it with an innovative, and creative measure by which he can subvert and reverse their plight."[24] By borrowing from Marx, Liberation Theologians incited mass contempt towards big business, big government and the rich who they regarded as being complicit in creating the repressive and deplorable life-style of the poor. Marxism, coupled with biblical judgments against injustices towards the poor, also proved to be an important motivator for socioeconomic, political, and religious reform. Through this, it was hoped the present generation of the poor would be elevated to a greater appreciative standing among the rest of society. With this, it was further hoped that segregation of the poor, as nonpersons, would be forever curbed. As this feeling of injustice, alienation and exploitation of the poor fermented, groups, known as *comunidades eclesiales de base,*[25] which consisted of fifteen to twenty families, led by laypersons, were started with the purpose of making the 'grass-roots' citizens aware of their deplorable conditions, and their basic human rights as taught in the scriptures.

Praxis – Catalyst for Change

Events during the middle of the last century forcefully pushed the Catholic Church to recognize the startling disparity of the deplorable social inequities among most of the third world nations, compared to those of Europe and North America. This awareness, coupled, with the conviction God empathizes with the poor, and copartners with them in the "fight" for change, stirred the Church to ask, "How, then, are the poor to live in their present crisis of segregation, deprivation, injustice and oppression so they may honourably gain what should be rightfully theirs?"

It was clear lasting, corrective reform for the impoverished and socially alienated would not be realized through the efforts of government or big business. But, despite the popularity and the enthusiasm of the *comunidades eclesiales de base,* advocates of Liberation Theology knew that an open and defiant revolution by the poor would also not better their plight. Reform, for the marginalized, would be best realized through praxis, the basic raw material of change as "thoughts, creeds, doctrines, faith and ethically good practices were 'married' to form the bridge of connecting the poor and the Church in a fight of solidarity."[26] Only this, the church said, would inaugurate a slow, but certain orthopraxis which would eventually bring healing to their plight. Praxis always emphasizes practical and corrective measures over theories, for it is through this that a resilient resolve for betterment of the poor will best be ignited. Stephen Bevans provides the following analysis of praxis:

> The praxis model employs a method that 'in its most profound sense is understood as the unity of knowledge as activity and knowledge as content.' It works on the idea that 'truth is at the level of history, not in the realm of ideas.' As practitioners of the praxis model began to reread the Bible and Christian tradition, they began to discover that the Bible is a product of struggles for human freedom; that Jesus message is not primarily about doctrines, but of structure-shaking attitudes and behaviour; that sin must be opposed not by compromise, by radical reordering of one's life. Social change – and the social location of the poor – can become a reality as people are transformed into action based on this deeper transforming knowledge of God.[27]

Movement towards change would be generated from the "grass-roots," and would be plausible as the marginalized recognized God was comforting, and co-working with them in their crisis. He would empower them to find liberty from their oppression as the Christian community determinately worked together in love and unity. Advancement for righteousness cannot be demanded. Rather, social amelioration will be achieved once Christians analyzed the biblical warrants for justice towards the poor, adopted a Christ-like spirit of love towards the offenders and each other, and strategized base-level changes in the local communities which will foster a better life-style, education, work ethic, and more humane treatment of the poor. Gustavo Gutierrez adds:

> Following Christ has become point of reference for the theological reflection taking place in Latin America. It is a aware that is preceded by the spiritual experience of Christians committed to the process of liberation. This

> encounter with God and the discipleship of the Lord - sometimes extending to surrendering one's life, to martyrdom – has been made more urgent and fruitful by the events of recent years. In context of the struggle for liberation motivated by love and justice for all, there has possibly opened a new way of following Jesus in Latin America even to the extent of seeing measurable, positive changes for the disenfranchised and marginalized.[28]

Through praxis the Church would hear the cries of the poor, as Christ does, and empower the collective body – priests and laity alike – to advocate and, where possible, to promulgate changes so the conditions of the disadvantaged might be improved. Liberation Theologians clearly encouraged all believers to labour intensely to this end, for those that are called of God cannot avoid this imperative for God promises judgment on those that do not fulfill it (Is 3:14-15). Proponents of Liberation Theology suggested praxis is best articulated when fellow Christians can place themselves in the "shoes" of the poor, and walk with them along the path of suffering. Then immediate, proactive concern for improvement will become an inseparable passion for all believers' daily life-style. Martin Luther King, Jr., according to John Wimberly, referenced to praxis in this manner. He contributes:

> Martin Luther King, Jr., a Liberation Theologian before the term was coined, saw himself and the African-American population in the United States when he read about the Hebrew slaves in Egypt being called and led to freedom by their God. Adopting this approach, the Bible stories no longer remain ancient events seated in the past. They are about people like us – people like those of Latin America who are labelled as nonperson. As preachers we need to encourage our brothers to identify with the poor of scripture so we can identify ourselves with the poor in our society. Then we will both love and help them see a new day with a better, privileged life-style that is rightly theirs already.[29]

Praxis is best cultured within society through dialogue with government, large business, the Church and the marginalized so a consensus for amends can be gained. God empathizes with the poor and marginalized, gives them strength to endure their plight, and gives them perseverance to contend for change, regardless how slow and difficult this may be. But, Liberation Theology contends unless praxis extends beyond the micro culture of the poor to touch the entire nation, it will be of no real effect because the disenfranchisement of the poor is grounded in the historical context of the whole nation. Change, envisaged among the *comunidades eclesiales de base* must filter up to all ranks of society, so the entire nation will realize spiritual, as well as socioeconomic and political reform. This one hope may have been the main reason Liberation Theologians have continued their struggle for improvement among the poor despite little, if any, proposed change has been realized over the previous fifty years. Their dream for Christians – regardless of their present socioeconomic status – is an unwavering confidence in God that He will adequately and timely supply their daily needs in ways unimaginable and bring a new, just world for them to enjoy through democratic elections throughout the upcoming years.

Problems with Liberation Theology

Whereas Liberation Theology may be complemented for its enthusiasm in advancing the cause of the poor, it would be an oversight to overlook several inherent problems with this model. These include the Exodus Motif, Triumphalism, Marxism, and Dialogue.

First, Liberation Theology maximizes, as its foundation, God called Moses to collectively incite the Hebrews to oppose the deplorable conditions under which they lived. Further, Liberation Theologians contend that God "fought with them" and helped them win their freedom from Pharaoh. Careful exegesis of the Exodus Motif shows they may have twisted the story to suit the second of their problems, i. e. Triumphalism - the poor will see better days!

An examination of the biblical Exodus readily teaches three contradictions to Triumphalism. First, God spoke individually to Moses, and ordained him to be advocate for Israel as its leader. Moses did not collectively incite the people to join him in open opposition to their plight. Rather, God, without the help of the

Hebrews, invoked plagues on Egypt and Pharaoh whereby He effected liberation from ill-treatment and emancipate them. God called Moses to obey and follow so He, and not Moses nor the people, could lead them out of bondage.

Second, it expounds "praxis" as the most plausible corrector of the poverty-stricken's plight because reform usually is best realized through initiatives actively and strategically implemented. A predisposition to this conduct is unbiblical and irrational. Jesus clearly indicated to Judas that his self-centred, bigoted concern for the poor was futile because the poor's plight, with all its unwarranted encumbrances, can never be eliminated (John 12:8).

An attempt to eradicate poverty – regardless how serious it might be – is also irrational because poverty is not a singular socioeconomic condition. Rather it is multifaceted, and with every impoverished person there are a number of mitigating factors that impede progression to a betterment of his or her social standing. The Christian community needs to be commended for desiring to offer a "hand up" instead of a "hand out." But, with this, the needy must take initiatives whereby they might better their income,[30] or graciously endure their plight as God empowers them awaiting the eschaton when full release from their impoverished status will be gained.

Third, Liberation Theology's suggestion the problem of poor can be resolved through dialogue with government and social agency is unfounded. It has been suggested the elitist "developmental programs," often conducted by governments or big business may be the primary instigator of poverty in Latin America. If this is true, it is doubtful the 'door' to dialogue with them would be open. Further, the economic resources in Latin America may be so limited that even though a consensus of agreement was reached, little more than what has already been accomplished can be realized. Liberation Theology's desire for dialogue may be construed as a simplified diversion from accepting honestly and realistically that the eradication of poverty is not feasible. It would be commendable for the Church to free humanity from the woes of poverty and suffering. This, however, is neither plausible nor possible. Therefore, instead of holding dialogue over an improbable result, perhaps it should reach out one family at a time, so it might educate and mentor those who are genuinely interested to improve their plight. Poverty will never be relinquished. However, as the aforementioned alternatives to Liberation Theology are enacted, the suffering of many will be lightened.

Fourth, Liberation Theology's alliance with Marxism is also troubling. Marxism contends social reform finds its meaning as the poor contend with the wealthy for a rightful piece of the wealth so their plight can be reversed. Theoretically, the concept is inviting. Realistically, it is problematic because rich investors arduously contend the capital invested has been "risk capital." The profits gained – regardless how large - are rightfully theirs. They further assert corporations help society by employing others, and by providing resources for their life necessities.

When Liberation Theologians suggest everyone in a society has the right to share the wealth of the rich, this extinguishes the entrepreneurship spirt risk takers possess. But, more drastic than this, it may increase a parasitic, codependent spirit in individuals who do not want to seek ways of bettering themselves This, is not the intention of Gustavo Gutierrez and other exponents of Liberation Theology. Instead, they sincerely hope the rich and poor will willingly pull their ideas, resources and energy so no one in South America will be in want economically, materially and socially.

Conclusion

Apart from the problems cited, Liberation Theology Latin American has proven to be a welcome reform for thousands of poor, disenfranchised, uneducated, and impoverished people. God's people are called to share each other's burdens, trials and afflictions by offering constructive care and counsel, and by helping with their financial resources wherever possible. Churches in North America, and other parts of the world that are extravagantly blessed materially, need to be touched with the afflictions of the poor in Latin American, evaluate their life-style, and sacrifice financially so that their brothers and sisters may find relief from their crisis as they live in hope for Christ's kingdom to come to earth.

Chapter 14

MS PowerPoint: Investigating Its Pro’s and Con’s

MS PowerPoint

MSPowerPoint

Discovering
Its
Usefulness . . .

If There Is Any!

Introduction

A new ministry aid, MS PowerPoint, has made itself known within both small and large churches. Individuals walking into the sanctuary usually notice a large projection screen displaying church weekly events or some other noteworthy advertisement. But, PowerPoint has not only made its presence known in the sanctuary. Visit the youth department, the adult Sunday School classes or the evening teaching sessions, and one will soon discover it has taken a significant, if not a dominant role, everywhere in the church. Without doubt, the "technological revolution" has touched the church. It may have become the controller of church worship, rather than a valued helper.

Value of PowerPoint

PowerPoint, in many ways, is a welcome addition to church ministry.

First, is worthwhile because it brings a single audience focus to the presentation. Because it is shown on large screens, in a moderately dim room, distractions that might be obvious using other media, are removed. Further, because the screen is the focus, it is likely the learning experience will also be more defined as the perimeters of conversation are delineated for the group.

Second, it facilitates speakers with the opportunity to share supportive maps, graphs, charts, and photographs to a large audience with little difficulty. No longer does the speaker appear at a meeting with a large stack of books, large, cumbersome drawings or charts, or a stack of stapled documents. Now, instead, he or she stores them on the computer. Whenever they are needed, he or she "pulls them up," and shows them with ease and confidence. John Goshen comments:

> Imagine a speaker wanting to speak about Jesus' miracles at Capernaum or Bethany. To adequately cover the materials he would need a globe of the world, a large map of Israel, and a model or a large photo of the temple at Capernaum so the audience would gain an adequate understanding of the area of the world he might want to discuss. Just think how difficult it would be, first, for the speaker to obtain all these articles, and second, how much more difficult it would be for him to set them out so a large audience can see and relate to them during the discussion. Now, with PowerPoint that's solved; the projector, the computer and the screen make it all possible. That's how PowerPoint articulates its power.[1]

PowerPoint, third, allows the speaker to be creative in his presentation. Instead of the presentation being a monologue, centered solely around the speaker's narrative or sermon, it now can be shaped into a multifaceted, multimedia production intermixed with videos, photographs, secondary speaker contributions, artwork, animations, or anything else the speaker might wish to use to strengthen the presentation and possibly, make it more appealing to the audience. Monologues, no matter how charismatic the speaker might be, or how intriguing the topic might be, because of the boredom inherent in them, eventually causes the listeners to "drift off into their own world." But, with PowerPoint, if the speaker is creative, the audience will never know for sure what's coming next. This expectation of "what's coming next" will motivate them to remain attentive throughout the presentation. With creative PowerPoint presentations, it is also likely the learning experience will be more enhanced than through other means of communication formerly used.

PowerPoint is a valuable educational tool. Whereas students were left to decipher what is significant, and what is not during learning sessions of 1960-1990, with PowerPoint's manipulative alternatives, significant texts can be coloured, bolded, underlined, enhanced with special fonts, or they can be brought in as overlays through text animations. Educators or pastors, using Office MS PowerPoint 2010 can construct their messages as puzzles, and produce an endless number of formats by which he or she can develop his or her material for the audience. And with PowerPoint, it can be assembled for varying age or interest groups with little adjustment. J. S. Broadley, pastor of Grace Baptist Church, comments:

> Whenever I want to speak on a passage where Paul wants us to construct our life after a biblical pattern, for example, the fruit of the spirit being an essential mark of the 'spirit walk,' I construct the form of a man walking one-piece at a time using the puzzle tool. The animation feature enables me to visually connect each piece before the audience as a progression. When the message is finished, my people will leave both with the assembly in progress, and the final product, fixed firmly in their mind. Regardless of what I've said, my message will have been received by the audience.[2]

Discredits of PowerPoint

Regardless how worthwhile and helpful PowerPoint might appear, it has limits as a ministry tool when it is used during worship.

First, PowerPoint is often used by individuals who have not been adequately trained in how it should be used to attain the best desired results from the presentation. Therefore, in many circumstances, unbecoming distracting animations, irrelevant drawings, graphs, or music, and lengthy quotes are used in a presentation. Because each frame is separate from the other, the presentation can become disconnected in its content. If this should happen – as it often does – then the audience will also become disconnected from the message. When this happens, regardless how much creative work has gone into developing PowerPoint, the intended positive, and favorable results desired may be minimized.

With these distractions, one might also add the possibility the speaker may not, during the presentation, be able to smoothly progress from one slide to the next. Often, inexperienced PowerPoint users are not adequately versed with using the control buttons to transition from one slide to the next. Because of this, the wrong frame is selected, or the desired frame may be skipped altogether. When this happens, two problems may arise. First, the presenter becomes frustrated, and makes added undesired transition errors, and second, the audience may be apprehensive the presentation has not adequately been rehearsed, and therefore, lose interest in it.

Second, although a PowerPoint may be well intended for a learning experience, it may become nothing more than "information transport." Education is a two-way learning experience, which includes communication between a "sender" and a "receiver." In most PowerPoint presentations, the "receiver" – student or congregant – is focused on the screen.[3] Even though a lecturer might be speaking, "the new Gnosticism of learning"[4] may make consuming what is seen more significant, meaningful and "spiritual" than that which is heard. If PowerPoint enables an audience to disconnect from physical speakers, what level of audience disconnect might there be from God as it becomes consumed with what is seen, rather than is heard? "This disconnect is very probable", says Robert Philips. He suggests:

> No longer are congregations brought together to partake in worship, they are now brought together to participate in worship with PowerPoint, as it presents the liturgy of song, scripture, and creed, being the referee as to what should be included in the worship service.[5]

PowerPoint, because it is a swift, continual moving narrative in worship, forcing the full, undivided attention of the audience, may become the "authoritative voice of God" in the service, rather than being a tool which helps the audience hear the voice of God. Whenever time for reflection about what has been heard or seen is withheld from the audience, there is a high probability the message will not be adequately received or understood.

Third, PowerPoint may provide the pastor with a sense of power. Since he or she is the speaker, and the designer of the presentation, he or she has full, uncontrolled power over what information the audience will hear and see. On many occasion, the pastor may select specific graphs, graphics, photos, or articles that reaffirm exactly the issue he or she desires to make. As this occurs, the input – both the verbal and visual content – now appear to "speak" with one, unified voice, even though they may not be directly associated one with one another.

Such may happen, for example, if a pastor desires to speak about the injustice Pharaoh showed to the Hebrew Children (Ex 1-14). To make his point, the speaker might show photos and clip art about the Hebrews Children's ill-treatment under Rameses I with reading scripture passages to support his claim. But, to impress on the audience that physical hurt on anyone is unjust, the speaker may think if he or she were to show a video clip about the suffering of children in Sudan during the Sudan War, this might embed his point on the audience better.

The problem, although both incidences are unjust, the pastor could be prejudicing the audiences understanding of what happened during the biblical Exodus as contrasted with what happened during the Sudan Crisis. During the suffering under Pharaoh, the Children were being instructed regarding God's faithful care and deliverance despite suffering. During the Sudan Wars, humanity was learning about the ill that befalls others when Kings, Prime Minister or Presidents seek personal prestige, power and position over the good of the community.

Fourth, PowerPoint may be a detractor from joint participation in the liturgy, and worship of the collective body within the church. Worship is a combined effort of prayer, song, confession, and affirmation of Christ's redemptive grace. PowerPoint, as the new tool, may fail in this area because it often redirects people to a fractured concentration on worship as they are required to listen, view, and meditate on what is being presented during a short period of time. While the author was visiting a church in Cochrane, Alberta the pastor asked the attendees to turn to a passage of scripture. Immediately the presentation started, the pastor read the passage, and moved on to the next two or three slides that introduced the message. Of note, as the pastor was speaking, many in the congregation were still trying to find the scripture passage which was the basis for the message. This swift, unannounced, disconnected and often abrupt, transition from slide to slide, could make what was intended as worship, nothing more than a matter of theatrics. As this happens, whole-hearted, concentrated meditation, and devotion required for valued and validated worship is quickly diminished or destroyed. Worship does not occur unless there is "dialogue with God and with each other in concert around His word, and the accepted common liturgy of the fellowship."[6]

Fifth, PowerPoint may provide a noticeable disconnect for congregants and scripture. In many churches scripture is projected onto the screen for public viewing or joint reading. No longer is it necessary for parishioners to bring their Bible to church, and turn to the biblical passage during the preaching of the gospel message. This personal disconnect, in public worship, can have serious consequences. If parishioners start believing the church, through PowerPoint, will adequately provide them scripture they should read, they may be tempted to abandon home, personal Bible reading week after week. As this occurs, believers may become impoverished in their knowledge and understanding of the gospel. Because of this, parishioners may start exemplifying a sub-standard Christian worldview that is displayed through carnal, ungodly, and unwholesome conduct and a lack of fellowship with like-minded saints.

Because of this possibility, churches that project scripture readings should, prior to the viewing, ask the congregants to open their Bible to the required passage, and follow along while the reading is done. A second alternative might be to have alternate scripture readings from selected passages with some being projected on the screen, and others not. The greater the personal, visual and hands-on encounter with scripture congregants have, the more connected to the Word they will feel. As personal connection with the Word increases through "hands on" and oral readings, the greater the meaning scripture will have to them. Jakob Spener, founder of the Pietist Movement (1649), strongly advocated daily, personal scripture reading. He states:

> How much good it would do if good friends would come together on a Sunday and instead of getting out glasses, cards, or dice would take up a book and read it for the edification of all, or would review something of the sermons that were heard. If, they should not be quite able to find their way

through, they would ask a preacher to clarify the matter. We preachers cannot instruct the people from our pulpits as much as is needful unless other persons from the congregation, who by God's grace, have a superior knowledge of Christianity, take the pains by the virtue of their universal priesthood, to work with and under us to correct and reform as much in their neighbours as they are able according to the measure of their gifts and their simplicity.[7]

And Christopher K. Lensch, in an article entitled, "The Public Reading of Scripture," strongly suggests that personal, daily reading of scripture is the parishioners faithful encounter with the truth of the Word through which they become sanctified (John 17:17). Personal participation of congregants in oral scripture reading during public worship, for Lensch, is imperative because it "awakens believers to the truth of the gospel as it is audibly stated, expressed, and sanctioned as truth." He adds:

> We believe the reading and hearing of God's Word is a means of grace. When it is attended by the Spirit Who gave it, inspired truth has irresistible power to sanctify and build up its hearers in the faith. Hearing the Word is an essential part of God's means of transforming us by the renewing of our minds so we might know His will. Note the Bible's self-authentication: Sanctify them by Your truth. Your word is truth." (John 17:17). God from the beginning chose you for salvation through sanctification by the Spirit and belief in the truth, to which He called you by our gospel" (2 Thess. 2:13-14). If God sanctifies His people through their personal reading of the Bible, how much more should our attention be given in a public worship service where the congregation gathers to honor God and receive grace. Hence the Bible's command to pastors in 1 Tim 4:13: "...give attention to [public] reading…." The original Greek word "reading" always means public, vocal reading."[8]

Sixth, PowerPoint can create disconnects in hymn and chorus singing. Usually, when songs and choruses are projected for public worship, only the words, and not the musical scores, are shown. The inherent problem with this is when few of the attendees -- other than the worship team -- know the melody the intended joyful rendition of the music may become bland and distorted. Jeremy S. Begbie comments about the need of musical scores being available to congregants during collective, public worship. He states:

> Musical notations provide singers with a map to how a song should be sung; abandon the notes, and you abandon the possibility of a song. Notes bring condition and direction to music. Dispose of the score, and you've disposed of the music. Without the score the sounds deployed have no connection with the spatio-temporal characteristics of the phenomena evoked by the physical language, and the intended masterpiece loses its essential worth and validity.[9]

Seven, PowerPoint may remove worshippers from the passive learning experience inherent in preaching and lecturing, but it does not enhance the possibility of learning. Vivid colours, dynamic graphics and animations more readily hold the participants interest in what is being presented, but because of the probable disconnect as the presentation moves from frame to frame, or because of the vast amount of information being presented in such a short time span, it is likely the engaged learning experience will be no greater than sitting and listening to a lecture of the same length. PowerPoint, like television, mesmerizes the viewers, induces passive participation with the medium, and lessens the learning experience. J. T. Mayes comments:

> Multimedia presentations have as their goal the achievement of engagement. The learner will be enticed, by the vividness or the fidelity of the presentation, to focus full attention on the task or on the flow of meaning. When sound and full-motion video on the computer can compete with domestic television, then we have achieved perhaps the first requirement of interactive learning. At least we have engaged the learner's interest. But, multimedia systems may even interfere with engagement, especially if the "bells and whistles" of the presentation have no direct correlation to the intended instructional content. Now, instead of being a benefit to learning, the multimedia system may be considered as merely a diversion from the lecture medium, and may sharply decrease, if not totally destroy, the opportunity for learning.[10]

Conclusion

PowerPoint is the new "game" in the market. Everyone is 'playing with it' to get their intended end. On the surface it looks that

PowerPoint is the best thing "since sliced bread." But, from the concerns mentioned, PowerPoint may not be all that it is proposed to be. Therefore it should be used on a limited basis after great consideration of the goal it may aid the speaker to reach without instilling a 'disconnect' to the hearers.

While PowerPoint may be a great aid for teaching within the church, the author strongly suggests its use during public worship should be minimized. The evidence presented, and available from other sources, indicates it is more of a hindrance to congregational worship, than an aid. The possible reason for it being a hindrance is t, with the slide transitions, animations, and extreme colour variants, may inculcate within the congregants a sense of theatrics, rather than a sense of worship. Such an exchange for worship should never occur within Christ's church because His "house is to be called, and revered, as a house of prayer: (Mark 11:17 cf. Isaiah 56:7). This commendation for the church remains as valid today as it was in His day.

PowerPoint should be prudently and cautiously used to aid the speaker make his point. It should never be used illegitimately as persuasive power to making his or her point. This should always be the work of the Holy Spirit as the speaker copartners with Him in administering kingdom knowledge to the people, through the preaching and teaching of the Word that is supplemented by skillful use of audio, text, graphics and the like in PowerPoint presentations Anything, other than this, could rightly be construed as a blatant abuse of modern technology.

Chapter 15

Baptist Pastoral

Leadership Training
in
Post-Communist Romania

Introduction

Donna and I have visited Romania eight times since 2001. During our visits we have talked with hundreds of Romanian pastors of large city, and small, isolated village churches. Not many westerners are familiar with the hardships pastors, who lived under Ceausescu's rule, faced. This paper is a historical sketch of the growth of the Baptist Union Fellowship, Romania, from 1909 to 1991.

From 1994 to December 25, 1989, whenever the western world received news about Romania, it usually was about oppression the nation suffered at the hands of Gheorghiu-Dej or Nicolae Ceausescu.[1] Although the entire nation faced immeasurable dictatorial controls, evangelical churches – in particular – suffered worse as educational programs were introduced to desensitize Christians from believing in God and to "destroy" the seditious, unwholesome influence evangelicals had – especially in the small, isolated villages. Not only would God no longer be worshipped, it was hoped He no longer would be thought about. Peter Dugulescu rightly concludes, "Romania's problems began in 1944 when Communists assumed leadership of the country, and declared it "a land without God."[2]

Of the two leaders, Gheorghiu Ceausescu proved to be the greater "albatross" for Romanian evangelicals. On gaining power in 1962,[3] he became threatened by the rapid growth of evangelical church congregations. Immediately he developed a disdainful disgust towards them. At his inaugural address he unabashedly stated that evangelicals were an imperialist enemy to the state. Within six months he limited the number of evangelical denominations that would be recognized by the government, strictly monitored the pastor's activities, and had them arrested "on the slightest suspicion" they were not complying with his orders. Necula Marian comments about Ceausescu's pastoral control:

> The cults (evangelicals) were a "legitimate target" for the Communist regime for a twofold reason: first, as another religious challenger to its ideological prominence; second, because they were labelled as agents to the imperialist camp. So, even if the constitution guaranteed the freedom of conscience and of confession, persecutions were an everyday reality for the members of these protestant cults. [4]

The height of Ceausescu's overwhelming hatred for evangelical churches was demonstrated in 1985 when border authorities confiscated twenty-four thousand Bibles which were being smuggled in from England. On receiving the report concerning the discovery, he became so incensed he had the "entire load ground to pulp and made into toilet paper."[5] Commenting on this travesty, with uncontrolled tears, Peter Vidu remarked, "That which thousands regarded as being more precious than food, one man regarded as nothing more than dung."[6]

Of the four religious denominations "recognized" by Ceausescu,[7] the Baptist Union Fellowship incurred the most vicious persecution. But, regardless how intense the oppression became, the attacks did not thwart its steadfast commitment to God or their zeal to establish new centres of worship. Under the cover of darkness, in homes or in village forests, pastors boldly preached the gospel.

Thousands came to faith in Christ despite the consequences that befell them. Peter Vidu comments on these events:

> My father was one of the preachers who would not surrender to Ceausescu's demands. When the Secretariat learned that his church was increasing in numbers, it withdrew his ministerial license and sent him to Muldova to work in a textile factory thinking that this would crush his zeal for ministry. However, on arriving, my father immediately began preaching Christ, and many villagers believed and repented. When they inquired about baptism, my father baptized them in nearby streams using the moonlight God provided. According to my father, the risk of being one of Christ's Ambassadors was nothing compared with the joy he discovered as he saw countless individuals come to Christ. So, day and night, he laboured to see God's kingdom be established in earth as it is in heaven.[8]

Background to the Romanian Baptist Union Fellowship

Although Baptists were known in Romania as early as 1869, the first recognized group had its beginnings in 1909 when a group of German Christians visited the nation, and started a mission church near Arad.[9] During the following four years, because of intense physical and verbal harassment by the Orthodox Priests, it made no further attempts to establish new churches. In 1913, however, Constantin Adorian,[10] an ethnic Romanian, felt God was appointing him to start a Romanian "fellowship church" in or near Bucharest. As a result of his faithfulness to the "call," the church – with another five or six supporters – was started within the year. By 1917, because of unexpected church growth, the pastors laid the foundation for the Baptist Union Fellowship, and in 1920 it became a reality. Today the Baptist Union Fellowship is Romania's largest religious sect consisting of over five hundred churches, two theological seminaries,[11] a Christian university,[12] and a hospice care centre.[13]

Clergy Training during Pre-communist Times

In the earliest days of ministry – 1913-1920 – Baptist pastors had no official theological training, so they started, and oversaw new churches, based on their "perceived call" to ministry. On weekends, or in evenings after working on farms, they visited nearby villages and boldly proclaimed what they had been taught by missionaries, or what they understood from reading the scriptures. When a new church was started, the "church planter" commissioned a trustworthy, competent, new believer to oversee the work, and then moved on to another village where he would start a new work.

The first "revivalist missionary and noteworthy church planter" at this time was Iosif Trifa. During his earliest days of ministry he was an Orthodox Priest. However, as he began understanding – through an illumination of the Holy Spirit – Christ was the Savior, he began preaching the need for people to repent, and follow God. His ministry among the Orthodox churches ended in 1922 when he was excommunicated from the Church for preaching repentance. Over a period of fifteen years – 1922-1937 – he established thirty-five Baptist churches, of which twenty-one still exist today.[14]

Although many new works were established during this time, their survival was doubted. Two major deterrents to their survival existed. First, relentless caustic and belittling verbal and physical attacks on Baptist pastors by the Orthodox priests often discouraged young and untrained workers from starting new works. If pastors did not succumb to the attacks, the priests would confront the converted and discourage them from attending the meetings by saying the evangelicals had entered into a battle for their souls, and "through their dubious and untested teachings they were leading them into deeper sin by causing them to leave the True Church and the spiritual care they had been promised by God's appointed priests."[15]

Second, charges by Pentecostal missionaries Baptist pastors willingly neglected preaching the full gospel about the Holy Spirit[16] greatly hindered church growth. Using this accusation as a foundation for starting new congregations, Pentecostal missionaries moved into nearby villages, and enticed Baptists to join them so they could "hear the whole truth, and nothing but the truth!"

Recognizing that most pastors could not counteract these charges, the Baptist Union opened Bucharest Bible Training Centre in

1914[17] to provide the much needed leadership training. The first "headmaster" was Ioseph Tson[18] who believed the accusations made by Pentecostals could be adequately addressed if pastors received intense Bible training. In 1935 the first one year training session was started with four students attending, and in 1945 a four-year Bachelor of Theology program was inaugurated. The first graduating class consisted of eighteen trained pastors that could be commissioned to full-time ministry throughout the major cities of Romania including Bucharest, Timisoara, Iash, and Oradea. Daniel Marin, Pastor of Grace Baptist Church, Zalau was one of those students. About his training at Bucharest Bible College he comments:

> The training was like manna from heaven; we were fed the Word of God. It was during this time we realized that we were gaining new energy and insight to understand our faith and to contend with those who were misrepresenting our work in the gospel. As we left Bucharest, we were convinced that we needed to impart the same bread to others. Therefore, as students of the Word and as commissioned pastors, we went to the people, empowered by the Holy Spirit, presenting the gospel, and many came to faith in Christ. The churches grew in numbers rapidly.[19]

Clergy Training during Communism

Because the Romanian Constitution guaranteed freedom of religion, and the right of peaceful, collective assembly,[20] Ceausescu sanctioned religious gatherings "twice a week in public places as long as the gatherings were conducted by an Orthodox priest, or by a licensed pastor who was in good standing with the Department of Cults."[21] To ensure the meetings were being conducted following stipulated, government regulations, and so he could know what was happening during the meetings, Ceausescu ordered members of the District Secretariat to attend every meeting and document the proceedings. Nothing was to be "hidden from him." Steve Friesen comments:

> Ceausescu's Department of Religious Affairs kept a tight rein on the churches. It strictly regulated the number and the schedule of worship services, and denied church building permits for years. No denomination officials could be elected without the Department's consent. The government, sometimes even required the election of certain people, and would occasionally intervene in a congregation's choice of its pastors or priests. Travel to international church conferences was possible only with the department's approval, and speakers had to submit their speeches to the department or the Secretariat in advance. The department also kept tabs on active lay people, and often had them harassed at work. Christian leaders, who were especially uncooperative, were sometimes threatened, jailed or physically injured.[22]

From 1964-1976, as Ceausescu became more suspect of the evangelical influence, he implemented more rigorous controls over pastoral leadership. First, he limited the number of pastoral training applicants nationwide, and disallowed further enrollment of new candidates until the class in progress graduated four years later. By doing so, he decreased the number of available, new pastors from twenty every four years, to five or six. In 1974 nineteen students were selected for candidate interviews. But, as Radu Tet states, "Only five were chosen and I, praise the Lord, was one of them."[23] In 1980, as Baptist pastors began to speak against Ceausescu's overbearing demands and refused to comply with them he, for the first time, closed Bucharest Bible College, and disallowed training of pastors for a period of four years. Added to this, he bribed or intimidated elderly and relatively poor pastors to renounce the pulpit and join his ranks as Secretariat Informers. Many, because of intimidation and financial need, yielded to his seductive plan. Peter Dugulescu comments:

> The saddest thing for the believers and ministers of the evangelical churches in Romania, in the forty-five years of Communism, and atheistic dictatorship was that those who were our nominal leaders had much more fellowship with the sons of darkness and with the atheists than with their brothers. Their obedience and dedication to God was

conditional, but their obedience to Communism was unconditional.[24]

Because of these two developments, the number of full-time, trained pastors overseeing congregations decreased rapidly. By 1984, because no new pastors were being trained, fewer than twenty percent of the Baptist Union Fellowship churches had licensed clergy.[25] Untrained, poor and tired farmers cared for the small local churches, while trained, and licensed ministers cared for four or five city churches weekly.

Although Ceausescu was convinced he had "crippled" pastoral leadership training by limiting candidate admission to Bucharest Bible College, he had, unknowingly, "opened the door" to an "underground clergy training" by trained and government certified pastors. Radu Tet explains the process followed:

> Access to formal pastoral training, indeed, was controlled by Ceausescu during my college years. But that does not mean pastoral training was limited to Bucharest. When we left, we took the message with us, and we imparted it to lay leaders. When they were adequately trained, they started new churches and past the message down-the-line. Ceausescu's limit on "college pastoral training" compelled us to do believer discipleship. This we accepted as Christ's great church building principle, and this we did. We taught one parishioner at a time how to disciple another so he would disciple another and another. When Ceausescu fell, we rejoiced over his death. But we also rejoiced because, during those days, we saw Christ's church grow in spite of the problems we faced.[26]

As Romanian pastors mentored lay leaders for leadership, pastors and teachers, from the School of Prophets in England, provided "remote, well-hidden, underground house training schools,"[27] in which students were sequestered for two or three weeks at a time to receive intensive leadership preparation. Regardless of the risk or danger, pastors throughout Romania gathered in numbers. By the Holy Spirit they subverted Ceausescu's plan to destroy Christ's church by receiving solid and balanced biblical instruction, and then fearlessly proclaiming the gospel wherever they went.

Ceausescu's noxious control over evangelical pastors came to its most unexpected demise on December 16, 1989 when, in Timisoara, the army tried to arrest Pastor Laszlo Tokes – Pastor of the Reformed Church in Timisoara – because he had not complied with an order to close a small, village church.[28] Despite the threats of pending military action, thousands of believers from villages surrounding Timisoara, gathered around him tightly so he could not be arrested. This collective support of one godly man was to be the catalyst behind the, sure and sudden, collapse of Ceausescu's twenty-five year demonic control over Romania's evangelicals.

Pastoral Leadership in Romania Today

As has been stated, during Ceausescu's dictatorship only four religious sects were recognized. However, since December 1989, seventeen were given authority to operate in Romania.[29] Of all the ministries certified by the Department of Cults, the Baptist Union Fellowship remains the largest evangelical denomination with over six hundred pastors throughout the country, preaching the gospel with little, or no hindrances. Membership in the Baptist Union now exceeds one hundred and seventy thousand converts,[30] and every ten to fifteen days a new Baptist mission church is being established throughout the nation.

Pastoral training is active at Bucharest Bible College and Seminary in Bucharest, and at Emanuel Baptist University in Oradea where courses in Theology, Homiletics, Spiritual Formation, and Leadership are taught. Both centres require students to spend one month each summer actively ministering in a village church, during which time they must preach no less than two times, and conduct an outreach program in the community. The reason behind this is that student pastors must learn servant leadership by ministering to the poor and the sick before taking on their own church. The quickest way for the leadership of the Baptist Union to discover if one is ready to minister on his own in a church, is to test him in a small, isolated village. Students who cannot show servant, shepherd leadership are not admitted to the next year of pastoral training at either seminary.

If individuals cannot attend either of these institutions, training can be received through Mission without Borders, in London, England or through Budapest Seminary, in Budapest, Hungary. Three times yearly representatives from these institutions visit Romania for two consecutive weeks and present modules in the areas of Theology, Church History, Bible, Homiletics, and Pastoral Care. On completing three years of study, graduates are licensed to pastor smaller established churches, or to plan new village churches under the supervision of an older and licensed pastor.

With these programs, a two-year presbyter/pastor course for potential pastors is available at Cluj Napoca's Babes Bolyai University. To qualify for training, candidates must present a letter of recommendation from their pastor, and must display leadership potential. On graduating, candidates receive a certificate from the Ministry of Education and Research allowing them to teach religion in public schools, or to pastor a mission church for a period not exceeding two years. To gain a permanent ministerial license, candidates must complete their pastoral training by attending one of the two seminaries in the country. A pastoral license is not granted to anyone if full pastoral training is not completed within five years of enrolling in the program.

Besides the basic pastoral training offered through the aforementioned institutions, many Romania pastors are now obtaining Master of Divinity and Doctor of Ministry degrees from government recognized institutions in nearby countries,[31] or by taking courses offered online by seminaries in the United States and Canada.[32]

Pastoral Leadership Problems

Although pastoral leadership is more accessible today than it was during the period of Communism, there are several problems that need to be examined.

First, there is little or no pre-screening of candidates for ministry. Although candidates enrolling at all Romanian seminaries must present, with their application, a personal vitae and a letter of recommendation from their pastor, they are not interviewed about their doctrinal convictions, or pulpit ministry call and conviction. Because of this, many candidates have graduated and have been licensed as pastors, but do not have the slightest understanding of what the "call to full-time ministry entails."

Second, pastoral training may be taken by many for the wrong reason. Unfortunately pastors are respected by most Romanian parishioners as being the "oracles of God." Because of this they are well supported economically, and are rarely asked to give an account of their weekly activities. Sometimes, therefore, pastors have been known to be the "preacher" on Sundays and Thursdays,[33] but a self-directed entrepreneur the rest of the week.

Third, most pastoral candidates are not trained in pastoral care. Because of this, few strong pastor/congregant interpersonal relationships are developed. This disconnect is most apparent during the Sunday services. Parishioners arrive for the services punctually at the hour of worship, and depart immediately at the close of worship with no other pastoral contact except a shake of the hand, and the voicing of, "pace" (peace).[34] Beyond this cordial exchange, no further contact is made by the pastor and congregant unless a distressing, urgent problem occurs. During a recent five week ministry tour of Romania,[35] I met only one pastor who visited his parishioners regularly at home or in the hospital.

There are three possible reasons for this gross lack of pastoral care. First, most clergy of small village churches do not live in the village where they pastor.[36] Instead, they usually live in the larger metropolis some distance from the church, and travel there only on Sunday or Thursday. Because of this, they have no contact with the parishioners beyond this. Second, most Baptist congregants, before their conversion, were registered members of the Orthodox Church. Because of this, they believe the pastor's role is to preach the weekly message, perform weddings and bury the dead, and nothing else. To request the pastor to visit them would be disrespectful. Rarely, therefore, does a parishioner seek pastoral care or counsel. Thomas J. Keppeler adds:

> The dominant leadership images that emerges from present Romanian churches is that of the preacher, and that, to a much lesser degree of pastor or shepherd. Those who are in

leadership are qualified on the basis of God through which the pastor vicariously influences the people to also study the Word, and influence others to Christ. Highly valued competencies are preaching and pastoral skills of encouraging, exhorting and evangelizing. Beyond these, nothing else is expected by Romanian congregations.[37]

Third, since pastoral candidates spend most of their training secluded, apart and separate from regular church life, it may be they are losing contact with the spiritual and social needs of the people to whom they minister. In light of this, it becomes difficult for the pastor "to be at home in the church"[38] and be participants with the people in their joys and discouragements.

Fourth, graduates are rarely equipped to deal with the numerous, unwelcome tensions present when dealing with angry and contentious Orthodox Priests. The slightest provocation of a priest may result in unexpected, costly legal expenses for the church. In Margine – a small village community – for example, the congregation was taken to civil litigation because the priest charged the pastor/overseer, Cosmin Marc with erecting the Baptist Church too close to the Orthodox graveyard. At a cost of thirty thousand dollars American, and a year and a half of interfaith tension, the issue was settled in favour of the Baptist Church. As Cosmin stated, "The protectionism of the Orthodox Church over the people of Romania is so strong it will do anything – reasonable or unreasonable – to ensure that not one of its supporters is lost to the evangelical scoundrels."[39] It is imperative that new pastors know how to contend with the Orthodox Priests. Otherwise, their fervency for ministry will be crushed within two or three years after licensing.

Fifth, new pastors – especially those in small, isolated villages – rarely receive mentoring or coaching by older and "more seasoned pastors. Larger city church pastors have far too many functions to care for, and usually are not willing to travel distances to mentor new pastors. According to many pastors, "mentoring is biblical, and it looks good on paper," but it is not possible because some of the missionary churches are "pastored" by visiting members of larger churches. There is no consistency in leadership, and therefore, there is no value in mentoring. Because of this, most young pastors/leaders are snatched away by discouraging encounters with the Orthodox which the newly appointed pastor is unlearned as to how to handle them. From the Baptist Union's perspective, it is better to have a new and unskilled pastor over a group than to have no one guiding them.

Sixth, college pastoral training is not supplemented by post-graduation, extended learning seminars. Annual National Baptist Fellowship Conferences and monthly District Fellowships are conducted regularly. But, usually, such meetings are held for only one day because village pastors need to travel a great distance to attend. During the most recent conference[40] held at Imanuel University, less than fifteen percent of the pastors attended because they could not afford the cost, or because they did not have someone to "cover their ministry responsibilities" while they were absent from the church.

If pastors are to remain proficient in their ministry skills, they need to be provided, once every four or five years, an opportunity to receive additional up-to-date instruction in ministry skills. Other professionals have access to extended learning. As the Under Shepherds of God's flock, tending to the people's eternal destiny, should not pastors be given the same opportunity?

And seventh, pastors need to be reminded "that the call to ministry is without repentance." During the years 1966-1989, Baptist pastors were intent on preaching the gospel and seeing new converts come to Christ regardless of the outcomes that might befall them. However, since religious freedom has come to the country, many pastors have been side tracked from gospel ministry to building new homes, new worship centres and running private, in-house businesses, rather than teaching the Word and doing evangelism. This new direction has been accepted because many Romanian pastors no longer believe people will attend church if there is not a well-designed and maintained building in which they can gather, or if the pastor is "poor."

Romanian pastors need to remember their former years. Along with this, they need to remember that Jesus promised, "Where two or three are gathered together in my name, there I am in the midst" (Jn 12:32). As pastors remind the people worship centres on

God, not on a building, they will gladly gather week after week. It is time to move on from building structures to teaching the love and provisional care of the Father so young and old may grow in Christ and in the ministry they are called to do.

God, by crushing Communism's debilitating control over His church, has opened the door for evangelism in Romania which has not been known before. Now, as never before, pastors need to be trained and committed so they can reach their community – in cities or in villages – to know Christ as Savior and Lord as they fulfill His commission, "Go ye into all the world and make disciples of all nations" (Matt 28:16).

Conclusion

Baptist Union churches endured untold hardships at the hands of Ceausescu and his cronies. God, faithfully, brought them through every one of them. His promise to His people is "He will build His church, and the gates of hell will never prevail against it" (Matt 16:18). To see God's kingdom come to earth, pastors in Romania must not – despite freedom from persecution – abandon their total dependence on God for their success. Instead, they must prostrate themselves in submission before God, listen for His direction, and in obedience with boldness from the Holy Spirit, attend to the call He has placed on their lives.

As this occurs, Baptist Union churches will become a powerful witness of God's continued love and care for His people, and many – even those of the Orthodox persuasion – will come to faith in Christ. Without complete surrender to God, and an unwavering obedience to His will, Baptist Union churches will be free to fellowship together, but they will not enjoy the blessing of God, the joy of increased repentance of the ungodly, and an increase in church membership that they knew during more trying days. God help the leaders of the Baptist Union to never forget the past so they can fervently complete God's call today!

Endnotes & Bibliography

Chapter 2

Endnotes

[1]. “Going with the flow” for the author, however, is limited to the action or cause being godly, moral, ethical and legal.

[2]. Partick Hans, ed., *The Collins English Dictionary* (Glasgow: William Collins & Sons Ltd., 1986), 4.

[3]. NB. *Emergency Contraception: The Morning after Pill* (accessed 28 February, 2004, http://www.morningafterpill.org/mapinfo1.html

[4]. Charles B. Clayman, ed., *The American Medical Association Encyclopedia of Medicine* (NY: Random House, 1989), 58.

[5.] Sheryl H. Blunt, “Catholic Report, Survival of the Unaborted”, *Christianity Today,* (Fall, November 13 1995), 91.

[6]. Clarence Taber, *Taber’s Cyclopedic Medical Dictionary,* (Toronto: Ryerson Press, 1963), c103 & d32.

[7]. Joyce Arthur, “Abortion in Canada,” *The Human Quest.* (accessed February 24th, 2004),
http://www.prochoiceactionnetworkcanada.org/aboutus/aboutus.shtml

[8]. James C. Fleck, “Canada Debates Abortion and Homosexuality”, *The Christian Century* (March 12, 1969), 354.

[9]. Henry Morgentaler, “A Letter to Pope John II from Henry Morgentaler” in *The Humanist* (Toronto: Doubleday, 1967), 45

[10]. Neil Arneston, “Morgentaler Against The Courts”, *The Abortion Crisis* (Toronto: Doubleday Canada, 1975), 62.

[11]. John Arnason, "Trudeau Legalizes Abortion?" *The Toronto Star,* (August 16, 1977): 7.

[12]. Charles Hartshorne, "Concerning Abortion: An Attempt at a Rational View," *The Christian Century,* (January 21, 1981), 44.

[13]. Francis Schaeffer, & Everett C. Koop, M.D., *Whatever Happened To The Human Race?* (Old Tappan, NJ: Fleming H. Revell Company, 1979), 193.

[14]. Elizabeth Liston, "The Woman after an Abortion", *Pro-Life News,* 21, no. 3 (March 1996): 6.

[15]. Andrew Bahm, Stanton Newman, John Weinman, Robert West, Chris McMainmus, *Cambridge Handbook of Psychology Health & Management* (Cambridge: University Press, 1997), 340

[16]. *Physical Consequences Of Abortion* (accessed 28 January 2004), http://www.straight-talk.net/abortion/consequences.html

[17]. Elizabeth Liston, 6.

[18]. Jill D. Chasse, "A Journey of Life in the Womb," *The World of The Fetus* (accessed March 3, 2004), http://www.jilldiana.homestead.com/fetus.htm.

[19]. Charles B. Clayman, 58.

[20]. Charles Hartshorne, 41.

[21]. F. Earle Fox, "Two Kinds of Personhood: A Reply to Grobstein", *Perspectives On Science & Christian Faith* (March 1993): 49.

[22]. Jean Garton, "Who Broke the Baby?" *ProLife News* 21, no. 1 (January 1996): 11-12.

[23]. John F. Kilner, Nigel M. de S. Cameron, David L. Schielermayer, ed., *Biothetics and the Future of Medicine: A Christian Appraisal* (Grand Rapids, MI: William B. Eerdmans, 1995), 189.

[24]. The Presbyterian Church Of Canada is against liberalizing abortion laws, but favours abortion when the mother's health is in danger; The United Church of Canada advocates abortion, but lessens the right of abortion for every day the fetus develops; The Anglican Church argues for abortion, but before it being allowed, individuals must first prove that fetus with life is present; The Unitarian Church, after a vote, concluded that 'abortion should be made available to every woman who chooses to exercise it; and the Roman Catholic Church forbids abortion for all other reasons except that the mother's health is in danger. James C. Fleck, 355

[25]. John Stott, *Involvement: Social and Sexual Relationships In The Modern World,* 2 Vols. (New Jersey: Fleming H. Revell Company, 1985), 2:193.

Bibliography

Arnason, John. "Trudeau Legalizes Abortion?" *The Toronto Star,* August 16, 1977.

Arneston, Neil. "Morgentaler against the Courts." *The Abortion Crisis.* Toronto: Doubleday Canada, 1975.

Arthur, Joyce, "Abortion in Canada." *The Human Quest.* Accessed February 24th, 2004. http://www.prochoiceactionnetwork canada.org/aboutus/aboutus.shtml

Bahm, Andrew, Stanton Newman, John Weinman, Robert West, and Chris McMainmus. *Cambridge Handbook of Psychology Health & Management.* Cambridge: University Press, 1997.

Blunt, Sheryl H. "Catholic Report, Survival of the Unaborted." *Christianity Today* (Fall November 13, 2000): 91-93

Chasse, Jill D. "A Journey of Life in the Womb." *The World of the Fetus.* Accessed March 3, 2004. http://www.jilldiana.homestead.com/fetus.html

Clayman, Charles B. Editor. *The American Medical Association Encyclopedia of Medicine.* NY: Random House, 1989.

Emergency Contraception: The Morning after Pill. Accessed 28 February, 2004. http://www.morningafterpill.org/mapinfo1.html

Fleck, James C. "Canada Debates Abortion and Homosexuality." *The Christian Century* 88. (1969): 973-75.

Fox, F. Earle. "Two Kinds of Personhood: A Reply to Grobstein." *Perspectives on Science & Christian Faith,* 45 (March 1993): 49-56.

Garton, Jean "Who Broke the Baby?" *Pro-Life News,* 21, no. 1. (January 1996): 37-45.

Hans, Partick. Editor. *The Collins English Dictionary.* Glasgow: William Collins & Sons Ltd., 1986.

Hartshorne, Charles. "Concerning Abortion: An Attempt at a Rational View." *The Christian Century* (January 21, 1981): 42-45.

Liston, Elizabeth. "The Woman after an Abortion." *ProLife News* 21, no 3 (March 1996): 1-12.

Kilner, John F., Nigel M. de S. Cameron, and David L. Schielermayer, Editors. *Biothetics and the Future of Medicine: A Christian Appraisal.* Grand Rapids, MI: William B. Eerdmans, 1995.

Morgentaler, Henry, "A Letter to Pope John II from Henry Morgentaler." In *The Humanist.* Toronto: Dobuleday, 1967.

Physical Consequences of Abortion. (Accessed 28 January 2004). http://www.straight-talk.net/abortion/consequences.shtml.

Schaeffer, Francis A. and C. Everett Koop. *Whatever Happened To The Human Race*? Old Tappan, NJ: Fleming H. Revell Company, 1979.

Stott, John. *Involvement: Social and Sexual Relationships in The Modern World,* 2 Vols. Ada, MO: Fleming H. Revell Company, 1985.

Taber, Clarence. *Taber's Cyclopedic Medical Dictionary.* Toronto: Ryerson Press, 1963.

Chapter 3

Endnotes

[1] Names used within this article are fictitious. There is no intent to connect this story to any person or company existing at the moment or at a previous time.

[2] Those that suggest that life begins with conception appeal to Psalm 51:5 where David claims that "in sin did his mother conceive him, and Psalm 139:14-21 where David states "my substance was not hid from thee when I was made in the secret place."

[3] The Anglican Church of Canada, the United Church of Canada and some Presbyterian Churches suggest that an abortion could be permitted in the first trimester in cases of rape, incest, or extreme medical circumstances where the mother's health is at stake.

[4] The Roman Catholic Church rigorously opposes abortion regardless of the circumstance, because it believes that all fetus at conception is fully human.

Lorraine Boettner, *Roman Catholicism* (Philadelphia: The Presbyterian & Reformed Publishing Company, 1968), 341.

[5] *Abortion - The Islamic View* (accessed April 6, 2005) http://www.bbc.co.uk/religion/ethics/abortion/relig_islam1.shtml

[6] Qur'an 17:32.

[7] Robert Gill, ed. *The Cambridge Companion to Christian Ethics* (Cambridge: Cambridge University Press, 2001), 63.

[8] Patrick Hans, ed. *The Collins English Dictionary* (Glasgow: William Collins & Sons Ltd., 1986), 4.

[9] William Werpehowski, "The Pathos and Promise Of Christian Ethics: A Study Of The Abortion Debate," *Horizons* (December 2, 1985): 290.

[10] Francis Schaeffer and Everett C. Koop, *Whatever Happened to the Human Race?* (Old Tappan, NJ: Fleming H. Revell company, 1979), 193.

[11] Revenue Canada, Child Services Branch - Provides applications for financial aid and child care services..

[12] Charles Hartshorne, "Concerning Abortion: An Attempt at a Rational View," *The Christian Century* (January 21, 1981): 44.

[13] John F. Kilner, Nigel M. De S Cameron, David L. Scheilermayer, *Biothetics and the Future of Medicine: A Christian Appraisal* (Grand Rapids, MI: Wm. B. Eerdmans, 1995), 189.

[14] Jean Gaston, "Who Broke the Baby?" *ProLife News* 21, no. 1. (January 1996): 11-12.

[15] John Stott, *Involvement: Social and Sexual Relationships in the Modern World,* 2 Vols. (Ada, MO: H. Revell Company, 1985), 2:193.

[16] "Christian Teachings against Abortion," *Tertullian Apolgeticus,* (accessed April 14, 2004) http://www.cpforlife.org/teaching_against_abortion.htm.

[17] John Calvin, *Institutes of the Christian Religion,* 2 Vols. Translated by Henry Beveridge (Michigan: Wm. B. Eerdmans Publishing Company, 1966), 1:346.

[18] A born-again medical doctor from White Rock, BC.

[19] Andrew Bahm, ed. *Cambridge Handbook of Psychological Health and Management* (Cambridge: University Press, 1997), 340.

[20] Elizabeth Liston, "The Woman after an Abortion," *ProLife News* 21, no. 3 (March 1996): 6.

[21] Willingdon Church located in Burnaby, BC has such a care centre for unwed mothers - women who had considered abortion, after coming here, have found a such a strong sense of acceptance and support that they have decided to carry the fetus to completion.

[22] Such an arrangement has been made for a young lady in Hay River, Northwest Territories, who has had a child out of wedlock. Although the arrangement is demanding on both the mother of the child and the grandmother, both feel that this short term sacrifice is better than having aborted the child.

Bibliography

Abortion - The Islamic View. Accessed April 6, 2005. http://www.bbc.co.uk/religion/ethics/abortion/relig_islam1.shtml.

Bahm, Andrew. Editor. *Cambridge Handbook of Psychological Health and Management.* Cambridge: University Press, 1997.

Calvin, John. *Institutes of the Christian Religion,* 2 Vols. Translated by Henry Beveridge. Grand Rapids, MI: Wm. B. Eerdmans Publishing Company, 1966.

Gaston, Jean. "Who Broke The Baby?" *ProLife News* 21, no. 1 (January 1996): 11-12.

Gill, Robert. Editor. *The Cambridge Companion to Christian Ethics.* Cambridge: Cambridge University Press, 2001.

Hartshorne, Charles. "Concerning Abortion: An Attempt at a Rational View." *The Christian Century* (January 21, 1981):44.

Hans, Patrick. Editor. *The Collins English Dictionary*. Glasgow: William Collins & Sons Ltd., 1986.

Kilner, John F. Nigel M. De S Cameron, and David L. Scheilermayer. *Biothetics and the Future of Medicine: A Christian Appraisal.* Grand Rapids, MI: Wm. B. Eerdmans, 1995.

Liston, Elizabeth. "The Woman after an Abortion." *ProLife News* 21, no. 3 (March 1996): 1-12.

Schaeffer, Francis and Everett C. Koop. *Whatever Happened to the Human Race?* Old Tappan, NJ: Fleming H. Revell Company, 1979.

Stott, John. *Involvement: Social and Sexual Relationships in the Modern World,* 2 Vols. Ada, MO: H. Revell Company, 1985.

Werpehowski, William. "The Pathos and Promise of Christian Ethics: A Study of the Abortion Debate." *Horizons* (December 2, 1985):290.

Chapter 4

Endnotes

1. Child Abuse: A Fact Sheet from the Department of Justice Canada, 1998.

[2]. R. Kim Oakes, *Child Abuse: A Community Concern* (NY: Brunner/Mazel, Publishers, 1982), 3.

[3]. Grant Robertson, *Parenting Issues in Family Crisis* (NY: Doubleday, 1976), 231.

[4]. Child Abuse Fact Sheet from the Department of Justice, Canada.

[5]. Ofelia Rodriguez-Srednicki, and James A. Thwaite, "Understanding and Reporting Child Abuse: Legal and Psychological Perspectives-Part One," *The Journal of Psychiatry and Law* 32, no. 3 (Fall 2004): 320.

[6]. Robert Emery, "Family Violence," *American Psychologist* 44, no. 2 (February 1989): 322.

[7]. Ken Blue, "Abuse," in The Complete Handbook of Everyday Christianity, edited by R. Paul Stevens (Downers Grove, IL: InterVarsity Press, 1997), 4-5.

[8]. G. M. Houk and M. C. King, "Child Maltreatment: Family Characteristics and Development Consequences," *Issues in Mental Health Nursing* 10, no. 3-4 (1989): 196.

[9]. Diane J. English, David B. Marshall, and Angela J. Stewart, "Effects of Family Violence on Child Behaviour and Health during Early Childhood," *Journal of Family Violence* 18, no.1 (February 2003): 44.

[10]. Lyle Larson, J. Walter Goltz, and Charles Hobart, *Families in Canada: Social Context, Continuities, & Changes* (Toronto, On: Prentice Hall, Canada, 1994), 491.

[11]. Lawrence M. Berger, "Income: Family Characteristics and Physical Violence towards Children," *Child Abuse and Neglect* 29, no. 2 (2005): 109.

[12]. Lisa Bethea, "Primary Prevention of Child Abuse," *Psychology Today* (November, 1994): 21.

[13]. L. M. Berger, 112.

[14]. Daphne B. Bugental and Patricia C. Ellerson, "A Cognitive Approach to Child Abuse Prevention," *Journal of Family Psychology* 16, no. 3 (December 2002): 243.

[15]. Christina Rodriguez and Britanny L. Price, "Attributions and Discipline History as Predictors of Child Abuse Potential and Future Discipline Practices," *Child Abuse & Neglect* 28, no. 8 (2004): 848.

[16]. Cindy Blackstock, Nico Trocme, and Marilyn Bennet, "Child Maltreatment Investigations among Aboriginal and Non-Aboriginal Families in Canada," *Violence against Women* 10, no. 8 (August 2004): 910.

[17]. Michelle D. DiLauro, "Psychosocial Factors Associated with Types of Child Maltreatment," *Child Welfare* 83, no. 1 (January/February 2004): 70

[18]. Maureen O. Marcenko, Susan P. Kemp, and Nancy C. Larson, "Childhood Experiences of Abuse, Later Substance Use, and Parenting Outcomes among Low-Income Mothers," *American Journal of Orthopsychiatry* 70, no. 3 (July 2000): 318

[19]. Collin Campbell, "Family Violence & Substance Abuse," *Fact Sheet: National Clearinghouse on Family Violence* (Health Canada 1993), 3.

[20]. Jean M. Goodwin, "Credibility Problems in Sadistic Abuse," *Journal of Psychohistory* 21, no. 4 (Spring 2004): 483.

[21]. Lloyd DeMause, "Why Cults Terrorize and Kill Children," *Journal of Psychohistory* 21, no. 4 (Spring 1994): 511.

[22]. Daniel Gottlieb Schreber, *Soul Murder* (NY: Nelson, 1994), 24.

[23]. Linda Lee Nelson, "Heart of A Child," *Christian Century* (September 26 - October 3, 2001): 23.

[24]. Lloyd DeMause, 505.

[25]. In Canada, child welfare laws require that all cases of suspected child abuse must be investigated to determine if a child is in need of protection.

[26]. Mark Davies, "Abuse," in *Thoughtful Parenting* (Downers Grove, IL: InterVarsity Press, 2002), 4.

[27]. Kathleen Mulryan, "How to Recognize and Respond to Child Abuse," *Nursing 2004* 34, no. 10 (2004): 55.

[28]. Rodriguez, 325.

[29]. S. Richard Sauber, "Facing Abuse Head On," *American Journal of Family Therapy* 35, no. 2 (2007): 35.

[30]. Claude M. Chemtob and John G. Carlson, "Psychological Effects of Domestic Violence on Children and Their Mothers," *International Journal of Stress Management* 11, no. 3 (2004): 225.

[31]. Tamas Treuer, Magdalena Koperdak, Sandor Rozsa, and Janos Furedi, "The Impact of Physical and Sexual Abuse on Body Image in Eating Disorders," *European Eating Disorder Review* 13, no.2 (March 2005): 110.

[32]. Alan Kazdin, Joanne Moser, Debra Colbus and Robin Bell, "Depressive Symptoms among Physically Abused and Psychiatrically Disturbed Children," *Journal of Abnormal Psychology* 94, no. 3 (August 1985): 298-299.

[33]. Linda Lee Nelson, 27.

[34]. Bunnie Riedel, "A Parent's View of Parental Rights," *Christian Social Action* (January 1997): 10.

[35]. John Stott, Involvement: *Social and Sexual Relationships in the Modern World,* 2 Vols. (New Jersey: Fleming H. Revell Company, 1985), 2:193.

[36]. Charles J. Scicluna, "The Church's Role in Child Protection," (accessed January 25, 2016) http://www.nems.va/en/news/full-text-of-msgr-sciclunas address on-the-churchs

[37] Gary W. Moon and David G. Benner, *Spiritual Direction and the Care of Souls* (Downers Grove, IL: InterVarsity Press, 2000). 66.

[38]. Rod Wilson, *Counselling and Community: Using Church Relationships to Reinforce Counselling* (NY: Word Incorporated, 1995), 178.

Bibliography

Berger, Lawrence M. "Income: Family Characteristics and Physical Violence towards Children." *Child Abuse and Neglect* 29, no. 2 (2005): 107-133.

Bethea, Lisa. "Primary Prevention of Child Abuse." *Psychology Today* (November, 1994): 21.

Blackstock, Cindy, Nico Trocme, and Marilyn Bennet. "Child Maltreatment Investigations among Aboriginal and Non-Aboriginal Families in Canada" *Violence against Women* 10, no. 8, (August 2004): 901-916.

Blue, Ken. "Abuse." In *The Complete Handbook of Everyday Christianity*. Edited by R. Paul Stevens. Downers Grove, IL: InterVarsity Press, 1997.

Bugental, Daphne B. and Patricia C. Ellerson. "A Cognitive Approach to Child Abuse Prevention" *Journal of Family Psychology* 16, no. 3 (December 2002): 243-258.

Campbell, Collin. "Family Violence & Substance Abuse." *Fact Sheet: National Clearinghouse on Family Violence.* Health Canada 1993.

Chemtob, Claude M. and John G. Carlson. "Psychological Effects of Domestic Violence on Children and Their Mothers." *International Journal of Stress Management* 11, no. 3 (2004): 209-226.

Child Abuse: A Fact Sheet from the Department of Justice Canada, 1998.

Davies, Mark. "Abuse." In *Thoughtful Parenting.* Downers Grove, IL: InterVarsity Press, 2002.

DeMause, Lloyd. "Why Cults Terrorize and Kill Children." *Journal of Psychohistory* 21, no. 4 (Spring 1994): 511.

DiLauro, Michelle D. "Psychosocial Factors Associated with Types of Child Maltreatment." *Child Welfare* 83, no. 1 (January/February 2004): 69-99.

Emery, Robert. "Family Violence." *American Psychologist* 44, no. 2 (February 1989): 321-328.

English, Diane J., David B. Marshall, and Angela J. Stewart. "Effects of Family Violence on Child Behaviour and Health during Early Childhood." Journal of Family Violence 18, no.1 (February 2003): 43-57.

Goodwin, Jean M. "Credibility Problems n Sadistic Abuse" *Journal of Psychohistory* 21, no. 4 (Spring 2004): 479-496.

Houk, G. M. and M. C. King. "Child Maltreatment: Family Characteristics and Development Consequences." *Issues in Mental Health Nursing* 10, no. 3-4 (1989): 193-208.

Kazdin, Alan, Joanne Moser, Debra Colbus and Robin Bell, "Depressive Symptoms among Physically Abused and Psychiatrically Disturbed Children." *Journal of Abnormal Psychology* 94, no. 3 (August 1985): 298-307.

Larson, Lyle, J. Walter Goltz, and Charles Hobart. *Families in Canada: Social Context, Continuities, & Changes*. Toronto, On: Prentice Hall, Canada, 1994.

Marcenko, Maureen O., Susan P. Kemp, and Nancy C. Larson. "Childhood Experiences of Abuse, Later Substance Use, and Parenting Outcomes among Low-Income Mothers." *American Journal of Orthopsychiatry* 70, no. 3 (July 2000): 316-326.

Moon, Gary W. and David G. Benner. *Spiritual Direction and the Care of Souls*. Downers Grove, IL: InterVarsity Press, 2000.

Mulryan, Kathleen. "How to Recognize and Respond to Child Abuse." *Nursing 2004* 34, no. 10 (2004): 55.

Nelson, Linda Lee. "Heart of A Child." *Christian Century* (September 26 - October 3, 2001), 23.

Oakes, R. Kim. *Child Abuse: A Community Concern*. NY: Brunner/Mazel, Publishers, 1982.

Riedel, Bunnie. "A Parent's View of Parental Rights." *Christian Social Action* (January 1997): 10.
Robertson, Grant. *Parenting Issues In Family Crisis*. NY: Doubleday, 1976.

Rodriguez, Christina and Britanny L. Price. "Attributions and Discipline History as Predictors of Child Abuse Potential and Future Discipline Practices." *Child Abuse & Neglect* 28, no. 8 (2004): 845-861.

Rodriguez-Srednicki, Ofelia, and James A. Thwaite. "Understanding and Reporting Child Abuse: Legal and Psychological Perspectives-Part One." *The Journal of Psychiatry and Law* 32, no. 3 (Fall 2004): 315-359.

Sauber, S. Richard. "Facing Abuse Head On." *American Journal of Family Therapy* 35, no. 2 (2007): 22-41.

Scicluna, Charles J. "The Church's Role in Child Protection." Accessed January 25, 2016 http://www.nems.va/en/news/full text-of msgr-sciclunas-address on-the-churchs

Schreber, Daniel Gottlieb. *Soul Murder.* NY: Nelson, 1994.

Stott, John. Involvement: *Social and Sexual Relationships in the Modern World,* 2 Vols. New Jersey: Fleming H. Revell Company, 1985.

Treuer, Tamas, Magdalena Koperdak, Sandor Rozsa, and Janos Furedi. "The Impact of Physical and Sexual Abuse on Body

Image in Eating Disorders." *European Eating Disorder Review* 13, no.2 (March 2005): 106-111.

Rod Wilson, *Counselling and Community: Using Church Relationships to Reinforce* Counselling. NY: Word Incorporated, 1995.

Chapter 5

Endnotes

[1]. Gary Collins, *Fractured Personalities, The Psychology of Mental Illness* (Lake Mary, FL.: Creation House, 1975), 27.

[2]. Robin B. Jarrett, "Guilt in Depressed Outpatients," *University of Texas Southwestern Journal,* 14, no 2 (Spring 2000): 37.

[3]. Lamont Satterly, "Guilt, Shame, and Religious Spiritual Pain," *Holist Nars Pract* 15, no 2 (January 2001): 31.

[4]. Kathleen Nader, "Guilt Following Traumatic Events," (accessed September 20, 2014) http://www.giftfromwithin.org/html/Guilt-Following-Traumatic-Events.html.

[5]. Roy F. Baumeiter, "Guilt: an Interpersonal Approach," *Psychological Bulletin* 115, no. 2 (1994): 245.

[6]. David Begum, "Guilt," *Counselling and Values*.29, no 2 (Jan 1997): 129.

[7]. Paul Gilbert, "Evolution, Social Roles, and the Differences in Shame and Guilt," *Social Research* 70, no. 4 (Winter 2003): 1209.

[8]. Patrick Hanks, ed. *The Collins English Dictionary,* (London & Glasgow: William Collins Sons & Co. Ltd., 1978), 1293.

[9]. Virginia S. Thatcher, ed. *The Webster Encyclopedic Dictionary of the English Language* (NY: Avenel Books, 1984), 673.

[10]. Christopher M. Faiver, Eugene M. O'Brien & R. Elliott Ingersoll, "Religion, Guilt, and Mental Health," *Journal of Counselling & Development* 37, no. 2 (Spring 2000): 158.

[11]. Roy J., *Saint Augustine, Treatises on Marriage and Other Subjects* (Washington, DC.: The Catholic of America Press, 1955), 29.

12. Gian V. Caprara ed., "Facing Guilt: Role of Negative Affectivity, Need for Reparation, and Fear of Punishment in Leading to Prosocial Behaviour and Aggression." *European Journal of Personality* 15, no. 3 (2001): 220.

[13]. Charles Villa-Vicenio, "The Burden of Moral Guilt: Its Theological and Political Implications," *Journal of Church and State* 39, no 2 (Spring 1997): 240.

[14]. Kathleen Nader, "Guilt Following Traumatic Events," (accessed September 14, 2004) http://www.giftfromwithin.org/html/Guilt-Following-Traumatic-Events.html.

[15]. Kathleen Nader.

[16]. Charles Villa-Vicenio. 241.

.

[17]. Becca Cowan Johnson, *Good Guilt, Bad Guilt And What to Do with Each* (Downers Grove, IL.: InterVarsity Press, 1969), 14.

[18]. Joy Ufema, "Insights on Death & Dying: Tortured by Guilt," *Nursing 2015* 34, no. 2 (September 2004): 74.

[19]. W. E. Vine, *An Exposition Dictionary of New Testament Words* (Westwood, NJ.: Fleming H. Revell Company, 1966), 224.

[20]. Ibid. Kathleen Nader.

[21] "Restitution and Other Legal Financial Obligations," in Council of State Government/American Probation and Parole Association under Cooperative Agreement Number 2009-SZ-B9-K001, (accessed December 16, 2015) https://csgjumticecenter.org/wp-content/uploads/2013/10/Factsheet-4.pdf

[22]. Karl Menninger, Whatever Became of Sin? (NY: Hawthorn Books Inc., 1977), 182.

[23]. George Arthur Buttrick, ed., "Sin," in *The Interpreter's Dictionary of The Bible: An Illustrated Encyclopedia* (Nashville, TN: Abingdon Press, 1984), 361.

[24]. Since God has allowed political parties to rise to power, it is the Christian's belief that people are to obey the legislated civic laws of a country, city, etc. even if they do not agree with what has been legislated. There is one qualification for disobeying civic law; that is when one must choose between obeying that which is of man, or that which is of God. In this situation obeying that which is of God always takes preeminence.

[25]. Word "they" exchanged for the word "we."

[26]. John E. MacArthur, Jr., *The Vanishing Conscience: Drawing the Line in a No-Fault, Guilt-Free World* (Dallas, TX.: Word Publishing, 1994), 19.

[27]. David says, "I acknowledge my sin - that of lying with Bathsheba - it is ever before me."

[28] Consequences, but no condemnation - believers who repent are freed from endless, haunting guilt pangs previously felt by ungodly.

[29]. Clyde M. Narramore, *Encyclopedia of Psychological Problems* (Grand Rapids, MI.: Zondervan Publishing House, 1966), 108.

[30]. Arthur H. Becker, *Guilt: Curse or Blessing?* (Minneapolis, MN.: Augsburg Publishing House, 1977), 75.

Bibliography

Baumeiter, Roy F. "Guilt, an Interpersonal Approach." *Psychological Bulletin* 115, no. 2 (1994): 243-267.

Becker, Arthur H. *Guilt: Curse or Blessing?* Minneapolis, MN: Augsburg Publishing House, 1977.

Begum, David "Guilt," *Counselling and Values* 29, no 2 (Jan 1997): 110-135.

Buttrick, George Arthur. Editor. "Sin." In *The Interpreter's Dictionary of the Bible: An Illustrated Encyclopedia.* Nashville, TN: Abingdon Press, 1984.

Caprara, Gian V. "Facing Guilt: Role of Negative Affectivity, Need for Reparation, and Fear of Punishment in Leading to Prosocial Behaviour and Aggression." *European Journal of Personality* 15, no. 3 (2001): 219-237.

Collins, Gary. *Fractured Personalities: The Psychology of Mental Illness*. IL: Creation House, 1975.

Deferrari, Roy J., *Saint Augustine, Treatises on Marriage and Other Subjects*. Washington, DC: The Catholic of America Press, 1955.

Favier, Christopher M., Eugene M. O'Brien and R. Elliott Ingersoll. "Religion, Guilt, and Mental Health." *Journal of Counselling & Development* 37, no. 2 (Spring 2000): 155-161.

Gilbert, Paul "Evolution, Social Roles, and the Differences in Shame and Guilt" *Social Research* 70, no. 4 (Winter 2003): 1205-1230.

Hanks, Patrick. *The Collins English Dictionary.* London: William Collins Sons & Co. Ltd., 1978.

Jarrett, Robin B. "Guilt in Depressed Outpatients." *University of Texas Southwestern Journal* 14, no 2 (Spring 2000): 32-45.

Johnson, Becca Cowan. *Good Guilt, Bad Guilt and What to Do With Each.* Downers Grove, IL: InterVarsity Press, 1969.

MacArthur, John E., Jr. *The Vanishing Conscience: Drawing the Line in a No-Fault, Guilt-Free World.* Dallas, TX: Word Publishing, 1994.

Menninger, Karl *Whatever Became of Sin?* NY: Hawthorn Books, Inc., 1977.

Nader. Kathleen "Guilt Following Traumatic Events." *Gift From Within.* (Accessed September 14, 2004).

http://www.giftfromwithin.org/html/Guilt-Following-Traumatic Events.html.

Narramore, Clyde M. *Enclopedia of Psychological Problems.* Grand Rapids, MI: Zondervan Publishing House, 1966.

Satterly, Lamont. "Guilt, Shame, and Religious Spiritual Pain." *Holist Nars Pract.* 15, no 2 (January 2001): 30-39.

Thatcher, Virginia S. *The Webster Encyclopedic Dictionary of the English Language.* NY: Avenel Books 1984.

Ufema, Joy. "Insights on Death & Dying: Tortured By Guilt." *Nursing 2015* 34, no. 2 (September 2004): 74-75.

Villa-Vicenio, Charles. "The Burden of Moral Guilt: Its Theological and Political Implications." *Journal of Church and State* 39, no. 2 (Spring 1997): 237-252.

Vine, W. E. *An Exposition Dictionary of New Testament Words.* Westwood, NJ: Fleming H. Revell Company, 1966.

Chapter 6

Endnotes

[1]. Oz Guinness, *The Gravedigger Files* (London: Hodder & Stoughton, 1983), 51.

[2]. George Holyoake, "The Reasoner," (accessed November 8, 2006) http://www.atheist.org/atheism/holyoake/holyoake.html.

[3]. Leslie Newbign, *The Gospel in a Pluralistic Society* (Grand Rapids, MI: Wm. B. Eerdmans Publishing Co., 2001), 211.

[4]. Ian Fisher, "Pope Warns against Secularization in Germany," *New York Times*, 10 September 2006, section 1.

[5] The term anthropocentric stresses that human beings are the most significant entity of the universe. With this it also infers that interpreting or regarding the world in terms of human values and experiences is the best means of knowing man's purpose for existence.

Sarah Boslaugh, "Anthropocentricism," in Encyclopedia Britannica (accessed December 18, 2015) http://www.britannica.com/topic/anthropocentrism.

[6] Bob Haskel, "The Use of Secular Methods in Ministry," *The Covenant Quarterly* (February 1977): 2.

[7]. Rodney Stark, "Secularization R. I. P.," *Sociology of 'Religion* 60, no. 3 (Spring 1999): 250.

[8]. Craig M. Gay, *The Way of the (Modern) World* (Grand Rapids, MI: Wm. B. Eerdmans Publishing Company, 1998), 99.

[9]. Kenneth Cragg, *The Secular Experience of God* (Harrisburg, PA: Trinity Press, International, 1998), 8.

[10]. S. W. Carruthers, *The Westminster Confession of Faith* (London: Free Presbyterian Publications, 2001), 4:2.

[11]. *The New Lexicon Webster's Encyclopedic Dictionary of the English Language: Canadian Edition* (NY: Lexicon Publications, 1972), 263.

[12]. Frank H. Littell, *Illustrated History of Christianity* (NY: Continuum International Publishing Company, 2001), 31.

[13]. Christopher Dawson, *Progress and Religion: An Historical Inquiry* (London: Sheed & Ward, 1934), 96.

[14]. F. L. Cross, *The Oxford Dictionary of the Christian Church* (Oxford: University Press, 1997), 1615.

[15]. Dawson, 164.

16. Keith Thomas, *Religion and the Decline of Magic* (NY: Hodder & Rowe Publishers, 1971), 29.

17. Bernard Russell, *History of Western Philosophy* (London: George Allen & Unwin Limited, 1965), 548.

18. C. S. Lewis, *The Abolition of Man* (San Francisco, CA: Harper Collins Publishers, 2001), 67.

19. Peter E. Glasner, *Sociology of Secularization: A Critique of a Concept* (NY: Routledge & Kegan Paul. 1977), 632.

20. Edward Craig, ed. *The Encyclopedia of Philosophy,* 2 Vols. (NY: Routledge Publications, 1998), 2:501-502.

21. More on this can be gained by reading Alex de Jong and Marc Shuilenberg's *From Genius to Scienius: Redefining Creativity in the Practice of Architecture* (accessed December 31, 2015), https://www.books.google.ca/books?id=tXBdOoZ-faYC&pg=RA2PA127&lpg=RA2PA127&dq=genius+who+accredit+God+helping+them&source=bl&ots=5XBFTvnbzF&sig=vyZajVS35uSZwqdEOD1N1xc4T6I&hl=en&sa=X&ved=0ahUKEwiUzbuAmYfKAhUM5GMKHQgzAusQ6AEIGzAA#v=onepage&q=genius%20who%20accredit%20God%20helping%20them&f=false, 1-5

22. By "spiritual quest" I do not mean Christian faith. Rather, I suggest this could refer to any metaphysical idea of worship to Zeus, Shiva, Zoraster or any other god man would create for himself. Secularism neutralizes God out of its activity. However, this does not mean that society is void of all spiritual awareness.

23. Tom Small, *Like Father, Like Son: The Trinity Imaged in Our Humanity* (Grand Rapids, MI: Wm. B Eerdmans Publishing Company, 2005), 112.

24. Steve Bruce, *God is Dead: Modern Secularization in the West* (Oxford: Blackwood Publishing House, 2002), 12.

25. R. Stark, 230.

[26]. Mankind may be able to actualize creative design, but unless God generates the idea for creativity in the mind, man can do nothing.

[27] *Christian Statistics: The Largest Christian Populations,* (accessed November 18, 2006) www.adherents.com/largecom/com_christian.html

[28]. Small, 120.

[29]. Henry C. Thiessen *Lectures in Systematic Theology* (Grand Rapids, MI: Wm. B. Eerdmans Publishing Company, 1967), 47.

[30] Wesley W. Nelson, "An Introduction to a Secular Evangelism," in *Covenant Quarterly* 59, no. 3 (August 2001): 4.

[31]. S. W. Carruthers, 188.

[32]. Stanley J. Grenz, *The Moral Quest: Foundations of Christian Ethics* (Downers Grove, IL: InterVaristy Press, 1997), 38.

[33]. Ferd. L. Wagner, *Most Evil is done by Good People Who do not Know They are Not Good* (Xulon Press, 2010), 11-13.

[34]. Newbigin, 215

[35]. 10 Reasons to Oppose Genetic Engineering (accessed December 31, 2015) http://nwrage.org/content/10-reasons-oppose-genetic-engineering.

[36]. Gay, 105.

[37]. William Barrett, *The Death of the Soul: From Descartes to the Computer* (NY: Anchor Publishing Company, 1986), 34.

[38]. Wolfhart Pannenberg, *Christianity in a Secularized World* (NY: The Crossroad Publishing Company, 1989), 30.

[39]. James Hitchcock, "Self, Jesus and God: The Roots of Religious Secularization," *Summons to Faith and Renewal: Christian Revival in a Post-Christian World* (Grand Rapids, MI: Servant Books, 1983), 26.

[40]. Blaise Pascal, *Pensees*, A. J. Krailsheimer, trans. (London: Penguin, 1993), 45.

[41]. Glenn F. Chestnut, "The Pattern of the Past: Augustine's Debate with Eusebius and Sallust," in *Our Common History as Christians: Essays in Honor of Albert C. Outler*, John Deschner, Leroy T. Howe, and Klaus Penzel, ed. (NY: Oxford University Press, 1975), p. 72.

[42]. Allister E. McGrath, "Evangelical Theology: The State of the Art," in *Evangelical Futures* (Grand Rapids, MI: Baker Book House, 1995), 33.

[43]. John G. Stackhouse, Jr., *Humble Apologetics* (Oxford: Oxford University Press, 2002), 181.

Bibliography

10 Reasons to Oppose Genetic Engineering. Accessed December 31, 2015 http://nwrage.org/content/10-reasons-oppose-genetic-engineering.

Barrett, William. *The Death of the Soul: From Descartes to the Computer.* NY: Anchor Publishing Company, 1986.

Boslaugh, Sarah. "Anthropocentricism." In Encyclopedia Britannica. Accessed December 18, 2015 http://www.britannica.com/topic/anthropocentrism.

Bruce, Steve. *God is Dead: Modern Secularization in the West.* Oxford: Blackwood Publishing House, 2002.

Carruthers, S. W. *The Westminster Confession of Faith.* London: Free Presbyterian Publications, 2001.

Chestnut, Glenn F. "The Pattern of the Past: Augustine's Debate with Eusebius and Sallust." In *Our Common History as Christians: Essays in Honor of Albert C. Outler.* Edited by John Deschner, Leroy T. Howe, and Klaus Penzel. NY: Oxford University Press, 1975.

Christian Statistics: The Largest Christian Populations. Accessed November 18, 2006 www.adherents.com/largecom/com_christian.html.

Cragg, Kenneth. *The Secular Experience of God.* Harrisburg, PA: Trinity Press, International, 1998.

Craig, Edward. Editor. *The Encyclopedia of Philosophy,* 2 Vols. NY: Routledge Publications, 1998.

Cross, F. L. *The Oxford Dictionary of the Christian Church.* Oxford: University Press, 1997.

Dawson, Christopher. *Progress and Religion: An Historical Inquiry.* London. Sheed & Ward, 1934.

Fisher, Ian. "Pope Warns against Secularization in Germany." *New York Times.* 10 September 2006.

Gay, Craig M. *The Way of the (Modern) World.* Grand Rapids, MI: Wm. B. Eerdmans Publishing Company, 1998.

Glasner, Peter E. *Sociology of Secularization: A Critique of Concept.* NY: Routledge & Kegan Paul. 1977.

Grenz, Stanley J. *The Moral Quest: Foundations of Christian Ethic.* Downers Grove, IL: InterVaristy Press, 1997.

Guinness, Os. *The Gravedigger Files*. London: Hodder & Stoughton, 1983.

Haskell, Rob. "The Use of Secular Methods in Ministry." *The Covenant Quarterly* 55.1 (1997): 3-13.

Hitchcock, James. "Self, Jesus and God: The Roots of Religious Secularization." In *Summons to Faith and Renewal:*

Christian Revival in a Post-Christian World Grand Rapids, MI: Servant Books, 1983.

Holyoake, George. "The Reasoner." Accessed November 8, 2006 http://www.atheist.org/atheism/holyoake/holyoake.html.

Lewis, C. S. *The Abolition of Man.* San Francisco, CA: Harper Collins Publishers, 2001.

Littell, Frank H. *Illustrated History of Christianity.* NY: Continuum International Publishing Company, 2001.

McGrath, Allister E. "Evangelical Theology: The State of the Art." In *Evangelical Futures.* Grand Rapids, MI: Baker Book House, 1995.

Nelson, Wesley W. "An Introduction to a Secular Evangelism." In *Covenant Quarterly* 59, no. 3 (August 2001): 3-10.

Newbigin, Leslie. *The Gospel in a Pluralistic Society.* Grand Rapids, MI: Wm. B. Eerdmans Publishing Co., 2001.

Pannenberg, Wolfhart. *Christianity in a Secularized World.* NY: The Crossroad Publishing Company, 1989.

Pascal, Blaise. *Pensees*. Translated by A. J. Krailsheimer. London: Penguin, 1993.

Russell, Bernard. *History of Western Philosophy.* London: Georg Allen & Unwin Limited, 1965.

De Jong Alex and Marc Shuilenberg. *From Genius to Scienius: Redefining Creativity in the Practice of Architecture.* Accessed December 31, 2015 https://www.books.google.ca/books?id=tXBdOoZ-faYC&pg=RA2PA127&lpg=RA2PA127&dq=genius+who+accredit+God+helping+them&source=bl&ots=5XBFTvnbzF&sig=vyZajVS35uSZwqdEOD1N1xc4T6I&hl=en&sa=X&ved=0ahUKEwiUzbuAmYfKAhUM5GMKHQgzAusQ6AEIGzAA#v=onepage&q=genius%20who%20accredit%20God%20helping%20them&f=false

Small, Tom. *Like Father, Like Son: The Trinity Imaged in our Humanity.* Grand Rapids, MI: Wm. B Eerdmans Publishing Company, 2005.

Stark, Rodney "Secularization R. I. P." *Sociology of 'Religion* 60, no. 3 (Autumn 1999): 249-273.

The New Lexicon Webster's Encyclopedic Dictionary of the English Language: Canadian Edition. NY: Lexicon Publications, 1972.

Thiessen, Henry C. *Lectures in Systematic Theology.* Grand Rapids, MI: Wm. B. Eerdmans Publishing Company, 1967.

Thomas, Keith. *Religion and the Decline of Magic.* NY: Hodder & Rowe Publishers, 1971.

Wagner, Ferd. L. *Most Evil is done by Good People Who do not Know they are Not Good.* Xulon Press, 2010.

Chapter 7

Endnotes

[1]. Howard Vanderwell, ed., *The Church of All Ages: Generations Worshipping Together* (Herndon, VA: The Alban Institute, 2008), 26.

[2]. Doug Brown, "United Families Dividing Churches," *Faith Pulpit* (Jan-March 2012): 16.

[3]. Brian Dauphinais, "The Age-Integrated Church," (accessed August 27, 2012) http://utmost-way.com/theintegratedchurcharticle.

[4]. Reb Bradley, "Our Philosophy of Age Integration," (accessed September 1, 2012) http://www.familyministries.com/HC_ages.htm.

[5]. Paul E. Engle, ed., *Who Runs the Church? 4 Views on Church Government,* (Grand Rapids, MI: Zondervan Publishing House, 2004), 227.

Bibliography

Bradley, Reb. "Our Philosophy of Age Integration. Accessed September 1, 2012. http://www.familyministries.com/HC_ages.htm.

Brown, Doug. "United Families Dividing Churches." *Faith Pulpit."* (Jan-March 2012): 10-16.

Dauphinais, Brian. "The Age-Integrated Church." Accessed August 27, 2012. http://utmostway.com/theintegratedchurcharticle. Engle, Paul E. Editor. *Who Runs the Church? 4 Views on Church Government.* Grand Rapids, MI: Zondervan Publishing House, 2004.

Vanderwell, Howard. Editor. *The Church of All Ages: Generations Worshipping Together.* Herndon, VA: The Alban Institute, 2008.

Chapter 8

Endnotes

[1]. The authorship of Isaiah and Hebrews is also questioned.

[2]. Leslie Newbigin, *The Light Has Come* (MI: Wm. B. Eerdmans Publishing Company, 1982), xii.

[3]. F. F. Bruce, Leslie Newbigin, Donald Guthrie, Blomberg, D. A. Carson, Westcott.

[4]. C. K. Barrett, Dodd, Khummel, Witherington.

[5]. F. F. Bruce, *The Gospel According to John* (Grand Rapids, MI: Wm. B. Eerdmans Publishing, 1983), 5.

[6]. F. F. Bruce 9.

[7]. Josephus alludes to the freedoms that were granted to the Jews in Tiberias during the time of Herod the Tetrarch, who gave favour to those who lived in Tiberias. One of the benefits, undoubtedly, would have been a guarantee of educations. John, having lived in Tiberias, undoubtedly would have qualified for this education.

Flavius Josephus, *The Complete Works Of Josephus,* translated by Wm. Whiston (Grand Rapids, MI: Kregel Publications, 1981), 278

[8]. Craig L. Blomberg, *The Historical Reliability of John's Gospel,* (Downers Grove, IL: InterVarsity Press, 2001), 35.

[9]. Adolf Deissmann, *Light From The Ancient Near East: The New Testament Illustrated By Recently Discovered Texts Of The Graeco-Roman World,* (Grand Rapids, MI: Baker Book House, 1965), 69.

[10]. Donald Guthrie, *New Testament Introduction,* (Downers Grove, IL: InterVarsity Press, 1979), 257.

[11]. Blomberg, 43.

[12]. D. A. Carson, *The Gospel According To John* (Grand Rapids, MI: Wm. B. Eerdmans Publishing Company, 1991), 76

.

[13]. B. F. Westcott, ed. A. Westcott, *The Gospel According To John: The Greek Text With Introduction Notes,* (Grand Rapids, MI: Baker Book House, 1980), li.

[14]. In the Synoptic narratives of the feeding of the five thousand (Matthew 14:21, Mark 6:44, and Luke 9:14), the writers only describe the activity and the results of the feeding of the large crowd. But John's account compliments their account by adding "now there was much grass in the place." The detail clarifies the account of the story. John is a detailed witness of Christ's earthly ministry, and such detail validates his authorship.

[15]. Joseph S. Exell, ed., *The Biblical Illustrator* (Grand Rapids, MI: Baker Book House, 1958), xiii.

[16]. The "Acts of John" appears to be the only available recorded documentation that verifies that in Ephesus, near the end of the first century AD, or near the early beginning of the second century AD, there lived an individual named, "John." It could well be that this is the Apostle John who settled in Ephesus for a short time prior to being exiled to the Isle of Patmos.

Montague R. James, "Acts of John," *The Apocryphal New Testament* (London: Oxford University Press, 1966), 238-327.

[17]. Virginia S. Thatcher, ed., *The New Lexicon Webster's Encyclopedic Dictionary of the English Language: Canadian Edition* (NY: Lexicon Publications, 1988), 703.

[18]. Specifically the eleven other disciples heard the title over and over again, possibly more times than is recorded in Scripture, knew to whom the title actually referred.

[19]. Lacoste Munn, "An Introduction to the Gospel of John," *The Southwestern Journal of Theology* 31, no. 1 (November 14, 1998): 7.

[20]. Jesus gives John and James, the sons of Zebedee, the pseudonym Boanerges, meaning Sons of Thunder, and there is no contention over this. In all probability, over time this pseudonym is what they were best identified by.

[21]. Craig S. Keener, *The Gospel according to John* (NY: Hendrickson Publishers, 2003), 88.

[22]. Charles E. Hill, "What Papias Said about John (And Luke): A 'New' Papian Fragment," *The Journal Of Theological Studies,* 49, no. 2 (October 1998): 588.

[23]. M. S. James, 229.

[24]. F. F. Bruce, 1.

[25] "The, other disciple, namely John, having come with Peter."

[26]. The passage states Jesus left Judaea heading to Galilee, possibly through the shortest and most direct route. John 4:4 then adds, "And He must needs go through Samaria". The "must needs" here cannot be interpreted to me that "he had a great desire" to go through Samaria. Rather, going through Samaria was an absolute necessity if Christ were to take the shortest and most direct route to Galilee. John's faithful accounting of this demonstrates he is an honest, faithful witness to the activities of Christ.

[27]. Abraham, 8:56; Moses, 5:46; the figures of the Good Shepherd, John 10; the association of manna coming down from heaven, 6:31-33 the image of the Passover Lamb not having any bones broken, 19:36, and the special relationship God had with Israel as His chosen people, 22:15, 18; 34:20; 35:19; 41:9; 69:4.

[28]. He went forth with his disciples over the brook Cedron, where there was a garden, into which he entered, and his disciples.

[29]. Judas then, having received a band of men and officers from the chief priests and Pharisees, cometh thither with lanterns and torches and weapons.

[30]. Then Simon Peter having a sword drew it, and smote the high priest's servant, and cut off his right ear. The servant's name was Malchus.

[31]. Howard M. Jackson, "Ancient Self-referential Conventions and Their Implications for the Authorship Integrity of the Gospel of John," *The Journal of Theological Studies* 50, no. 1 (April 1999); 5.

[32]. John using either the "royal we" or the "inclusive we" claims to be a witness to the activity of Christ, and in Revelation 1:11 he states that he was to "write in a book, whatever he witnesses and send it unto the seven churches which are in Asia; unto Ephesus, and unto Smyrna, and unto Pergamos, and unto Thyatira, and unto Sardis, and unto Philadelphia, and unto Laodicea. The parallel construction between these two books provides sufficient collaboration that the one who wrote John or Revelation also had to be the author of the other book.

[33]. Ignatius, (30-107 AD) and a contemporary of John, the son of Zebedee, either living in Jerusalem or Judaea, accepts John as author of the book.

F. L. Cross, ed., *The Oxford Dictionary Of The Christian Church*, (London: Oxford University Press, 1971), 676.

[34]. Blomberg, 23.

[35]. Kenneth Scott Latourette, *A History of Christianity* (NY: Harper & Rowe, Publishers, 1953), 76.

[36]. Guthrie 45.

[37]. Franklin H. Littell, *Illustrated History of Christianity* (NY: Continuum, 2001), 45. It is believed that Eusebius lived at approximately 342 AD.

[38]. C. Hill, 589.

[39]. Justo L. Gonzalez, *The Story of Christianity* (San Francisco, CA: Harper Collins Publishers, 1984), 29.

[40]. F. F. Bruce, 2.

Bibliography

Blomberg, Craig L. *The Historical Reliability of John's Gospel.* Downers Grove, IL: InterVarsity Press, 2001.

Bruce, F. F. *The Gospel according to John.* Grand Rapids, MI: Wm. B. Eerdmans Publishing, 1983.

Carson, D. A. *The Gospel according to John*. Grand Rapids, MI: Wm. B. Eerdmans Publishing Company, 1991.

Cross, F. L. Editor. *The Oxford Dictionary of the Christian Church*. London: Oxford University Press, 1971.

Deissmann, Adolf. *Light from the Ancient Near East: The New Testament Illustrated by Recently Discovered Texts of the Greco-Roman World.* Grand Rapids, MI: Baker Book House, 1965.

Exell, Joseph S. Editor. *The Biblical Illustrator.* Grand Rapids, MI: Baker Book House, 1958.

Gonzalez, Justo L. *The Story of Christianity.* San Francisco, CA: Harper Collins Publishers, 1984.

Guthrie, Donald. *New Testament Introduction.* Downers Grove, IL: InterVarsity Press, 1979.

Hill, Charles E. "What Papias Said about John (And Luke): A 'New' Papian Fragment." *The Journal of Theological Studies.* 49, no. 2 (October 1998): 582-629.

Jackson, Howard M. "Ancient Self-referential Conventions and Their Implications for the Authorship Integrity of the Gospel of John." *The Journal of Theological Studies,* 50, no. 1 (April 1999): 1-34.

James, Montague R. "Acts of John." In *The Apocryphal New Testament.* London: Oxford University Press, 1966.

Josephus, Flavius. *The Complete Works of Josephus.* Translated by Wm. Whiston. Grand Rapids, MI: Kregel Publications, 1981.

Keener, Craig S. *The Gospel According to John.* NY: Hendrickson Publishers, 2003.

Latourette, Kenneth Scott. *A History of Christianity.* NY: Harper & Rowe, Publishers, 1953.

Littell, Franklin H. *Illustrated History of Christianity.* NY: Continuum, 2001.

Munn, Lacoste. "An Introduction to the Gospel of John." *The Southwestern Journal of Theology* 31, no. 1 (November 14, 1998): 7-41.

Newbigin, Leslie. *The Light Has Come.* MI.: Wm. B. Eerdmans Publishing Company, 1982.

Thatcher, Virginia S. Editor. *The New Lexicon Webster's Encyclopedic Dictionary of the English Language: Canadian Edition.* NY: Lexicon Publications, 1988.

Westcott, B. F. *The Gospel According To John: The Greek Text with Introduction Notes.* Edited by A. Westcott. Grand Rapids, MI: Baker Book House, 1980.

Chapter 9

Endnotes

[1] Jurgen Moltmann, *The Trinity and The Kingdom* (Minneapolis, MN: Fortress Press, 1993), 9.

[2]. Charles Van Engen, *God's Missionary People* (Grand Rapids, MI: Baker Book House, 2004), 105.

[3]. Mortimer Arias, *Announcing the Reign of God* (Eugene, OR: Wimp & Stock Publishers, 1984), 3.

[4]. Greg Ogden, *Transforming Discipleship* (Downers Grove, IL: InterVarsity Press, 2003), 231.

[5]. "The Holy Spirit and the Evangelist," in *Decision* (October 2000), 13.

[6]. R. J. Sider, *Churches that Make a Difference* (Grand Rapids, MI: Baker Book House, 2002), 134.

[7]. Charles Van Engen, 187-188.

[8]. He also actively convicts the ungodly of sin, of righteousness, and of judgment to come.

[9.] C. Sumner Wemp, "Practical Steps to Personal Evangelism," *Fundamentalist Journal* 3, no. 2 (February 1984): 32.

[10]. Charles Ringma, *Catch The Wind* (Vancouver, BC: Regent College Publishing, 1994), 40.

[11]. Ibid. 41.

[12]. George G. Hunter III, *How To Reach Secular People* (Nashville, TN: Abingdon Press, 1992), 110.

[13]. R. Paul Stevens, *The Other Six Days* (Grand Rapids, MI: Wm. B. Eerdmans Press, 1999), 39.

[14]. Ringma, 52.

[15]. Bruce Milne, *Know The Truth* (Downers Grove, IL: InterVarsity Press, 1998), 88.

[16]. R. C. H. Lenski, *The Interpretation of John's Gospel* (Minneapolis, MN: Augsburg Publishing, 1943), 259.

[17]. R. J. Sider, 132.

[18]. William B. Frazier, "Guidelines for a New Theology of Mission," *Mission Trends* 1 (NY: Paulist Press, 1972), 30.

[19]. Jim Wallis, *God's Politics* (San Francisco, CA: Harper Publishing, 2005), 194.

[20]. Ringma, 51.

[21]. R. J. Sider, 141.

[22]. Moltmann, 121.

[23]. Karl Barth, *The Gottingen Dogmatics: Institutes of the Christian Religion,* 2 Vols. (Grand Rapids, MI: Wm. B. Eerdmans Publishing Company, 1994), 1:24.

[24]. Darrell L. Guder, ed., *Missional Church: A Vision for the Sending of the Church in North America* (Grand Rapids, MI: Wm. B. Eerdmans Publishing Company, 1998), 229.

[25]. Ringma, 60.

Bibliography

Arias, Mortimer. *Announcing the Reign of God.* Eugene, OR: Wimp & Stock Publishers, 1984.

Barth, Karl. *The Gottingen Dogmatics: Institutes of the Christian Religion,* 2 Vols. Grand Rapids, MI: Wm. B. Eerdmans Publishing Company, 1994.

Frazier, William B. "Guidelines for a New Theology of Mission." *Mission Trend* 1. NY: Paulist Press, 1972.

Guder, Darrell L. *Missional Church: A Vision for the Sending of the Church in North America.* Grand Rapids, MI: Wm. B. Eerdmans Publishing Company, 1998.

Hunter III, George G. *How to Reach Secular People.* Nashville, TN: Abingdon Press, 1992.

Lenski, R. C. H. *The Interpretation of John's Gospel.* Minneapolis, MN: Augsburg Publishing, 1943.

Milne, Bruce. *Know The Truth.* Downers Grove, IL: InterVarsity Press, 1998.

Moltmann, Jurgen. *The Trinity and the Kingdom.* Minneapolis, MN: Fortress Press, 1993.

Ogden, Greg. *Transforming Discipleship.* Downers Grove, IL: InterVarsity Press, 2003.

______, *Unfinished Business: Returning the Ministry to the People of God*. Grand Rapids, MI: Zondervan, 2003.

Ringma, Charles. *Catch the Wind.* Vancouver, BC: Regent College Publishing, 1994.

Sider, R. J. *Churches that Make a Difference.* Grand Rapids, MI: Baker Book House, 2002.

Stevens, R. Paul. *The Other Six Days.* Grand Rapids, MI: Wm. B. Eerdmans Publishing Co., 1999.

"The Holy Spirit and the Evangelist." *Decision* October 2000.

Van Engen, Charles. *God's Missionary People.* Grand Rapids, MI: Baker Book House, 2004.

Wallis, Jim. *God's Politics.* San Francisco, CA: Harper Publishing, 2005.

Wemp, C. Sumner, "Practical Steps to Personal Evangelism." *Fundamentalist Journal* 3, no. 2 (February 1984): 31-33.

Chapter 10

Endnotes

[1] James Nichols, "Disputation XLIV," in *The Writings of James Arminius,* 3 Vols. (Grand Rapids, Michigan: Baker Book House, 1956), 3:109-110.

[2]. Robert A. Peterson, "Preservation, Perseverance, Assurance, and Apostasy," *Presbuterion: Covenant Seminary Review* 22, no. 1 (Spring 1996): 32.

[3.] John Calvin, "Reply by John Calvin to the Letter by Cardinal Sadolet to the Senate and People of Geneva," in *Calvin's Institutes* (Grand Rapids, MI.: Wm B. Eerdmans Publishing, 1966), 2:42.

[4]. James Hastings, *A Dictionary of the Bible,* 3 Vols. (NY: Charles Scribner's Sons, 1900), 3:754.

[5]. John Flavel, "Concerning the Work of the Spirit, as the Internal, and Most Affectual Mean of the Application of Christ," Sermon IV in *The Works of John Flavel,* 6 Vols. (London: The Banner of Truth Trust, 1968), 2:78. See also "The First Branch of Christ's Prophetical Office, Consisting in the Revelation of the Will of God," Sermon IX in *The Works of John Flavel* 1:120-123.

[6]. Robert L. Reymond, *A New Systematic Theology of the Christian Faith* (Nashville, TN.: Thomas Nelson Publishers 1997), 782.

[7] Augustus H. Strong, *Systematic Theology: A Compendium* (Valley Forge, PA: The Judson Press 1907), 845.

[8]. Robert Shank, *Life in the Son: A Study of the Doctrine of Perseverance,* introduced by William Adams (Springfield, MA: Westcott Publishers, 1964), 52.

[9]. Geoffrey W. Hodge, ed., *The International Standard Bible* (Grand Rapids, MI.: William B. Eerdmans 1900.) 1:332

[10]. "Of the Assurance and Grace of Salvation," in *Westminster Confession of Faith* (Glasgow: Bell and Bain Ltd., 2000), 75.

[11]. "Of the Perseverance of the Saints," in *Westminster Confession of Faith* (Glasgow: Bell and Bain Ltd., 2000), 73.

[12]. Rudolph Bultman, "peiqw," in *Theological Dictionary of the New Testament,* 8 Vols., edited by Gerhard Kittel (Grand Rapids, MI.: Wm. B. Eerdmans Publishing Company, 1966), 1:4.

[13]. Georg Bertram, "Katergazomai," in *Theological Dictionary of the New Testament,* 8 Vols., edited by Gerhard Kittel (Grand Rapids, MI.: William B. Eerdmans Publishing Company,1967), 6:635.

[14]. Alvin L. Baker, "Eternal Security Understood," *Fundamentalist Journal* 3, no. 8 (September 1984): 19.

[15]. A. A. Hodge, *A Commentary in the Confessions of Faith* (Pater Noster Row, London: T. Nelson & Sons, 1870), 24.

[16]. Fanny J. Crosby, "Blessed Assurance," in *Broadman Hymnal* (Nashville, TN: Broadman Press 1956), 120.

[17]. John Flavel, *The Works of John Flavel,* 6 Vols. (London: The Banner of Truth Trust, 1968), 6: 451.

[18]. Kurt Aland, Matthew Black, Carlo M. Martini, Bruce M. Metzger, and Allen Wikgren, *The Greek New Testament* (Deutsche Bibelgesellschaft Stuttgart) 1983.

[19]. Samuel Bagster, "Katergarvzesqe," in *Analytical Greek Lexicon* (London: Bagster and Sons Ltd. 1958), 223.

[20]. *Faith and Order*: *Baptism, Eucharist and Ministry,* III (Geneva & World Council of Churches, 1983), 4.

[21]. Joel R. Beeke, *Assurance of Faith: Calvin, English Puritanism, and the Dutch Second Reformation* (NY: Peter Lang, 1994), 125.

[22] Michael W. Holmes, "The Letter of Polycarp to the Philippians," in *The Apostolic Fathers,* translated by J. B. Lightfoot and J. R. Harmer (Grand Rapids, MI.: Baker Book House, 1989), 127-128.

[23].Lewis A. Drummond, *Spurgeon: Prince of Preachers*, foreword by Carl F. Henry (Grand Rapids, MI.: Kregel Publications 1992), 574-575.

Bibliography

Aland, Kurt, Matthew Black, Carlo M. Martini, Bruce M. Metzger, and Allen Wikgren. *The Greek New Testament*. Deutsche Bibelgesellchaft Stuttgard, 1983

Bagster, Samuel. *Analytical Greek Lexicon.* London: Bagster and Sons Ltd., 1958.

Baker, Alvin L. "Eternal Security Understood." *Fundamentalist Journal* 3, no. 8 (September 1984): 18-20.

Beeke, Joel R. *Assurance of Faith: Calvin, English Puritanism, and the Dutch Second Reformation.* NY: Peter Lang, 1994.

Bertram, Georg. "Katergazomai." In *Theological Dictionary of the New Testament,* 8 Vols. Edited by Gerhard Kittel. Grand Rapids, MI: William B. Eerdmans Publishing Company,1967.

Bultman, Rudolph. "peiqw." In *Theological Dictionary of the New Testament,* 8 Vols. Edited by Gerhard Kittel. Grand Rapids, MI.: Wm. B. Eerdmans Publishing Company, 1966).

Calvin, John. "Reply by John Calvin to the Letter by Cardinal Sadolet to the Senate and People of Geneva." In *Calvin's Institutes.* Grand Rapids, MI: Wm B. Eerdmans Publishing, 1966.

Crosby, Fanny J "Blessed Assurance." In *Broadman Hymnal*. Nashville, TN: Broadman Press, 1956.

Drummond, Lewis A., *Spurgeon: Prince of Preachers.* Foreword by Carl F. Henry. Grand Rapids, MI: Kregel Publications. 1992.

Faith and Order: Baptism, Eucharist and Ministry, III. Geneva & World Council of Churches. 1983

Flavel, John. *The Works of John Flavel,* 6 Vols. London: The Banner of Truth Trust, 1968.

Hastings, James. *A Dictionary of the Bible*, 3 Vols. NY: Charles Scribner's Sons, 1900.

Hodge, A. A. *A Commentary in the Confessions of Faith.* Pater Noster Row, London: T. Nelson & Sons, 1870.

Hodge, Geoffrey W. Editor. *The International Standard Bible,* 3 Vols. Grand Rapids, MI: William B. Eerdmans, 1900.

Holmes, Michael W. *The Apostolic Fathers.* Translated by J. B. Lightfoot and J. R. Harmer. Grand Rapids, MI: Baker Book House, 1989.

Nichols, James. *The Writings of James Arminius,* 3 Vols. Grand Rapids, MI: Baker Book House, 1956.

"Of the Assurance and Grace of Salvation." In *Westminster Confession of Faith.* Glasgow: Bell and Bain Ltd., 2000.

"Of the Perseverance of the Saints." In *Westminster Confession of Faith..* Glasgow: Bell and Bain Ltd., 2000.

Peterson, Robert A. "Preservation, Perseverance, Assurance, and Apostasy." *Presbuterion: Covenant Seminary Review* 22, no. 1 (Spring 1996): 32.

Reymond, Robert L. *A New Systematic Theology of the Christian Faith.* Nashville, TN: Thomas Nelson Publishers, 1997.

Shank, Robert. *Life in the Son, A Study of the Doctrine of Perseverance.* Springfield, MO: Westcott Publishers, 1964.

Strong, Augustus H., *Systematic Theology: A Compendium*. Valley Forge, PA: The Judson Press, 1907.

Chapter 11

Endnotes

[1] Jaroslav Pelikan, *The Illustrated Jesus Through The Centuries* (London: Yale University Press, 1997), 143.

Pope Pious XI preferred to refer to Francis of Assisi as "the second Christ." However, such a designation fringes on the "shores of blasphemy," for regardless of how notable an individual is, one should never attempt to rob Christ of his solitary place of glory. See also G. K. Chesterton, St. Francis of Assisi, 135.

[2]. The actual date as of yet has not been finalized.

[3]. "The Franciscan Experience," *Franciscan Institutional Outreach* (accessed October 10, 2004) http://198.62.75./www1/ofm/fra/FRAlife1.html.

[4]. Henry H. Milman, "St. Francis," in *History of Latin Christianity; Including that of the Popes to the Pontifices of Nicholas V* (London: John Murray Press, 1855), 261.

[5]. Ibid, 261.

[6]. Justo L. Gonzalez, *The History of Christianity: The Early Church to the Dawn of the Reformation,* 2 Vols. (San Francisco, CA: Harper Collins Publishers, 1984), 1:302.

[7]. Margaret Mehren, "Francis of Assisi: Reconciliation with God, Humanity, and Creation," Missionalia 19, no. 3 (November, 1991), 184.

[8]. F. Lenord, "Francis of Assisi," in *Encyclopedia of Church History* (NY: Harper & Row Publishers, 1956), 328.

[9]. "St. Francis and St. Clare: Life and Times," *The Franciscan Experience* (accessed October 10, 2004) http://198.62.75./www1/ofm/fra/FRAlife1.html.

[10]. Alcuin F. Shields, "The Gospel Pattern in the Franciscan Concept of Community, 1209-1517," *The Journal of Religious Thought* 1, no. 2 (Spring/Summer 1944): 108.

[11]. Kenneth Scott Latourette, *A History of Christianity* (NY: Harper & Row Publishers, 1953), 429.

[12]. Marion A. Habig, *St. Francis of Assisi: Writings and Early Biographies* (Chicago, IL: Franciscan Herald Press, 1972), 147.

[13]. Marion A. Habig, 148.

[14]. Lawrence Cunningham, "The Vitality of the Franciscan Spirit," *Christian Century* 93, no. 32 (2001): 866.

[15]. Shields, 108.

[16]. F. L. Cross, "Francis of Assisi," in *The Oxford Dictionary of the Christian Church* (London: Oxford University Press, 1958), 521.

[17]. G. K. Chesterton, *St. Francis of Assisi* (London: Hodder & Stoughton Limited, 1934), 59.

[18]. Ibid. 60.

[19]. F. L. Cross, 522.

[20]. Pelikan, 145.

[21]. Richard Rohr, "A Life Pure and Simple: A Franciscan Reflection on a Saint," *Sojourners* (December, 1981): 14.

[22]. Henry H. Milman, 263. We know that 'poverty' was used by Francis as an allegory, by which he renounced the romantic energies towards wealth that had been awakened in the twelfth century, and not as a forthright condemnation of material gain. The Franciscan Monks, as the Order grew, purchased land for the monasteries and churches which they possessed without guilt.

[23]. Kenneth R. Himes, "The Little Poor Man," Sojourners (December 1981): 19.

[24]. Frederick Sontag, "Who are the Truly Poor?" *Journal of the Evangelical Theological Society* 39, no. 4 (December 1996): 612.

[25]. Elgin S. Moyer, *Who was Who in Church History?* (Chicago, IL: Moody Press, 1968), 149.

[26]. Elizabeth W. Grierson, *The Story of St. Francis of Assisi* (Milwaukee, MO: The Moore Publishing Co., 1912), 66.

[27]. "Franciscan Order," *Catholic Encyclopedia* (accessed October 10, 2004) http://198.62.75./www1/ofm/fra/FRAlife1.html, 3.

[28]. G. K. Chesterton, 123.

[29]. Ewert H. Cousins, "Francis of Assisi and Irreligious Dialogue," *Dialogue and Alliance* 5, no 2 (September 1991): 22.

[30]. Cousins, 22.

[31]. It is not absolutely clear if these were three totally separate "Rules" or whether they were three "Associated Rules" which added new rules to the previous one. K. S. Latourette and G. K. Chesterton suggest these were enlargements of former rules; I am inclined to agree with them.

"Saint Francis the Regula Bullata of 1223," (accessed October 15, 2004) http://www.san-francesco.org/gegola_eng.html.

[32]. Grierson, 74.

[33].Regula Bullata 1223.

[34]. "Franciscan Order," *Catholic Encyclopedia* (accessed October 26, 2004) http://www.newadvent.org/cathen/06217a.html, 3.

[35]. Theodore Maynard, *Richest of the Poor: The Life of Saint Francis of Assisi* (NY: Echo Books, 1967), 272-273.

[36]. Regis J. Armstrong, ed., *Francis of Assisi: Early Documents,* 2 Vols. (NY: New City Press, 2000), 2: 640-641.

[37]. Susan Saint Sing, *A Pilgrim in Assisi* (NY: St. Anthony Press, 1981), 46.

[38]. The incident of Francis stripping himself of his clothing and abandoning family identity to be identified with Christ alone, strongly implies Francis had no other life than that which he found in Christ.

[39]. Margaret Mehren, 190.

[40]. I acknowledge that Christ's was vicarious in order to bring humankind unto salvation, and that Francis's death was not. However, Francis's death could well be a catalyst to bring individuals to faith in Christ as they critically examine the foundation for his life of servitude, and willful obedience in all things to the God he loved.

[41]. "Franciscan Missions," Franciscan Mission Opportunities (accessed October 15, 2004) http://www.wtu.edu/franciscan/pages/misc/mission.html.

Bibliography

Armstrong, Regis J. Editor. *Francis of Assisi: Early Documents,* 3 Vols. NY: New City Press, 2000.

Chesterton, G. K. *St. Francis of Assisi.* London: Hodder & Stoughton Limited, 1934.

Cousins, Ewert H. "Francis of Assisi and Irreligious Dialogue." *Dialogue and Alliance* 5, no. 2 (September 1991): 20-33.

Cross, F. L. "Francis of Assisi." In *The Oxford Dictionary of the Christian Church,* London: Oxford University Press, 1958.

Cunningham, Lawrence. "The Vitality of the Franciscan Spirit." *Christian Century* 93, no. 32 (2001): 865-868.

"Franciscan Order." *Catholic Encyclopedia.* Accessed October 10,

2004. http://198.62.75./www1/ofm/fra/FRAlife1.html.

Gonzalez, Justo L. *The History of Christianity: The Early Church to the Dawn of the Reformation,* 2 Vols. San Francisco, CA: Harper Collins Publishers, 1984.

Grierson, Elizabeth W. *The Story of St. Francis of Assisi.* Milwaukee, MO: The Moore Publishing Co., 1912.

Habig, Marion A. "Writings of St. Francis." In *St. Francis of Assisi: Writings and Early Biographies*. Chicago, IL: Franciscan Herald Press, 1972: 30-54.

Himes, Kenneth, R. "The Little Poor Man." *Sojourners* (December 16, 1981): 19.

Latourette, Kenneth Scott. *A History of Christianity,* 2 Vols. NY: Harper & Row Publishers, 1953.

Lenord, F. "Francis of Assisi." In *Encyclopedia of Church History.* NY: Harper & Row Publishers, 1956.

Maynard, Theodore. *Richest of the Poor: The Life of Saint Francis of Assisi.* NY: Echo Books, 1967.

Mehren Margaret. "Francis of Assisi: Reconciliation with God, Humanity, and Creation." *Missionalia* 19, no. 3 (November 1991): 183-191.

Milman, Henry H. *History of Latin Christianity: Including that of the Popes to the Pontifices Of Nicholas V,* 2 Vols. London: John Murray Press, 1855.

Moyer, Elgin S. *Who Was Who in Church History?* Chicago, IL: Moody Press, 1968.

Pelikan, Jaroslav. *The Illustrated Jesus through the Centuries.* London: Yale University Press, 1997.

Rohr, Richard. "A Life Pure and Simple: A Franciscan Reflects on a Saint." *Sojourners* (December, 1981): 13-16.

Shields, Alcuin F. "The Gospel Pattern in the Franciscan Concept of Community, 1209-1517." *The Journal of Religious Thought* 1, no. 2 (Spring/Summer 1944): 106-116.

Sing, Susan Saint. *A Pilgrim in Assisi.* NY: St. Anthony Press, 1981.

Sontag, Frederick "Who Are The Truly Poor?" *Journal of the Evangelical Theological Society* 39 no. 4 (December 1996): 609-615.

"St. Francis and St. Clare: Life and Times." *The Franciscan Experience.* (Accessed October 10, 2004). http://198.62.75./www1/ofm/fra/FRAlife1.html.

Chapter 12

Endnotes

[1]. Gerald R. Cragg, *The Church and the Age of Reason* 1648-1789 (NY: Penguin Books, 1974). 98.

[2]. F. E. Stoeffler, *The Rise of Evangelical Pietism* (Leiden: E. J. Brill Co., 1965), 183.

[3]. Kenneth Scott Latourette, *A History of Christianity* (London: Harper & Row, 1953), 896.

[4]. Jakob Spener, trans. Theodore G. Tappert, *Pia Desideria* (NY: Fortress Press, 1964), 44.

[5]. Justo L. Gonzalez, *The Story of Christianity* (San Francisco, CA: Harper Collins: 1985), 205.

[6]. *Encyclopedia Britannica,* 22 Vols. (NY: William Benton Publishers, 1970), 21:1061.

[7]. F. E. Stoeffler, 184.

[8]. E. E. Cairns, *Christianity through the Centuries* (Grand Rapids, MI: Zondervan Publishing House, 1954), 413.

[9] Ronald J. Gordon, "Rise of Pietism in 17th Century Germany," *European Origin of the Church of the Brethren* (accessed February 16, 2004), http://www.cob-net.org/pietism.htm.

[10]. Jakob Spener, Ibid., 64.

[11]. E. H. Broadbent, *The Pilgrim Church* (London: Pickering & Inglis Limited, 1963), 270.

[12]. Jakob Spener, 104.

[13]. Johnathan Storm, "Problems and Promises of Pietism Research," in *Church History* (Grand Rapids, MI: Wm. B. Eerdmans, 1998), 71.

[14]. Jakob Spener, 103.

[15]. Peter C. Erb, ed., *Pietists, Selected Writings* (NY: Paulist Press, 1983), 53.

[16]. Jakob Spener, 91.

[17]. Ronald R. Fuerehan, "The Roots and Fruits of Pietism," *Pieper Lectures,* 1998 (accessed: January 15, 2004) http://www.issuesetc.org/resource/archives/feuerhhn .htm, 7.

[18]. Peter C. Erb, 55.

[19]. Joyce Irwin, "German Pietists and Church Music in the Baroque Age," *The American Society of Church History*. 54, no. 1(March 1985): 38-39.

[20]. Jakob Spener, 107. His discussion throughout this section, (105-112), implores professors to guide 'pastors in training' to their true end of their calling which is to be able to equip all parishioners to effectively live out the life Christ has called them to. Head knowledge is nothing, Spener implies, if it cannot be lived out with immediate and lasting godly consequences.

[21]. Ibid, 108.

[22]. Ibid, 93.

[23]. Peter C. Erb, 53.

[24]. Jakob Spener, 96.

[25]. Peter C. Erb, 37-38.

[26]. Ernest E. Stoeffler, "Can These Bones Live?" *Christian History Magazine* 5, no. 2 (1996): 16.

[27]. Ernest E. Stoeffler, 15.

[28]. Gary R. Sattler, "Moving On Many Fronts," *Christian History Magazine* 5, no. 2 (1986): 20.

[29]. German Parish Life in London (accessed February 10, 2004), http://www.bl.ukcollections/georex10.html 14.

Bibliography

Broadbent, E. H. *The Pilgrim Church.* London: Pickering & Inglis Limited, 1963.

Cairns, E. E. *Christianity through the Centuries.* Grand Rapids, MI: Zondervan Publishing House, 1954.

Cragg, Gerald R. *The Church and the Age of Reason* 1648-1789. NY: Penguin Books, 1974. *Encyclopedia Britannica,* 21. NY: William Benton Publishers, 1970.

Erb, Peter C. Editor. *Pietists, Selected Writings.* NT: Paulist Press, 1983.

Fuerehan, Ronald R. "The Roots and Fruits of Pietism." *Pieper Lectures,* 1998. Accessed January 22, 2004. http://www.issuesetc.org/resource/archives/feuerhhn .htm.

German Parish Life In London. (Accessed February 10, 2004). http://www.bl.uk./collections/georex10.html.

Gonzalez, Justo L. *The Story of Christianity,* San Francisco, CA: Harper Collins: 1985.

Gordon, Ronald J. "Rise of Pietism in 17th Century Germany." *European Origin of the Church of the Brethren.* Accessed February 16. 2004. http://www.cob-net.org/pietism.htm.

Irwin, Joyce. "German Pietists and Church Music in the Baroque Age." In *The American Society of Church History.* 54, no. 1 (March 1985).

Latourette, Kenneth Scott. *A History of Christianity.* London: Harper & Row, 1953.

Sattler, Gary R. "Moving On Many Fronts." In *Christian History Magazine.* 5, no. 2 (1986).
Spener, Jakob. *Pia Desideria.* Translated by Theodore G. Tappert. NY: Fortress Press, 1964.

Stoeffler, Ernest E. "Can These Bones Live?" *Christian History Magazine.* 5, no. 2 (1986).

_______________. *The Rise of Evangelical Pietism.* Leiden: E. J. Brill Co., 1965.

Storm, Johnathan. "Problems and Promises Of Pietism Research." In *Church History.* Grand Rapids, MI: Wm. B. Eerdmans, 1998.

Chapter 13

Endnotes

[1]. Deanne William Ferm, *Third World Liberation Theologies* (NY: Orbis Books, 1986), 3.

[2]. John Patrick Koyles, "A Yoderian Appraisal of Latin American Liberation Theology," *Asbury Theological Journal* 57, no. 2 (Fall 2002): 26.

[3]. Ferm, 4.

[4]. Tom Hanks, "Liberation Theology after 25 Years: Passé or Mainstream?" *Anvil* 10, no. 3 (1983): 4.

[5]. F. L. Cross, *Oxford Dictionary of the Christian Church* (Oxford: University Press, 1977), 978.

[6]. James V. Schall, "Liberation Theology in Latin America: Theology as Institutionalized Poverty," in *Liberation Theology* (Grand Rapids, MI: Baker Book House, 1984), 91.

[7]. Dianne Stinton, "Africa, East and West," in *An Introduction to Third World Theologies,* ed. John Parratt (Cambridge: University Press, 2004), 115-116.

[8]. Kenneth Scott Latourette, *A History of Christianity* (NY: Harper and Row, Publishers, 1953), 430-431.

[9]. Paul E. Sigmund, "Latin American Catholicism's Opening to the Left," *Review of Politics* 35, no. 1 (January 1973): 72.

[10]. Christopher Rowland, "Introduction: The Theology of Liberation," *The Cambridge Companion to Liberation Theology* (Cambridge: University Press, 1999), 5.

[11]. Sherron K. George, "From Liberation to Evangelization: New Latin American Hermeneutical Keys," *Interpretation* 55, no. 4 (2001): 368.

[12]. Reuben R. Rodriguez, "Becoming a Church for the Poor: Towards a Reformed Spirituality of Liberation," *Koinonia* 12, no. 2 (2001): 154.

[13]. Peter C. Phan, "Method in Liberation Theologies," *Theological Studies* 61, no. 1(January 2000): 41.

[14]. Daniel M. Bell, Jr., "Men of Stone and Children of Struggle: Latin America Liberationists at the End of History," *Modern Theology* 14, no. 1, (January 1998): 116.

[15]. William A. Dyrness, *Learning About Theology from the Third World* (Grand Rapids, MI: Academic Books, 1990), 97.

[16]. Rodriguez, 156.

[17]. F. Van der Hoff, "Latin American Liberation Theology," *Missiology: An Ecumenical Introduction* (Grand Rapids, MI: Wm. B. Eerdmans Publishing Company, 1995), 355.

[18]. Others have chosen the Babylonian Exile Model also as a paradigm by from which Liberation Theology gains incentive to labour intensively for freedom from depravation and marginalization incurred by the poor.

[19]. Wilford Harrington, "*Jesus the Liberator*: Nazareth Liberation Theology (Luke 4:16-30)," *Catholic Quarterly Review* 59, no. 1 (1997), 171.

[20]. Henry Hart Milman, *History of Latin Christianity: Including that of the Popes to the Pontificate of Nicolas V* (London: John Murray Publications, 1855), 263.

[21]. John A. Broadus, "Matthew," *An American Commentary on the New Testament,* 2 Vols. (Valley Forge: The Judson Press, 1954), 1:510.

[22]. Ferm, 5.

[23]. Robert V. Andelson and James M. Dawsey, "From Wasteland to Promised Land: Liberation Theology for a Post-Marxist World," (accessed 9 March 2007) http://www.landreform.org/wp7.htm.

[24]. F. L. Cross, 978.

[25]. J. B. Labanio, "Liberation Theology," in *Dictionary of Mission: Theology, History, Perspectives,"* ed. Karl Muller, Theol Sundermeier, Stephen Bevans and Richard H. Bliese (NY: Orbis Books, 1997), 279.

[26]. John L. Markey, "Praxis in Liberation Theology: Some Clarifications," *Missiology* 23, no. 2 (April 1995): 180.

[27]. Stephen B. Bevans, *Models of Contextual Theology: Faith and Cultures* (NY: Orbis Books, 2006), 72-73.

[28]. Gustavo Gutierrez, "The Task and Content of Liberation Theology," in *The Cambridge Companion To Liberation Theology,* ed. Christopher Rowland (Cambridge: University Press, 1999), 30

[29]. Wimberly, 5.

[30]. Scripture, which Liberation Theology uses as its basis for justice for the poor, strongly emphasizes "if a person does not willingly work, he or she should not be given food" (2 Thess 3:10). Poor, anywhere, should expect some aid for relief from governments, churches, and other such like organizations. But integrity in trying to better one's self, despite difficult times, is shown by individuals seeking ways they might improve their conditions and then "chasing after them!"

Bibliography

Andelson, Robert V. and James M. Dawsey. "From Wasteland to Promised Land: Liberation Theology for a Post-Marxist World." Accessed March 9, 2007 http://www.landreform.org/wp7.htm.

Bell, Jr., Daniel M. "Men of Stone and Children of Struggle: Latin America Liberationists at the End of History" *Modern Theology* 14, no. 1, (January 1998): 113-141.

Broadus, John A. "Matthew." *An American Commentary on the New Testament,* 2 Vols. Valley Forge: The Judson Press, 1954.

Bevans, Stephen B. *Models of Contextual Theology: Faith and Cultures.* NY: Orbis Books, 2006.

Cross, F. L. *Oxford Dictionary of the Christian Church.* Oxford: University Press, 1977.

Dyrness, William A. *Learning about Theology from the Third World.* Grand Rapids, MI: Academic Books, 1990.

Ferm, Deanne William. *Third World Liberation Theologies.* NY: Orbis Books, 1986.

George, Sherron K. "From Liberation to Evangelization: New Latin American Hermeneutical Keys." *Interpretation* 55, no. 4 (2001): 367-377.

Gutierrez, Gustavo. "The Task and Content of Liberation Theology." In *The Cambridge Companion to Liberation Theology.* Edited by Christopher Rowland. Cambridge: University Press, 1999.

Hanks, Tom. "Liberation Theology after 25 Years: Passé or Mainstream?" *Anvil* 10, no. 3 (1983): 25.

Harrington, Wilford. "*Jesus the Liberator*: Nazareth Liberation Theology (Luke 4:16-30)." *Catholic Quarterly Review* 59, no. 1 (1997): 165-184.

Koyles, John Patrick ."A Yoderian Appraisal of Latin American Liberation Theology." *Asbury Theological Journal* 57, no. 2 (Fall 2002): 25-40.

Labanio, J. B. "Liberation Theology." In *Dictionary of Mission: Theology, History, Perspectives."* Edited by. Karl Muller, Theol Sundermeier, Stephen Bevans and Richard H. Bliese. NY: Orbis Books, 1997.

Latourette, Kenneth Scott. *A History of Christianity.* NY: Harper and Row, Publishers, 1953.

Markey, John L. "Praxis in Liberation Theology: Some Clarifications." *Missiology* 23, no. 2 (April 1995): 175-195.

Milman, Henry Hart. *History of Latin Christianity: Including that of the Popes to the Pontificate of Nicolas V.* London: John Murray Publications, 1855.

Phan, Peter C. "Method in Liberation Theologies." *Theological Studies* 61, no. 1(January 2000): 40-63.

Rodriguez, Reuben R. "Becoming a Church for the Poor: Towards a Reformed Spirituality of Liberation." *Koinonia* 12, no. 2 (2001): 144-160.

Rowland, Christopher. "Introduction: The Theology of Liberation." *The Cambridge Companion to Liberation Theology.* Cambridge: University Press, 1999.

Schall, James V. "Liberation Theology in Latin America: Theology as Institutionalized Poverty." In *Liberation Theology.* Grand Rapids, MI: Baker Book House, 1984.

Sigmund, Paul E. "Latin American Catholicism's Opening to the Left." *Review of Politics* 35, no. 1 (January 1973): 61-76.

Stinton, Dianne. "Africa, East and West," in *An Introduction to Third World Theologies.* Edited by John Parratt. Cambridge: University Press, 2004.

Van der Hoff, F. "Latin American Liberation Theology." *Missiology: An Ecumenical Introduction.* Grand Rapids, MI: Wm. B. Eerdmans Publishing Company, 1995.

Chapter 14

Endnotes

[1]. John Groshen, "Power within PowerPoint," *Christianity Today* (November 1997): 36.

[2]. J. S. Broadley, "Putting It All Together: One Piece at a Time," *The Churchman* (October 1994): 75.

[3] Quentin J. Shultze, "Faith, Education, and Communication Technology," *Journal of Education & Christian Belief* 8, no. 1 (September 2004): 7.

[4]. Kathy Sierra, "Creating Passionate Users: Stop Your Presentation before it Kills Again", *The Canadian Educator* (Fall 2005), 22.

[5]. Robert Philips, "Correlating PowerPoint to Worship," *Christianity Today* (Fall 2004): 76.

[6]. Q. J. Shultze, 27.

[7]. Ronald J. Gordon, "Rise of Pietism in 17th Century Germany," *European Origin of the Church of the Brethren* (accessed February 16, 2004) http://www.cob-net.org/pietism.htm.

[8] Christopher K. Lensch, "The Public Reading of Scripture," *Western Reformed Seminary Journal* 7, no. 1 (February 2000): 19.

[9] Jeremy S. Begbie, *Theology, Music and Time* (Cambridge: University Press, 2005), 25.

[10]. Jane Webster & Hayes Ho, "Audience Engagement in Multimedia Presentation," *The Data Base in Information Systems* 28, no 2 (Spring 1997): 71.

Bibliography

Begbie, Jeremy S., *Theology, Music and Time.* Cambridge: University Press, 2005.

Broadley, J. S., "Putting it All Together: One Piece at a Time." *The Churchman* 42, no. 3 (October 1994): 72-78.

Groshen, John, "Power within PowerPoint." *Christianity Today* (November, 1997): 17.

Lensch, Christopher K. "The Public Reading of Scripture." *Western Reformed Seminary Journal* 7, no. 1 (February 2000): 19-22.

Philips, Robert, "Correlating PowerPoint to Worship" *Christianity Today* (Fall 2004):27-34.

Shultze, Quentin J., "Faith, Education, and Communication Technology." *Journal of Education & Christian Belief* 8, no. 1 (March 2004): 9-21.

Sierra, Kathy, "Creating Passionate Users: Stop Your Presentation before it Kills Again." *The Canadian Educator* (Fall 2005).

Webster, Jane, & Hayes Ho. "Audience Engagement in Multimedia Presentation." *The Data Base in Information Systems* 28, no. 2 (Spring 1997): 63-77.

Chapter 15

Endnotes

[1]. "Ceausescus," (accessed July 3, 2006) http://wwww.ceausescu.org

[2]. June Matthews, "Romanian Revolutionary Hero," *The Alabama Baptist* (December 22, 2005): 7.

[3]. "Ceausescu," in *Encyclopedia Britannica,* 18 Vols. (NY: Harper Publishing, 2005), 3:137.

[4]. Necula Marian, "Studia Politica," *Romanian Political Science Review* 1, no 3 (2004): 522.

[5]. Mark Elliott, "Lazio Tokes: Timisoara and the Romanian Revolution," *Occasional Papers on Religion in Eastern Europe* 10, no. 5 (October 1990): 23-24.

[6]. Quote supplied by Reverend Peter Vidu, Biserica Emanuel Baptista in October, 2003 while I was on my second speaking tour.

7. Greek Orthodox, Greek Catholic, Apostolic Pentecost and Baptist which were registered with the Department of Cults, and which were licensed by the Secretariat.

8. Ibid. Because of Peter's father's determination to preach the gospel regardless of the consequences that might befall him, Peter also dedicated himself to preaching the gospel. For four years Peter was under constant surveillance by the Secretariat. Eventually he was dismissed from his job as an engineer, and locked in a room for four hours a day to read magazines because of his faith.

9. Ioan Bunaciu, *Istoria Bisericilor Baptiste din Romania* (Bucharest: Faclia Publishing House, 2006), 145-152.

The author presents a detailed commentary of the history of the Baptist Union Fellowship, starting from 1909 – district by district. Information provided for me in this paper was translated by Chip Smetu, a student at Immanuel Baptist University during my visit June 1st-July 6th, 2006.

10. "Baptist Union of Romania," *Wikipedia"* (accessed July 16, 2006) http://www.en.wikipedia.org/wiki/Baptist-Union-of-Romania

11. Bucharest Baptist Seminary offers only theological training.

12. Emanuel Baptist University – Oradea – A multifaceted Christian Liberal Arts university offering courses in theology, business management, Hospice and music.

13. Emanuel Hospice providing free medical care to clients throughout the county of Bihor.

14. Ioan Bunaciu, 151.

15. Alexander F. C. Webster, "Evangelicals versus Orthodox in Romania," *The Christian Century* 30, no. 64 (June 1990): 560.

16. Mihai Dumbravenu, "Pentecostalism din Romania," *Apostolic Training Manual.* Information provided by Pastor Nelu Molnar of Bethel Pentecostal Church, Zalau. Pentecostals accused Baptist pastors of not believing in signs and wonders, and not recognizing spiritual ministry gifts in the laity. When the laity felt they could not do ministry in Baptist churches, they moved to the Pentecostal churches where they were welcomed wholeheartedly, and given opportunity to utilize their gifts immediately.

17. Ioan Bunaciu, 155.

[18]. Peter Dugulescu, *Repenters* (Timisoara: Jesus, The Hope of Romania Publishers, 2003), 19.

[19]. Comment provided by Pastor Daniel Marin of First Baptist Church during my visit of June 1st-July 10th, 2006. Daniel is the most senior Romanian pastor actively preaching in Romania. He received his training at Bucharest Bible College in 1944 and pastored "according to the rules of the Secretariat" from 1964 to 1989.

[20]."Constitution 1948, Number 7."remained the basic law until October 13th, 2007 when a new Constitution came into effect. Today pastoral licensing is still processed through the Department of Cults, but the rules for training have been changed radically. The information for this paper was obtained from the Government Office in Timisoara on July 4th, 2006.

[21]. Department of Cults now has offices in every major city. Pastors in Romania may preach in any evangelical church, perform weddings and funerals once a license is obtained. Ministers visiting Romania must work in a registered denominational church under direction of the Lead Pastor of the Church. The head office for the Department of Cults still is in Bucharest.

[22]. Steven Friesen, "Renewal: Reorganization for Romanian Churches," *The Christian Century* 107, no. 6 (1990): 172-173

[23]. Radu Tet, Pastor of Magesti Baptist Church shared his testimony over a lunch at his home. His days of training at Bucharest, while Ceausescu ruled, were very difficult and demanding. Later, during public ministry, he was constantly under the scrutiny of the Secretariat's officers and former Baptist ministers who "sold themselves" to Ceausescu as informants of pastoral activity.

[24]. Duguslescu, 177.

[25]. Peter Popovich, "The Romanian Church Persecuted," *Baptist Union Fellowship Monthly* (Oradea: Rompflair Press, 1990), 27.

[26]. Radu Tet, Email received July 24th, 2006 in response to my request for information about pastoral training he received while at Bucharest Bible College in 1966.

[27]. Petre Cimpreu, "Inside Communist Romania," *Adventist Review* (Fall 1979): 23 This article may be view, in its entirety by visiting http://archives.adventistreview.org/2001-1524/story1.html.

[28]. Petre Cimpreu, 21.

[29]. The Department of Cults, at the time accepted the Jehovah's Witness, Mormons, as well as several evangelical denominations, including the Evangelical Mennonite Missionary Alliance and the Nazarene Church to be licensed.

[30]. "Baptist Union of Romania," Wikipedia (July 16, 2006).

[31]. Dr. Marius Ianc, Pastor at Ciacova received his Doctor of Ministry degree in May, 2016 from Covenant Theological Seminary, Creve Coeur Missouri and Adi Vidu received his Doctor of Philosophy degree from Oxford University, England. Daniel Lacotos, Pastor of Bacau Baptist Church regularly attended TCM International Institute in Vienna to complete his Master of Divinity degree by taking "in-house study sessions" for two weeks, twice a year. Regularly, Romanian pastors are taking courses at seminaries around the world because of the relaxation of travel visas by Bucharest.

[32]. Romanian pastors have attended Regent College, Vancouver since 1990.

[33]. Pastors in smaller, village churches find it more convenient to live in the bigger cities because of schooling for their children, shopping and cheaper housing. Village homes usually include farmland which pastors do not attend to, so they find no reason – other than ministry – to be there.

[34]. This Romanian greeting is said by Romanian parishioners on arriving and leaving the worship service or during the week as they meet in the marketplace, school and the like.

[35]. August 8th-September 6th, 2015.

[36]. Constantin Petrus, pastor of Tileagd Baptist Church – 37 KM from Oradea lives in Oradea. Florein Negrut, pastor of Piesti Baptist Church, also lives in

Oradea. Both pastors drive the distance for services and do not practice regular congregant home visits.

[37]. Thomas J. Keppeler, "Images of the Church and Leadership: Reflections on Church Leadership Education in Romania," *Christian Education Journal* 2NS, no. 1 (Spring 1998): 49

[38]. R. Paul Stevens and Phil Collins, *The Equipping Pastor: A Systems Approach to Congregational Leadership* (Lanham, MD: Rowman & Littlefield Publishers, 1993), 8.

[39]. Story related to me by Baptist Union Fellowship Missions Pastor at Biserica Emanuel Baptista in Oradea the afternoon I spoke at the Magine Mission Church in October 2006.

[40]. September 4th, 2015.

Bibliography

"Baptist Union of Romania." *Wikipedia"* Accessed July 16, 2006 http://www.en.wikipedia.org/wiki/Baptist_Union_of_Romania

Bunaciu, Ioan. *Istoria Bisericilor Baptiste din Romania* (Bucharest: Faclia Publishing House, 2006.

"Ceausescu," in *Encyclopedia Britannica,* 18 Vols. NY: Harper Publishing, 2005.

"Ceausescus." Accessed July 3, 2006 http://wwww.ceausescu.org.

Cimpreu, Petre. "Inside Communist Romania." *Adventist Review* (Fall 1979): 23

Dugulescu, Peter. *Repenters.* Timisoara: Jesus, The Hope of Romania Publishers, 2003.

Dumbravenu, Mihai. "Pentecostalism din Romania," *Apostolic Training Manual.*

Elliott, Mark. "Lazio Tokes: Timisoara and the Romanian Revolution" *Occasional Papers on Religion in Eastern Europe* 10, no. 5 (October 1990): 22-28.

Friesen, Steven. "Renewal: Reorganization for Romanian Churches." *The Christian Century* 107, no. 6 (1990): 172-178.

Keppeler, Thomas J. "Images of the Church and Leadership: Reflections on Church Leadership Education in Romania." *Christian Education Journal* 2NS, no. 1 (Spring 1998): 45-56.

Marian, Necula. "Studia Politica." *Romanian Political Science Review* 1, no 3, (2004): 519-540.

Matthews, June. "Romanian Revolutionary Hero." *The Alabama Baptist* (December 22, 2005): 7.

Popovich, Peter. "The Romanian Church Persecuted." *Baptist Union Fellowship Monthly.* Oradea: Rompflair Press, 1990.

Stevens, R. Paul and Phil Collins. *The Equipping Pastor: A Systems Approach to Congregational Leadership.* Lanham, MD: Rowman & Littlefield Publishers, 1993.

Tet, Radu. Email received July 24th, 2006.

Webster, Alexander F. C. "Evangelicals versus Orthodox in Romania." *The Christian Century* 30, no. 64 (June 1990): 560-561.

71804R00164

Made in the USA
Charleston, SC
02 April 2016